Franciscans
and the
Protestant Revolution
in England

Franciscans and the Protestant Revolution In England

FRANCIS BORGIA STECK, O. F. M.

MEDIATRIX PRESS

MMXXI

ISBN: 978-1-953746-86-3

Imprimi permittitur.
SAMUEL MACKE, O. F. M.
Minister Provincialis.

Nihil Obstat.
P. L. BIERMANN, *Censor Librorum.*

Imprimatur.
✠ GEORGIUS GULIELMUS MUNDELEIN,
Archiepiscopus Chicagiensis.
Die 2. Martii, 1920.

© Mediatrix Press
All rights reserved. *Franciscans and the Protestant Revolution in England* was originally published by Franciscan Herald Press in 1920, and is in the public domain. Editorial changes and typography ©Mediatrix Press. No part of this work may be reproduced in electronic or physical format without the permission of the publisher, except for reviews in blogs, journals, or classroom use. No part of this version may be placed on archive.org.

Mediatrix Press
607 E. 6th Ave.
Post Falls, ID 83854
www.mediatrixpress.com

TABLE OF CONTENTS

FOREWORD xvi

PART FIRST
UNDER THE TUDORS 1509-1603

CHAPTER I: INTRODUCTORY
Fr. William of England, a disciple of St. Francis—The first Franciscans arrive in England: Fr. Agnellus of Pisa and his eight companions—The first friaries: Canterbury, London, Oxford, Northampton, Cambridge—Marvelous expansion of the province—Character of the English Franciscans—Two remarkable features regarding the development of the province—Influence with the masses—In the service of State and Church—In the field of letters. 1

CHAPTER II: CALM BEFORE THE STORM
Early reign of Henry VIII—Religious conditions in England—Attitude toward papal supremacy—The king, a dutiful child of the Church—The reform movement in the Order of St. Francis—Its bearing on the Province of England—The king well disposed toward the Franciscans. 29

CHAPTER III: FIRST RUMBLINGS OF THE STORM
Henry seeks divorce from Catherine of Aragon—He repudiates her and marries Anne Boleyn—The Franciscans and the king's "secret affair"—Fr. William Peyto publicly rebukes the king and his court—Fr. John Elstow and Dr. Curwin—The two friars before the king—Banished. 37

CHAPTER IV OUTBREAK OF THE STORM
Henry's divorce and the question of papal

supremacy—The crisis—The king usurps spiritual supremacy over the Church in England—Meets with opposition from the Franciscans—Contemplates rigorous measures against them—A favorable opportunity—Elizabeth Barton, the Holy Maid of Kent—Her revelations and the king's divorce—Two of her adherents: FF. Richard Risby and Hugh Rich—The "public penance"—The two friars defend the Pope's spiritual supremacy—Accused of high treason—The first martyrs for the faith. 47

CHAPTER V RAGING OF THE STORM, 1534-1536
Franciscans continue to oppose the king's divorce and his usurped supremacy—Fr. Pecock's sermon—First step toward the suppression of their province—Cromwell, vicegerent and vicar general—Hilsey and Browne, "grand visitors" of all mendicant friars—Their instructions—They visit the Franciscans at Richmond and Greenwich—Visitation of Southampton—Loyalty of the friars—All Franciscans arrested and imprisoned—Their friaries in the hands of the king—Subsequent lot of the ejected friars—Some released from prison and banished—Many succumb to the hardships of prison life. 55

CHAPTER VI: RAGING OF THE STORM (CONT.), 1536-1538
Disaffection among the people—The Pilgrimage of Grace—Share of the Franciscans in the northern rising—Renewed hostilities against them—Three Franciscan martyrs: Ven. Antony Brookby, Ven. Thomas Cort, Ven. Thomas Belchiam. 69

CHAPTER VII: ST. THOMAS MORE, FRANCISCAN TERTIARY
Early youth — At Oxford — Professional studies — With the Carthusians — More's public and private life — The impending storm — He resigns the chancellorship — Poverty and distress at Chelsea — Efforts of Anne Boleyn and Cromwell to ruin the ex-

chancellor—Measures of the king against him — More rejects the Acts of Succession and Supremacy — In the Tower — His loyalty put to severe tests—Brought to trial — Found guilty of high treason and sentenced to death — His last days in prison — Beheaded on Tower Hill. 79

CHAPTER VIII: CATHERINE OF ARAGON, FRANCISCAN TERTIARY
The Spanish princess—Departure for England—Sudden death of Prince Arthur, her consort—She marries his brother Henry—Eighteen years of marital happiness—The king's infidelity—The divorce question—Catherine and the papal commission—Before the ecclesiastical court at Blackfriars—The queen's appeal to Rome admitted—Henry retaliates—Catherine insulted and disowned—Her secluded life at the More—At Buckden—At Kimbolton Castle—Bodily and mental suffering—Royal supremacy—Within sight of the scaffold—Her last illness and violent death—An estimate of her character. 109

CHAPTER IX: BLESSED JOHN FOREST, O.F.M.
Birth and parentage—Enters the Franciscan Order—Doctor of Oxford—Provincial of England—Espouses the queen's cause—Fr. Richard Lyst, traitor and spy—Blessed Forest and the king—Attempt to remove Forest from the provincialship—Staunch defender of papal supremacy—Imprisoned, tried, condemned to death—Martyrdom delayed—With the Conventuals in London Entrapped in the confessional—Before the Privy Council—Once more in Newgate—Tried for heresy—Sentenced to die at the stake—His alleged submission—Drawn on a hurdle to Smithfield—The friars and the bishop—Dreadful torture and death. 145

CHAPTER X: DEATH AND DESTRUCTION, 1538-1547
Renewed measures against the Franciscans—Three martyrs: FF. Antony Brown, John Waire, and Hemmysley—The Conventual friars—Their poverty—During the first years of the religious upheaval—The royal visitors—Wholesale robbery and vandalism—Subsequent lot of the Conventual houses and of the ejected friars. 177

CHAPTER XI: DIVINE RETRIBUTION, 1547-1558

Last days of Henry VIII—Remorse and despair—His death—The prophecy of Fr. Peyto fulfilled—Reign of Edward VI—Efforts to introduce Lutheranism—Further confiscation and spoliation of religious houses—The "Funus Scoti et Scotistarum" at Oxford—Reign of Mary the Catholic—England reunited with the Church of Rome—Franciscans again at Greenwich, London, and Southampton—Their activity and influence—Death of the queen. 193

CHAPTER XII: UNDER THE LAST TUDOR, 1558-1603
Queen Elizabeth's perfidy—Excommunicated by the Pope—The persecution against Catholics revived—Queen Elizabeth and the Franciscans—The friars expelled and banished—One of the exiles, a martyr—Franciscans in England during Elizabeth's reign—Fr. John Storrens martyred in 1572—Venerable Godfrey Buckley, O.F.M.—At first a secular priest—Joins the Franciscans in Rome—On the English mission—Seized and imprisoned—Tried and condemned to death for being a priest—His martyrdom. 205

PART SECOND
UNDER THE STUARTS 1603-1649

CHAPTER I: THE SECOND ENGLISH PROVINCE
Its founder: Fr. John Gennings—His remarkable

conversion from Protestantism—Priest and missionary in England—He enters the Franciscan Order—First steps toward the restoration of the English Province—Action of the general chapter in its behalf—A friary at Douai in Flanders—The province canonically established—Fr. John Gennings, the first provincial—Franciscan missions in England—Extent of the province before 1649—Character of the friars—Their activity against Protestantism. 227

CHAPTER II: VEN. WILLIAM WARD, FRANCISCAN TERTIARY

Troublous reign of Charles I—Puritan animosity against "Papists"—William Ward, a Protestant at Oxford—Returns to the old faith—Ordained priest—Seized on his return to England—Three years in prison—Thirty years of unceasing toil and hardship—A true follower of St. Francis—In Newgate for being a priest—Sentenced to death—Martyred at Tyburn. . 245

CHAPTER III: FR. CHRISTOPHER COLMAN, O. F. M.

Of Catholic parentage—Student at the Jesuit College in Douai—Returns to England—The Catholic gentleman—Joins the Franciscans in Douai—Ordained priest—Summoned to England—Arrested and released—Missionary labors—The persecution revived—Fr. Christopher one of the first to he seized—In Newgate—Condemned to death—Execution delayed and prevented by the war—Sufferings and death in prison. 255

CHAPTER IV: VENERABLE JOHN BAPTIST BULLAKER, O.F.M.

Studies with the Jesuits at Saint-Omer and at Valladolid—Desires to become a Franciscan—Enters the Order—Novitiate and years of study—Joins the English Province—Departs for England—Arrested and

imprisoned at Plymouth—In Exeter jail—Before the judges—Conveyed to London for trial—Liberated—Twelve years of missionary labors—Betrayed and captured while saying Mass—Court proceedings against him—Tried for being a priest—Condemned to death—Martyrdom at Tyburn.
.... 265

CHAPTER V: VENERABLE PAUL HEATH, O.F.M.

Of Protestant parentage—Student at Cambridge—Religious doubts—Conversion—Enters the Franciscan Order at Douai—Novitiate and years of study—Esteemed by the brethren—The scholar—The priest—The religious—Eager to join the English missionaries—Permission finally granted—Arrives in London—In Compter prison—Before the mayor and the commissioners of parliament—In Newgate—Before the judges—Sentenced to death—Martyred at Tyburn. 285

CHAPTER VI: VENERABLE FRANCIS BEL, O.F.M.

Of wealthy Catholic parents—Student at Saint-Omer and at Valladolid—Ordained priest—Seeks admission into the Franciscan Order—Novitiate and profession—Summoned to the English Province—Priestly zeal in Flanders—Provincial of Scotland—Missionary in England—His character—Arrested as royal spy—Suspected of being a priest—Conveyed to London for trial—Before the commissioners of parliament—In Newgate—His trial—Guilty of treason—Condemned to death—Last days in Newgate—Drawn to Tyburn—Martyrdom.
.... 305

CHAPTER VII: VENERABLE MARTIN WOODCOCK, O.F.M.

His Protestant father and Catholic mother—He embraces the old faith—Student at Saint-Omer and at Rome—Joins the Capuchins in Paris—Dismissed from the Order—Serious doubts regarding his vocation—Received into the Franciscan Order at Douai—Ordained priest—Longs to joint the missionaries in England—Permission at last granted—Arrested on arriving in England—Sufferings in prison—Before the judges—Sentenced to death for being a priest—Martyrdom............................ 323

CHAPTER VIII: CONCLUSION
Franciscans in prison during the Commonwealth—Early reign of Charles II—Peace and prosperity—Death of Fr. John Gennings—Activity and influence of the friars—The Maryland Mission—Franciscans and the Titus Oates Plot—Two martyrs: Ven. John Wall and Ven. Charles Mahoney—Four die in prison—Ominous signs—Fall of King James II—Franciscans forced to flee from the continent—Many of their number seized and imprisoned—Peace restored—The province at the height of prosperity—Two Franciscans die in prison: FF. Paul Atkinson and Germanus Holmes—Decline of the province—Subversive State laws—The French Revolution—Franciscans flee to England—Their number gradually decreases—The province canonically dissolved. 335

BIBLIOGRAPHY...................................... 347

DEDICATED
to the
Sacred Memory
of
VENERABLE JOHN DUNS SCOTUS,
the
Most Illustrious Member
of the
First Province
of
English Franciscans

FOREWORD

IN the following pages, an attempt is made to relate the story of the English Franciscans during the first century of the Protestant Revolution. Among the causes commonly assigned, even by Catholic historians, for the rapid spread of Protestantism in Europe is the inactivity and degeneracy of the so-called old Orders at the time when the conflict began. This serious charge loses much of its significance if we remember that for forty years these old Orders bore the brunt of the attack against the overwhelming forces of the enemy. The fact, too, that more than 150 members of these old Orders played a prominent role in the Council of Trent shows that their laxism and indifference could not have been so great after all. As to the Franciscan Order in particular, it may suffice to call to mind that of the above-mentioned 150 religious 85 were sons of St. Francis, and that, furthermore, between the years 1520 and 1620, more than 500 Franciscans shed their blood for the faith in the various countries of Europe.

To disprove the above charge in the case of the Franciscans in England, and at the same time to afford wholesome reading for all admirers of St. Francis and his Order, the present volume is placed before the public. As history clearly testifies, the popular mind of England in the beginning of the religious upheaval was deeply imbued with the truly Catholic spirit of the great Saint of Assisi. And perhaps nowhere at the time were his followers of the First Order so highly esteemed by all classes of society as in England. They enjoyed the confidence of the king not less than of the masses. Their life and activity were intimately bound up with the affairs of the higher circles and with the needs and aspirations of the lower classes. The former sought their favor and support, while the latter looked to them for guidance and consolation.

The writer has endeavored to recount their labors and sufferings for the Catholic faith in England in a popular way and with due regard to the postulates of modern historical criticism. Without claiming this to be the first treatment of the

The Franciscans and the Protestant Revolution

subject in English, he would designate as the special feature of his work the fact that it is a critical compilation of practically everything so far written on this matter. From the bibliography the reader can form an idea of the time and labor expended in gathering, sifting, and arranging the available material. The writer shall deem himself amply rewarded for his pains if his work, be it ever so imperfect, will help to make better known one of the many glorious chapters of the history of the Order to which he has the privilege of belonging.

Feast of St. Francis of Assisi, October 4, 1919.
F. B. S.

PART FIRST
UNDER THE TUDORS
1509-1603

CHAPTER I
INTRODUCTORY

Fr. William of England, a disciple of St. Francis—The first Franciscans arrive in England: Fr. Agnellus of Pisa and his eight companions—The first friaries: Canterbury, London, Oxford, Northampton, Cambridge—Marvelous expansion of the province—Character of the English Franciscans—Two remarkable features regarding the development of the province—Influence with the masses—In the service of State and Church—In the field of letters.

O realize the terrible calamity that befell the English Franciscans during the first century of the Protestant Revolution, the reader must know something of their history prior to the outbreak of the storm. For this reason, we shall devote the first chapter of our narrative to an account of their arrival on English soil and of the subsequent development and activity of the province. Though necessarily brief and incomplete, it will show how, throughout the centuries, the sons of St. Francis, by their sanctity and learning as well as by their zeal for the spiritual and temporal welfare of the realm, enjoyed the confidence of the English nation, so that in the beginning of the upheaval they were the most popular and influential religious in England.

Among the first disciples and companions of St. Francis was Fr. William, an Englishman by birth.[1] He was esteemed by his brethren both for his learning and for his extraordinary piety. His soul had deeply imbibed the spirit of the Seraphic Father, and it was very likely owing to his burning zeal for immortal souls, that the newly founded Franciscan Order found its way to England. During the second general chapter, which was held at Whitsuntide, in 1219, at Our Lady of the Angels, or

---

[1] The *Martyrologium Franciscanum* of Fr. Arturus commemorates him on March 7, in these terms: "At Assisi in Umbria, Blessed William, Confessor, a man of extraordinary perfection, who for his sanctity and miracles was widely known in life and after death."

Porziuncola, near Assisi, Fr. William petitioned St. Francis to let also England share the blessings of his new foundation. Accordingly, the Saint directed Blessed Agnellus of Pisa, who was then custos of the French Franciscans and guardian of the friary in Paris, to undertake the expedition to England. He vested him with the authority of provincial and drew up an obedience which read:

To Brother Agnellus of Pisa of the Tuscan Province of the Order of Minors, Brother Francis of Assisi, Minister General, though unworthy, salutation. By the merit of wholesome obedience, I command thee to go to England and there to exercise the office of Minister Provincial. Farewell.[2]

Trusting in Divine Providence and fortified with the blessing of his holy Father, Blessed Agnellus accompanied by eight friars set out for the new mission field. Of his companions, Fr. Richard of Ingworth was a priest, Fr. Richard of Devonshire a cleric in minor orders, and Fr. William of Esseby a youthful but very pious novice; these three were, like their leader, Englishmen by birth. The other five selected for the expedition were lay brothers; viz., FF. Henry of Cervise, Lawrence of Beauvais, William of Florence, Melioratus, and James Ultramontanus.[3] After staying a few months with their brethren in France, the little band of nine friars continued their journey to Normandy and received a hearty welcome from the monks of Fescamp. Supplied by these with the necessary means, they embarked for Dover in Kent, where they landed,

---

[2] In his *Annales Minorum* (an. 1219, num. 32), Wadding remarks that as a perpetual memorial of the founding of the English Province, the Franciscan friary of Mount La Verna at his time preserved a picture of Blessed Agnellus of Pisa holding his obedience in his hands. The saintly friar died in 1232 (1233); he was enrolled among the Blessed by Pope Leo XIII. The Franciscan Order celebrates his feast on May 7.

[3] Eccleston, *Liber de Adventu Minorum in Angliam* in *Analecta Franciscana*, Vol. I, p. 218.

probably on May 3, 1220.[4] Thence they proceeded to

---

[4] Historians do not agree as to the date of the arrival of the first Franciscans in England. Eccleston, a member of the Order who lived about the year 1340, says that they arrived on September 10, 1224. "In the year of the Lord 1224," he begins his narrative, "in the time of the Lord Pope Honorius, namely in the same year in which the Rule of St. Francis was approved by him, in the eighth year of the Lord King Henry, son of John, on Tuesday after the feast of the Nativity of the Blessed Virgin, which that year fell on Sunday, the Friars Minor first arrived in England." The precision and accuracy with which the statement is made (September 8, the day of the feast, was actually a Sunday in 1224) would settle the question once for all, as it did for Leland, Wood, and most English historians, were it not that other writers of repute and a number of indirect evidences speak against the date. Thus Wadding *Annales Minorum* (an. 1220, num. 58) maintains that the first friars arrived on May 3, 1220, adducing Marianus of Florence (d. 1537) as his authority. Others who assign the year 1220 are Matthew Paris (d. 1259), Marcus of Lisbon (d. 1591), Francis Harold (d. 1685), and Parkinson (d. 1728). Some historians assert that the friars arrived about four years after the coronation of King Henry III. Thereby they by no means settle the question, because the King was crowned twice, in 1216 and in 1220. Matthew Paris, who lived in England at this time as chronologist of the King, declares, under the year 1243, that the Franciscans "began to build their first habitations *scarce four and twenty years ago* (See Parkinson, *Antiquities of the English Franciscans*, p. 6). Again, in 1260, St. Bonaventure drew up an official list of the provinces till then founded in the Order, in which, apparently observing the order of their foundation, he places among those on this side of the Alps the one in France first and the one in England second (See *Annales Minorum*, an. 1260, num. 14). This seems to show, as Parkinson points out (ibidem, p. 7), that the Order had a province in England before 1221, since that year others were erected. Furthermore, in Glassberger's *Chronica* (*Analecta Franciscana*, Vol. II), we read on page 28: "At the general chapter which was held that same year (1223) at St. Mary of Porziuncola, Fr. Caesarius was relieved of his office as minister (provincial of Germany), which he had held for two years, and Fr. Albert of Pisa, *who had just returned from England,* was appointed in his stead." (See also Parkinson, ibidem, pp. 11, 65.) Finally, we find that in two instances Eccleston apparently contradicts his statement as to the arrival of the first friars in England. Regarding Fr. Lawrence of Beauvais, one of the companions of Blessed Agnellus, he relates the following (Analecta *Franciscana*, Vol. I, p. 219): "He in the beginning (of the province) labored unceasingly according to the Rule; and having later returned to Blessed Francis, he merited frequently to see him and to be consoled by his conversations; finally, the holy Father most freely gave him his tunic, and

Canterbury, about ten miles northwest, and knocked on the portals of the Benedictine priory of the Holy Trinity. The monks had probably been apprised of their coming, since the friars found no difficulty in identifying themselves and receiving food and lodging.

Leaving his brethren at the priory, Fr. Agnellus went to the king and, as was required at the time, presented the credentials drawn up and signed by the Pope.[5] Henry III had already heard of St. Francis and of the holy life he and his followers were leading. Hence he received the provincial with every mark of esteem and readily permitted the friars to settle in Canterbury. Thanking the Benedictines for their kindness, the Franciscans

---

having delighted him with his sweetest blessing sent him back to England." Now, St. Francis died on October 3, 1226. Hence, if Fr. Lawrence came to England in 1224, then all that is told of him must have taken place within the brief space of two years. Again, Eccleston concludes the second chapter of his narrative with the words: "It is worthy of note that in the second year of the administration of Fr. Peter (of Tewkesbury), the fifth minister of England, namely *in the thirty-second year since the arrival of the brethren in England,* there were in the English province 1,242 friars living in 49 places." Although the old chroniclers do not give the years of Fr. Peter's administration, Father Cuthbert *(The Friars and how they came to England,* p. 141) assumes that the year suggested in Eccleston's note is 1251. If this is correct, then it is clear that the first Franciscans did not arrive in England in 1224.

[5] The credentials which St. Francis obtained from the Pope read: "Honorius, Bishop, Servant of the servants of God, to Archbishops, Abbots, Deans, Archdeacons, and other prelates of church—Whereas Our beloved sons, Brother Francis and his companions of the life and institute of Friars Minor, despising the vanities of the world, have made choice of a way of life deservedly approved by the Roman Church, and sowing the seeds of the word of God, are traveling after the example of the Apostles through divers nations: We entreat you all, and exhort you in the Lord and command you, by the Apostolic letters addressed to you, that, whensoever members of said institute bearing these presents shall think fit to come to you, you receive them as Catholics and true believers; and that, for the honor of God and the respect you owe to Us, you show them favor and courtesy. Given at Rome on the third day of the ides of June, in the third year of Our Pontificate."—*Annales Minorum,* Vol. I, an. 1219, num. 28.

Introductory

took up their temporary abode in the Poor Priests' Hospice, where they remained till the following September.

In that month, the Archbishop of Canterbury, Cardinal Stephen Langton, who ever after proved a devoted friend and protector of the friars, raised the provincial to the dignity of the priesthood and conferred subdeaconship on Fr. Richard of Devonshire. Soon after these ordinations, Blessed Agnellus commissioned Fr. Richard of Ingworth and Fr. Richard of Devonshire with two lay brothers, FF. Henry and Melioratus, to establish houses in London and Oxford, while he with the four remaining friars remained at Canterbury, in order to begin the erection of the first friary on English soil.[6] Alexander, the master of the Poor Priests' Hospice, had presented them with a plot of ground and urged the citizens to contribute toward the erection of a house for them. His appeal was not in vain, and soon a neat little friary was ready to receive the sons of St. Francis. From Antony Wood, the Oxford antiquary, we learn that the friars held this place in the name of the Canterbury Corporation, since their Rule forbade them to possess temporalities. In this house, which was later dedicated to St. Francis, the friars lived for almost fifty years, laboring for the spiritual welfare of their generous benefactors and educating their boys in the adjoining school. In 1270, John Diggs, a civil official of Canterbury, had the friars take up their abode on Bennewith, an island in the double channel of the river Stour. It was this friary which late in the fifteenth century was given to the reformed members of the province, and which they inhabited till the time of its suppression under Henry VIII.

When Fr. Richard with his three companions arrived in London, the people vied with one another in giving them a hearty reception. After spending a fortnight with the

---

[6] Our chief sources of information regarding the erection of the first friaries are Eccleston and Parkinson.

Dominicans at Holborn,[7] the Franciscans went to Cornhill, where John Travers, Sheriff of London, had procured and fitted out a house for their use. So greatly were the citizens edified at the charming simplicity and self-denial of the friars, that they soon had a more spacious and comfortable home to offer them. John Irwin, a prosperous merchant of the city and afterwards a lay brother of the Order, presented them with a tract of land in the Shambles of St. Nicholas, a place where the poor and destitute were especially numerous. Here in the space of five years, through the charity of the people and the city officials, a church and a friary were erected.

Leaving the two lay brothers in London, Fr. Richard of Ingworth and Fr. Richard of Devonshire, about the feast of All Saints of the same year, 1220, set out for Oxford, where, at the time, King Henry was holding court. Being strangers in the country, they lost their way. Night was coming on, and they knew not where to turn for lodging. Finally, they came to a manor house that belonged to the Benedictine Abbey of Abbington. They knocked at the neighboring priory, and the porter, though astonished at their strange dress and strange story, was civil enough to admit them. But the prior, from a rather unworthy motive, treated the poor friars harshly and turned them out into the night. They had not gone far, when one of the monks, taking pity on them, had them called back, set refreshments before them, and led them to a hayloft, where they might rest their weary bones. That night, the good monk had a dreadful dream. He saw how Christ sitting in judgment commanded the inhospitable prior and monks of Abbington to be strangled, and how he himself found rescue in the fond embrace of St. Francis. On awaking, he hastened to the prior and found him struggling with death. Now he related his dream to the assembled brethren. All were filled with fear, especially when they went to the barn and found that the friars had gone.

---

[7] It is probable that the Dominicans had come to England in 1219. See Parkinson, p. 16.

Some time later, both the prior and the abbot of Abbington joined the ranks of St. Francis.[8]

After spending a week with the Dominicans at Oxford, they answered the summons of Richard Miller, a wealthy citizen, who offered them a little house situated near the parish church of St. Ebbe. During the ensuing Christmas season, Blessed Agnellus visited Oxford and appointed Fr. William of Esseby guardian. In the following summer, the friary was enlarged. It is said that the king himself broke ground for the new building, and that men of high standing in the realm, not only advanced the work by generous alms, but also lent manual assistance, carrying stones and mortar to the masons. The king also ordered that the friary be built as near as possible to the royal palace, that he might the more easily communicate with the friars. In this convent, which grew in dimensions as years went on, the sons of St. Francis dwelt till 1539, when it was demolished by order of Henry VIII. For three centuries, the clerics of the Order were sent there to study and to attend the famous university of Oxford, so that we may justly term this friary the nursery of Franciscan learning and the most famous convent in the English province.

Thus, before the end of the year 1220, the Franciscans had established themselves at Canterbury, London, and Oxford. Meanwhile, as is very probable, other friars, hearing of the cordial reception accorded Blessed Agnellus and his companions, took heart and set out for England.[9] Among these were Fr. Albert of Pisa, brother of Blessed Agnellus, Fr. Henry of Pisa and FF. Peter and Thomas, both of Spanish birth. With their arrival, the provincial was able to found new houses. Accordingly, FF. Richard of Ingworth and Richard of Devonshire went to Northampton and obtained lodging in a

---

[8] This incident is related by Antony Wood. See Parkinson, p. 14.

[9] Parkinson, p. 11. The fact, as the author observes, may explain the divergency of opinion among historians regarding the date when the first Franciscans arrived in England.

hospital in the parish of St. Giles, until a friary was ready to receive them. The first guardian of this foundation was Fr. Peter the Spaniard. Not long after, the Franciscans settled in Cambridge. For a time they lived in an old synagogue that adjoined the city prison. But finding the noisy surroundings an obstacle to the proper discharge of their religious exercises, they purchased with the ten marks sent them by the king a plot of ground near by, on which the people erected for them a little oratory "as a carpenter may build in a day." Fr. Thomas of Spain became the first guardian of this place.

The next twenty-five years saw Franciscan friaries spring up in all parts of England. From Eccleston we learn that in the second year of the provincialship of Fr. Peter Tewkesbury, probably 1251, they were 49 in number. At the general chapter, in 1260, the English Province was registered as comprising seven custodies.[10] At the end of the next century, Fr. Bartholomew of Pisa, in his celebrated *Liber Conformitatum*,[11] enumerated these same seven custodies, adding the names of the friaries which at the time amounted to 60. The names of the custodies with their respective friaries are as follows:

1. *London*, nine friaries; viz., London, Canterbury, Winchelsea, Southampton, Ware, Lewes, Chichester, Salisbury, Winchester;
2. *York*, seven friaries; viz., York, Doncaster, Lincoln, Boston, Beverley, Scarborough, Grimsby;
3. *Cambridge*, nine friaries; viz., Cambridge, Norwich, Colchester, Bury St. Edmunds, Dunwich, Walsingham, Yarmouth, Ipswich, Lynn;
4. *Bristol*, nine friaries; viz., Bristol, Gloucester,

---

[10] *Annales Minorum*, Vol. II, an. 1260, num. 14.

[11] *Analecta Franciscana*, Vol. IV, pp. 545 seq. In his *Annales Minorum* (Vol. IV, an. 1400, num. 13), Wadding places side by side three lists of English friaries as he found them in three ancient codices. While the three codices have 7 custodies, but two have 60 friaries, the third registering only 58.

Introductory

Bridgewater, Hereford, Exeter, Carmarthen, Bodmin, Dorchester, Cardiff;

5. *Oxford*, eight friaries; viz., Oxford, Reading, Bedford, Stamford, Nottingham, Northampton, Leicester, Grantham;
6. *Newcastle*, nine friaries; viz., Newcastle, Dundee, Dumfries, Haddington, Carlisle, Hartlepool, Berwick, Roxburgh, Richmond;
7. *Worcester*, nine friaries; viz., Worcester, Preston, Broughton,[12] Shrewsbury, Coventry, Chester, Hereford,[13] Hamely,[14] Stafford.

In the following towns, friaries were erected probably in the course of the fifteenth century;[15] at least they are not on the lists drawn up by Bartholomew of Pisa and by Wadding:

Anglesey (Llanfaes near Beaumaris) in Wales,
Aylesbury in Buckinghamshire,
Brougham in Westmoreland,
Greenwich in Kent,
Ludlow in Shropshire,
Maidstone in Kent,
Newwark in Nottinghamshire,
Penrith in Cumberland,
Plymouth in Devonshire,
Pontefract in Yorkshire,
Stoke in Somersetshire,
Warrington in Lancashire,

---

[12] Here Parkinson places Bridgenorth.
[13] Parkinson says Litchfield.
[14] Lancaster, according to Parkinson.
[15] See Parkinson, Part II, pp. 37 seq.

Becmachen on the Isle of Man.[16]

If the historian of to-day finds it difficult to reconcile contradictory statements as to the religious houses that constituted the English Province, he will try in vain to determine the number of friars that belonged to the province. Among the first to join it were, according to Eccleston, FF. Solomon, William of London, Joyce of Cornhill, John, and Philip; then certain Masters of the university as Walter de Burgh, Richard the Norman, Vincent of Coventry, Adam de Marisco; and finally two Benedictines and four knights.[17] How rapidly the province increased in membership, may be judged from the fact that thirty-two years after the arrival of the first Franciscans, it numbered 1,242 friars.[18] To some extent, the number of friaries existing in 1260 permits us to form an estimate of the number of religious who inhabited them. Professor Little reckons that shortly before the Black Death, the English Province numbered some 2,000 friars.[19] But their ranks were greatly thinned, when the dreadful plague visited the country. This fact is confirmed by Gasquet, when he writes, "Of the Franciscans at Winchester and Southampton, only three clerics could be presented for ordination in 1347 and 1348. And before the death of the Bishop which occurred in 1359, only two more were presented."[20]

It was, no doubt, this marvelous growth of the province that induced Matthew Paris, who died in 1259, to write regarding the friars, "All England was soon filled and replenished with these men, and not only the larger towns and cities, but the

---

[16] This last friary is mentioned by Thaddeus, *The Franciscans in England*, p. 16, who adds, on the authority of Tanner and Dugdale, that it was founded in 1373.

[17] Eccleston in *Analecta Franciscana*, Vol. I, pp. 221 seq.

[18] Ibidem.

[19] Little, *Studies in English Franciscan History*, p.71

[20] Gasquet, *Black Death*, p. 132.

Introductory

very villages and hamlets frequented by them."[21] Parkinson says that "their exemplary lives and disinterested comportment gained so upon all ranks of people, that their Order increased to an almost incredible number of friars, and their convents were built and enlarged in due proportion."[22] The same historian brings the names of about 350 English Franciscans who, during the three centuries before the so-called Reformation, distinguished themselves either by their sanctity or by their activity and influence as provincials, preachers, bishops, legates, or as lecturers and doctors at Oxford, Cambridge, and Paris. Casually, he mentions groups of friars; for instance, when he says under the year 1220 that "many Englishmen petitioned to be admitted into the Order," and again, on the authority of Harpsfield, remarks that "many of the Benedictine monks, of the Augustinian friars, nay and of the very Carthusians petitioned and were admitted into the Order of St. Francis."[23] Finally, it is worthy of special notice that, excepting the pioneers of the province, nothing at all is recounted regarding the lay brothers whose secluded life did not bring them before the public and into the annals of the province. From all this it may justly be inferred that the English Franciscans were very numerous, and that Brewer has reason to call the expansion of the province "an instance of religious organization and propagandism unexampled in the annals of the world."[24]

The early Franciscans in England were men of sterling piety and of untiring zeal for the spiritual and temporal welfare of the people. Complete detachment from earthly comforts combined with a cheerful and winning disposition won for them the esteem and confidence of all classes. In selecting their

---

[21] See Parkinson, p. 30.

[22] Ibidem, p. 17.

[23] Ibidem, p. 18.

[24] *Monumenta Franciscana*, Vol. I, Preface, p. XLI.

field of labor, the friars made no distinction between rich and poor, high and low, so that serf and outcast vied with king and noble in welcoming them in their midst and in providing them with the necessaries of life. At the ordination of Fr. Solomon, as Eccleston relates, the archdeacon called upon him with the words, "Brother Solomon, of the Order of the Apostles, may step forth," thereby unwittingly forecasting the future activity of the province.[25] For, as history shows, in their private life and in their exterior labors, the sons of St. Francis in England were true apostles sent to instruct and confirm the people in their faith and to imbue them with the true spirit of Christ. By word and example they showed the masses how to love God and their immortal soul above all things, how to submit to lawful authority in Church and State, how to foster love and harmony among themselves, how to forgive injuries, how to sympathize with sufferers, in a word, how to realize in their daily transactions those ideals of Christian perfection that have the promise of eternal life.

From the scanty records that escaped the vandalism of the sixteenth century, it is clear that the English Franciscans were ardent adherents of Lady Poverty. Penniless they came to England and penniless they lived and labored there. Their first friaries, erected almost without exception in the poorest and meanest quarters of the cities, were little better than hovels. "In all instances," Brewer maintains, "the poverty of their buildings corresponded with those of the surrounding district: their living and lodging no better than the poorest among whom they settle."[26] But even these humble dwellings the friars refused to possess as their own, declaring that they held them in the name of corporations. Likewise, in the beginning at least, they fairly rejected all lands and revenues, and depended for their subsistence on the liberality of the people whom they served. If it is certain that in after years wealthy benefactors

---

[25] Eccleston in *Analecta Franciscana*, Vol. I. p. 222.

[26] *Monumenta Franciscana,* Vol. I, Preface, p. XIX.

bequeathed landed property and annual incomes to them, it is equally certain that these were not welcomed, must less sought for, by the friars and were received by them only as alms to which they should have no legal claim.

Many interesting and edifying anecdotes are related, showing how the friars loved and practiced the vow of poverty. In London, for instance, the partitions of their original friary were filled out with dried grass. Before settling in Oxford, Blessed Agnellus gave orders that the walls of the infirmary were not to exceed a man's height; neither did this friary have a guest room until the time of Fr. Albert of Pisa, who was provincial in 1223. At Shrewsbury, Fr. William Nottingham, the fourth provincial, commanded that the stone walls in the dormitory be removed and mud walls put in their stead. The friars at Cambridge did not even have mantles to shield themselves against the cold. At another place, Fr. Solomon was, on one occasion, "so starved with cold that he believed himself nigh unto death; and the brethren having not wherewith to warm him, holy charity suggested to them a remedy; for all the brethren gathered together and huddled about him."[27]

This extreme poverty and lack of every comfort did not make the friars sullen and inaccessible. On the contrary, as they were poor and unassuming in their habits, so they were jovial and winning in their dealings with others. Their very poverty often proved a source of merriment and geniality. Thus Eccleston tells us how one evening, as was customary on days of fast, the brethren were gathered around the kitchen fire to drink of the beverage which, most probably, had been sent them by some benefactor. But the amount was not sufficient for all, so that "he esteemed himself fortunate who could in a friendly way seize the cup from another." At another time it happened that two brethren came to one of the friaries on a visit. Having no refreshments to place before them, the guardian procured a measure of ale on credit. Now, when the

---

[27] Eccleston in *Analecta Franciscana,* Vol. I, passim.

jug was passed around, the members of the community indeed put it to their lips, so as not to embarrass their guests; but they did not drink of its contents, because they feared there was not enough for all. At Oxford, the young friars had to be severely reprimanded for laughing out of season.[28] And Fr. Peter of Tewkesbury once told a Friar Preacher that he thought bodily health depended on three things; viz., food, sleep, and fun.[29]

A remarkable feature of the development of the province is the fact that so many persons of exalted station in the English realm were instrumental in erecting the friaries.[30] Henry III proved a constant friend and benefactor of the Franciscans; and it was in great part owing to his long reign that they gained so firm a footing and made such rapid progress on English soil. At least six of the first friaries were founded either entirely or partly by him. In this work he was seconded especially by Cardinal Stephen Langton, Archbishop of Canterbury, and by Dr. Henry Langton, the Cardinal's brother. The chief founder of the house at Worcester was the Earl of Warwick; while the one at Preston owed its founding to Edward of Lancaster, the brother of Henry III. The Bishop of Litchfield invited the friars to his episcopal city and had a house built for them. Similarly, at Salisbury, it was the bishop who erected the Franciscan friary on the site presented for that purpose by the king. About 1233, the Countess of Leicester set up a convent for them at Ware. Edward I, in the third year of his reign, built a spacious friary at Cambridge, and, in 1288, another at Libourne in Aquitaine, France. Here we may also mention that during the Hundred Years War between England and France, the English Franciscans had several houses both in France and in Scotland. The one at Bordeaux, for instance, was built by Edward III. Queen Margaret, consort of Edward I, caused the old church in

---

[28] Ibidem, passim.

[29] Cuthbert, *The Friars and how they came to England*, p. 236, from a marginal note in the Cottonian MMS. edition of Eccleston.

[30] The following facts are taken principally from Parkinson.

London, which had been erected about a century before by the lord mayor, to be torn down and replaced by a new one, she herself contributing 2,000 marks. At York and Lincoln, Henry Lacy, Earl of Lincoln, together with his chaplain was their principal benefactor, while at Scarborough and Colchester it was again the king, Edward II, who gave freely toward their support. His son, Edward III, founded or endowed the four houses at Walsingham, Berwick, Greenwich and Maidstone. About the same time, through the munificence of Edward, the Black Prince, a friary was founded at Coventry.

We have already mentioned that the Franciscans had scarcely settled in England when men from every station in life asked to be admitted into their ranks. It is surprising, indeed, how many in the course of time exchanged their wealth and worldly distinction for the poor and lowly living of the friar.[31] Before their entrance into the Order, Fr. William had been in the service of the Lord Justiciary of England; Fr. Zarmestre, a distinguished knight; Fr. Matthew Gayton, a wealthy and influential esquire. With Fr. Vincent of Coventry came his brother Henry and later William of York, both eminent doctors of the university. In 1230, Robert of Hendred, abbot of the Benedictine monastery at Abbington, gave up his costly raiment for the humble garb of St. Francis. His example attracted John of Reading, abbot of the celebrated monastery of Canons Regular at Osney, near Oxford. In 1239, Ralph of Maidstone followed in the footsteps of these two prelates and, after resigning his episcopal see of Hereford, joined the Order and led a retired life in the friary at Gloucester. Many doctors and professors of Oxford and Cambridge took the habit during the first half of the fourteenth century. Among them Parkinson mentions John Winchelsey, Reginald Lambourne, John Lisle, John Waler, Oliver Stanwey. In 1325, Lord Robert Fitzwater entered the Order; in 1343, Lord Baron Lisle; and in 1347, Sir Robert Nigram, a famous knight. Finally, in 1386, William

---

[31] What follows is likewise based chiefly on Parkinson.

Scharshille, and in 1426, a certain Clopton, who had both held the office of Lord Chief Justice of England, renounced the honor and preferments of the world and became followers of the Poor Man of Assisi.

The activity and influence of the English Franciscans during the pre-Reformation period fills one of the brightest pages of the history of the Order. About the year 1228, Robert Grosseteste, Bishop of Lincoln, wrote to Pope Gregory IX:

> Your Holiness may be sure that inestimable blessings are reaching our people through the said (Franciscan) friars. For they illuminate our whole land with the bright light of their preaching and teaching. Their saintly manner of living strongly incites to contempt of the world and voluntary poverty, to preserving humility even amid dignity and power, to maintaining complete submission toward prelates and toward the Head of the Church, to patience amid tribulation, to self-denial amid riches, and, in a word, to the exercises of every virtue. Oh, if your Holiness could see with what devotion and humility the people run to hear from them the word of life, to confess their sins, to be instructed in the rules of living, and how the clergy and the regulars have improved by imitating them, you would indeed say that the light has risen unto them that sit in the region of the shadow of death! The zeal of your Holiness will therefore provide that, so great a light having been extinguished or darkened, which the true light may avert, the ancient darkness of error and sin, already greatly dispelled by the rays of their light, may not overshadow and envelop the land which before others is especially dear to you.[32]

History tells us how during the succeeding centuries the friars merited this enviable eulogy.

When the Franciscans began to live and labor in England, serious and critical problems confronted the State as well as the Church. The crusades had introduced new ideas on society and politics, which gradually undermined the feudal system of the Middle Ages. Especially among the country folk, till then happy

---

[32] Felder, *Studien im Franziskanerorden*, p. 271.

and prosperous under the benign influence of the monastic institutions, a spirit of independence and discontent was plainly visible. In the towns whither they fled, their spiritual needs could not be sufficiently provided for by the limited number of secular clergy, while their own inexperience in matters commercial and industrial soon put them at the mercy of the wealthy and selfish merchant class. Add to this the constant clashes between popular rights and royal pretensions, and it is easy to understand how in the towns the lower classes soon fell a prey to poverty, ignorance, and vice, and even began to drift away from the Church.

Here then the sons of St. Francis found an extensive field for action. From their humble friaries, erected in the poorest and meanest districts of the populous towns, they went forth like angels of peace to proclaim their message of love and penance to all, and thus in time bridged over the gulf that lay between the upper and the lower classes. We are told that, on Sundays and holydays, they would assist the neighboring parish priests in administering the sacraments, preaching the word of God, and catechizing the children. At other times, they would preach on the open street, where crowds eagerly drank in their words of instruction and consolation. The outcasts of society, who in the suburbs were leading a life of spiritual desolation and bodily squalor, seem to have had a special claim on their loving solicitude. By word and example they showed the neglected poor how to serve God even in poverty and distress, taught the wealthy the proper use of temporal goods, and exhorted all to live in peace and harmony and in loyal submission to rightful authority. "The effect of such men upon the neglected masses of the population may easily be imagined. ... Lessons of patience and endurance fell with greater persuasion and tenderness from lips of men who were living and voluntary examples of what they taught."[33] If in later years, especially at the outbreak of the Protestant Revolution the

---

[33] *Monumenta Franciscana*, Vol. I, Preface, p. XXVIII.

English nation at large was devoted to the Holy See, it must be ascribed in great part to the sons of St. Francis, who were ever the fearless preachers and defenders of papal supremacy.

As a means of popular instruction and edification, the mystery and miracle plays were earnestly fostered by the friars. "In organizing and acting miracle plays," Howlett writes, "the Franciscan friars took a decided lead, and so far was it reckoned in late times one of the recognized callings of the Order that the corporation registers of York tell us that in 1426 William Melton, of the Order of Friars Minor, 'Professor of Holy Pageantry and a most famous preacher of the Word of God,' made arrangements respecting the Corpus Christi play in that city, evidently as manager of the performance."[34] The celebrated Coventry cycle of forty-eight plays is entirely their work. On appointed days, large crowds would gather at Coventry and in the neighboring towns to witness these representations of the Old and New Testament. "These pageants," Dugdale informs us, "were sacred representations wherein were exhibited the histories of the Old and New Testaments, the persons therein mentioned being brought upon the stage, and whom the poet, according to his fancy, introduced talking to one another in old English metre, composed by the Friars Minor, and acted by their direction."[35]

Although information is very meager regarding their activity during the Black Death, which devastated Europe in the first half of the fourteenth century, we may form an estimate, if we call to mind that their friaries stood in the neglected and unhealthy districts where the plague naturally raged most fiercely. What Howlett asserts regarding the Franciscan Order in general is also true of its members in England. "It is not disputed," he writes, "that in the awful visitations of the Black Death in the fourteenth century, the Franciscan Friars in different parts of Europe perished literally

---

[34] Ibidem, Vol. II, Preface, p. XXVIII.

[35] See *Franciscan Annals* (Pantasaph, England), Vol. XL, p. 168.

Introductory

by the thousands through their devoted attentions to the sick and dying."[36] That many of the English Province fell victims to their charitable ministrations may be also gathered from the fact that, as we have stated above, so few clerics could be presented for ordinations in the years immediately following the dreadful visitation.

In their zeal for the welfare of the people, the friars knew no distinction of creed or nationality. A striking instance of this we find toward the end of the thirteenth century. Growing complaints against the Jews, made especially by the merchant class, caused Edward I to take severe measures against them. When the persecution was at its height and a general massacre had been decreed, the Franciscans intervened and, by promising to work for the conversion of the Jews, succeeded in obtaining from the king a revocation of the decree. "For," as Parkinson explains, "the Franciscans had generally showed themselves so free from all mercenary regards, that they seemed to have no other interest in this world, besides working out their own salvation and laboring to contribute to that of their neighbor." In later years, Fr. Nicholas de Lyra, himself of Jewish extraction, worked zealously for the conversion of Jews in England. By his writings and sermons, it is said, he brought six thousand of his people to the fold of Christ.[37]

This heroic and disinterested zeal for the social uplifting of the lower and middle classes could not escape the notice of the wealthy and powerful. The activity of the English friars in State and Church affairs is perhaps unexampled in the history of the Order. Hardly were they settled in Canterbury, when Henry III appointed Bl. Agnellus of Pisa to his Privy Council. In 1232, when Richard, the Earl Marshal, was heading a rebellion of the barons against the king, this friar as the king's plenipotentiary treated with the powerful Earl and persuaded him to accept the king's proposals of peace and to put an end to the bloody

---

[36] *Monumenta Franciscana*, Vol. II, Preface, p. XXXIV.

[37] Parkinson, pp. 99, 161.

strife.[38] Fr. Adam de Marisco was on intimate terms with Simon of Montfort and with Robert Grosseteste, Bishop of Lincoln. His letters show what an influence he had on the efforts of these two men for the ecclesiastical and political welfare of the country.[39] It is not improbable that in Franciscan circles those principles of civil liberty first were clearly formulated which had already been laid down in the celebrated Magna Charta, and which in time led to the constitutional monarchy of England.[40] The letters show also how their author encouraged and counseled the Bishop of Lincoln in reforming the clergy of his large diocese. In 1241, after a meeting of the English bishops at Oxford, Franciscan and Dominican friars were sent to France, in order to rouse the people against Emperor Frederic II, and to remonstrate with him for ill-treating the Pope.[41] "Many other Franciscans," says Parkinson, "were employed in the several expeditions of the English to the holy wars; they being esteemed the most proper persons for that work, both because they were famous preachers and inured to mortifications and hardships, and likewise disengaged from any interest of this world."[42] Thus, for instance, Prince Edward, son of Henry III, selected Fr. Robert Turneham to accompany him on a crusade against the Turks and to serve as chaplain of the army he had fitted out for the expedition.[43]

About the year 1286, Edward I appointed Fr. John of Stamford, who had been chosen for the archbishopric of Dublin, Lord Lieutenant of Ireland, and later he sent him as ambassador

---

[38] Ibidem, pp. 9, 34.

[39] Brewer published these letters in *Monumenta Franciscana* as he found them in the Cottonian MMS. They are of historical interest and importance, since they throw abundant light on the activity and influence of the early English Franciscans.

[40] Holzapfel, *Geschichte des Franziskanerordens*, p. 234

[41] Gasquet, *Henry III and the Church*, p. 200.

[42] Parkinson, p. 98.

[43] Ibidem, p. 87.

to the imperial court. This same king placed such confidence in the loyalty and discretion of Fr. William of Gaynesborough, that in 1295 he sent him together with Fr. Hugh of Manchester to the King of France, in order to settle some disagreement concerning English territory in Aquitaine. Later, Fr. William, who had meanwhile become Bishop of Worcester, was again employed by Edward in negotiating the marriage between the Black Prince, the heir of the English throne, and Isabel, the daughter of Philip the Fair of France.[44] Repeatedly, in the course of Parkinson's narrative, we find the names of Franciscans whom the kings of England selected as their confessors and advisers.

After the civil war, in the beginning of the fifteenth century, a great disaster befell the friars. We mention this incident only to show how little they cared for royal favors when truth and justice came in question. When it was rumored that Richard II, who had been dethroned and murdered, was still among the living and ready to reclaim his throne, the friars credited the report and openly espoused his cause. This so exasperated the usurper Henry IV of Lancaster, that he had several of their number cast into prison. When Fr. Richard, guardian of Leicester, was asked by an official what he would do if the dead king were really alive, he answered that he would fight for him till death. This bold reply cost him his life. Subsequently, eleven more friars were imprisoned and executed for the same reason. After matters had cleared up, however, and Henry IV realized that the Franciscans had acted in good faith and from the start had been willing to acknowledge him their king provided Richard were dead, he reinstated them in their former favor and gave orders that they should be no longer molested for the stand they had taken.[45]

In 1235, and again in 1240, the provincial of the English Franciscans received a letter from the Pope urging the friars to

---

[44] Ibidem, pp. 98, 125.

[45] Ibidem, p. 185.

use their influence in behalf of the crusades; and in 1254, Pope Innocent IV appointed two of their number to collect subsidies for the Holy Land.[46] In fact, the Popes not less than the kings repeatedly employed them in this noble cause. Again, how high they stood in the estimation of Church and of State dignitaries, we see from the fact that so large a number were vested with episcopal dignities in England, Ireland, Scotland, Wales, and Italy. Parkinson brings the names of at least thirty-five friars who became bishops. Of these, the most distinguished for sanctity, learning, and influence was Fr. John Peckham, whom Pope Nicholas III appointed Archbishop of Canterbury and Primate of England. In 1246, Fr. John Anglicus became papal legate in England with full powers over all prelates of the realm. A few years later, this same office was held by Fr. John of Kent and by Fr. Adam de Marisco. In 1441, the Holy See granted Henry VI permission to have Franciscans reside constantly at court and to send them to foreign rulers on important State affairs. During the Exile of the Papacy, Fr. Thomas Travesham and Fr. Walter Cotton, two men of exceptional learning, were summoned to Avignon by Benedict XII and appointed papal plenipotentiaries.[47]

In their loyalty to the Church and their zeal for the propagation and preservation of the faith in England, the Franciscans did not entirely forget the foreign missions. As early as 1238, Fr. Adam of Exeter was sent by Pope Gregory IX to preach the gospel among the Saracens; but he died before reaching his destination. In 1337, a certain Fr. William, likewise of the English Province, suffered cruel martyrdom for the faith at the hands of the Saracens, at Salmastre in Persia. Finally, in 1392, Fr. Roger of England, engaged on the missions among the Tatars in Asia, was sent by the Vicar Apostolic to the Pope to

---

[46] *Annales Minorum,* Vol. I, an. 1235, num. 27; an. 1240, num. 20; Vol. II. an. 1254, num. 42.

[47] Parkinson, pp. 67, 72, 199, 154, 155.

solicit more missionaries.[48]

When John Wyclif was perverting England by his heretical teaching, the Franciscans of Oxford were among the first to oppose him. Learned theologians assembled at Oxford in 1381, and Fr. John Tyssington, a leading doctor of the university, was foremost in condemning Wyclif's doctrine regarding the Blessed Eucharist. The following year, on May 18, an ecclesiastical court was held at Blackfriars in London. Here again five Franciscan doctors of Oxford and Cambridge were among the signers of the twenty-four conclusions against the heretic. After the death of Wyclif, Thomas Arundel, Archbishop of Canterbury, held a convocation at St. Paul's in London, and publicly condemned the eighteen heretical propositions which Fr. William Woodford had drawn up from Wyclif's famous *Trialogue*.

Equally zealous in this affair was Fr. Thomas Wolward. Finally, when a second synod was held at St. Paul's, in 1408, to check the spread of the heresy, Fr. William Butler was chosen to preach before the distinguished assembly.[49]

Volumes could be written on what the English Franciscans achieved in the field of letters. We must confine ourselves to a few facts and names. "The English nation has given to the Franciscan Order a greater number of eminently learned men than all the other nations taken together. Yes, if we consider only the leaders of the Minorite schools, they all with the exception of St. Bonaventure belong to England."[50] Beginning with Oxford, almost all the friaries erected before 1254 had their school. In that year, the province numbered 33 or 34 lecturers, a fact which, as Felder points out, seems to imply that most of the friaries at the time were in need of them. Wood's incomplete catalog registers 67 Franciscans who had been public professors at Oxford before 1350; and according to

---

[48] Ibidem, pp. 41, 154, 180.

[49] Ibidem, pp. 178, 181, 182, 183, 191.

[50] Felder, p. 316.

another catalog, 72 had been similarly engaged at Cambridge before the middle of the fifteenth century.[51] All these were doctors of divinity, while many of them exerted immense influence as regents and chancellors of the two universities. Again, English Franciscans were summoned to teach at foreign seats of learning. "Lyons, Paris and Cologne," writes Brewer, "were indebted for their first professors to the English Franciscans at Oxford. Repeated applications were made from Ireland, Denmark, France, and Germany for English friars."[52]

Under their influence, theology and philosophy as well as the liberal arts were, not only greatly promoted, but also turned to practical account. Parkinson remarks that many English friars wrote commentaries on Sacred Scripture. And Brewer finds it remarkable "that the friars, the most ardent upholders of scholastic theology, are precisely the men who constitute the most popular preachers of the age." The friars were the first to treat medicine and physics empirically; they gave a new impulse to higher mathematics; while by their zeal for the classics, they paved the way for the Christian Humanism of the subsequent Renaissance period.[53] English friars were also instrumental in founding Baliol College at Oxford, Pembroke College at Cambridge, and a lecture hall at Paris. It was probably through their efforts that the art of printing was introduced at Oxford as early as 1463, and that, in 1474, the works of Duns Scotus were printed and published for the first time in England.[54] "In the thirteenth century," says Digby, "the Dominicans and Franciscans surpassed all their predecessors in zeal for writing and collecting books." At an early date, the Franciscans had two libraries at Oxford, one for the brethren and another for the secular professors and students of the

---

[51] Parkinson, pp. 28, 62.

[52] *Monumenta Franciscana*, Vol. I, Preface, p. LXXXI.

[53] Felder, pp. 412 seq.

[54] Parkinson, pp. 77 seq., 205.

university. Many of the volumes had been bequeathed to them by Bishop Grosseteste, while the large number of Greek and Hebrew works had been purchased from the exiled Jews.[55]

Among the English Franciscans who were esteemed as profound and influential scholars, Ven. John Duns Scotus and Fr. Roger Bacon undoubtedly hold the place of honor. The former, known as the Subtle Doctor, is the founder of the Franciscan school of Scholasticism. But he is chiefly revered as the Doctor of Mary. When the question of the Immaculate Conception of the Blessed Virgin was dividing the most eminent theologians of the time, it was he who boldly proclaimed this prerogative of the Mother of God—a doctrine which some 550 years later was solemnly declared a dogma of the Catholic Church. Fr. Roger Bacon is justly styled the father of experimental philosophy. As his numerous writings amply testify, there was literally no field of science that he did not cultivate. In the natural sciences, he was far in advance of his time. At the unveiling of a statue to his memory, five years ago, a speaker declared this distinguished friar to be "one of the most eminent as well as one of the most mysterious men that science has produced." It is related that for some marvelous invention of his, he was accused of witchcraft. The friar readily submitted the case to the ecclesiastical authorities in Rome. Needless to say, he was found innocent of the charges; whereupon the Pope publicly exonerated him, adding that his "only fault was being wiser and more knowing than others of his time."[56] Fr. Haymo of Faversham, at the command of Gregory IX, revised the Roman breviary and missal. Fr. Alexander of Hales, the teacher of St. Bonaventure and of St. Thomas, was the first to systemize Catholic theology. Whatever may be advanced to discredit the name of Fr. William Occham, every historian will agree with Holzapfel in reckoning this friar among the greatest scholars of the Order, on account of the far-

---

[55] Digby, Mores Catholici, Vol. IV, p. 139; Parkinson, p. 59.

[56] Parkinson, p. 111.

reaching influence he exerted on higher learning. The first noteworthy encyclopedia of the Middle Ages, entitled *De Proprietatibus Rerum,* was compiled by Fr. Bartholomew, surnamed Anglicus. It was the standard work down to the sixteenth century and was translated into several languages.[57] Fr. John Somer was probably the first to visit the north pole and to measure the lands there with his astrolabe.[58] One of the most influential advocates for the restoration of Catholic unity in the Church during the Great Western Schism was Fr. Nicholas Fackingham.[59] Of the many Franciscans who, besides those already mentioned, deserve special notice, we select a few; viz., FF. Henry of Oxford, Adam of York, Ralph Rose, John of London, Hugh of Newcastle, John Canon, Adam of Lincoln, Thomas Eccleston, John Hilton, Richard Middleton, John Lathbery, Robert Column, William Goddard, Robert Finningham, John Kynton, and Henry Standish. All these were doctors of divinity and eminent writers on Catholic theology and philosophy.

Such then was the activity of the English Franciscans prior to the Reformation, as widespread and vigorous as it was salutary and providential. "The English Franciscans," Parkinson justly declares, "were no lazy drones, but active good religious men, and spent their time well, to the edification of their neighbor, as well as for their own improvement. Some of them indeed were wholly taken up in contemplation and prayer, but others in study and in teaching, others in preaching and instruction, and assisting the people in both spiritual and corporal works of mercy, others in writing out the labors of their learned brethren and all principally, in the constant exercise of religion and a fervorous tendency towards Christian

---

[57] Holzapfel, pp. 229, 288, 289, 276. Regarding Fr. William Occham, see *Archivum Franciscanum Historicum,* Vol. VI.

[58] See *Franciscan Annals* (Pantasaph, England), Vol. XLIII, pp. 90 seq.

[59] Parkinson, p. 188. See also *Archivum Franciscanum Historicum,* Vol. I, pp. 577-600.

perfection."[60] Cherished by high and by low, they had decked the shrine of St. Francis with the flowers of sanctity and the laurels of learning. Now the time was at hand when they should gather in also the palms of martyrdom and join the glorious ranks of those "who are come out of great tribulation, and have washed their robes, and have made them white in the blood of the Lamb."

---

[60] Parkinson, Preface, p. V.

CHAPTER II
CALM BEFORE THE STORM

Early reign of Henry VIII—Religious conditions in England—Attitude toward papal supremacy—The king, a dutiful child of the Church—The reform movement in the Order of St. Francis—Its bearing on the Province of England—The king well disposed toward the Franciscans.

ELDOM were political and religious conditions more auspicious anywhere than in England when Henry VIII (1509-1547) ascended the throne. During the reign of his father, Henry VII, whose victory over Richard III at Bosworth put an end to the bloody War of the Roses, royal ascendancy gained a firm hold on the minds and hearts of the English. Though taxations had been heavy and frequent, the people at large submitted when they recalled the horrors of the recent war. And now that the first of the Tudors had died leaving the State treasury well filled, they pinned their hopes for brighter days on his youthful successor.

Endowed with rare qualities of mind and body, the prince of eighteen summers fully vindicated their most sanguine hopes. Shortly after his accession, he espoused, with papal dispensation, Catherine of Aragon, the maiden widow of his brother Arthur. This only raised him in the esteem of the people; the popularity of the fair and pious princess was naturally extended to him. What further assured him of popular favor was the fact that he confirmed the general pardon granted by his predecessor, and, not only offered compensation to those who had been wronged during the preceding reign, but ordered the arrest and punishment of those who had been the chief abettors of the late king's rapacity.[1] His military success in France and Scotland likewise augured well for the future. In

---

[1] Lingard, *History of England,* Vol. IV, p. 169.

short, politically his reign promised to be an era of peace at home and of prestige abroad; and as far as religious conditions were concerned, no one ever fancied that within twenty-five years a dreadful upheaval would take place in the realm.

The assertion often made by non-Catholic historians that on the eve of the Reformation religious life in England was at a very low ebb, conflicts with the latest researches; and to say that the religious revolution was but the inevitable outcome and culmination of Lollardism is utterly unwarranted.[2] Long before Henry's rupture with Rome, the heresy of Wyclif had sunk into the grave with the heretic himself. It is true that in the beginning of the sixteenth century there were serious evils in the Church of England that needed curing. Of these the most baneful was undoubtedly the worldly and mercenary spirit that prevailed among the nobility and the higher clergy. Generally speaking, however, historians to-day agree that the lower classes cherished and practiced their faith. Gasquet remarks that "religion on the eve of the Reformation was intimately bound up with the whole life of the people, animating it and penetrating it at every point." This refutes the oft-repeated charge that also the lower clergy, regular as well as secular, were wanting in virtue and zeal and that in consequence they had forfeited the respect and confidence of the people. It was Blessed Thomas More who argued that, if religious conditions among the laity were good, corruption among the clergy could not have been so general.

Unshaken was also the belief of the English nation in the spiritual supremacy of the Pope. Of course, the full import of this doctrine was then not so clearly defined as it is to-day. Repeatedly, disputes arose between the Church and the State, especially regarding ecclesiastical immunities and exemptions. Although it was again principally among the upper classes that loyalty to the Holy See was not what it should have been, certain it is that the nation as such recognized only one

---

[2] See Gasquet, *The Eve of the Reformation*, pp. 184 seq.

supreme head in the Church, namely the Bishop of Rome. The theory of royal supremacy did not emanate from the convictions of the people, but from the pride and covetousness of the crown.[3]

As to the king himself, history assures us that during the first years of his reign he was singularly well disposed toward the Church and humbly submissive to her doctrine and discipline. It is thought that he had been destined for the sacred ministry, but that this plan had to be abandoned on the premature death of his elder brother Arthur. Be this as it may, Henry's thorough training not only in Christian humanism but also in theology under the direction of Cardinal Fisher made him a man of firm religious convictions. Although he was of a gay and chivalrous disposition, delighting in the sports and jousts and other popular amusements of the time, there is nothing on record that points to a base and corrupt heart. When on a hunt, he was wont daily to hear three holy Masses, and on other days often four or five. Every day he assisted at Vespers and Compline in the Queen's chapel. He seems to have fostered a great devotion to the Blessed Virgin, in whose honor, it is said, he told his beads every day. In 1505, and again in 1510, he made a pilgrimage to Our Lady's shrine at Walsingham. Spelman relates that he walked barefoot to this place from Baseham, a distance of three miles, that he presented the shrine with a precious necklace, and that at his own expense he had new windows put in the chapel. It is known, too, that in 1522 he accompanied Emperor Charles V on a pilgrimage to Canterbury, where the two monarchs, having attended high Mass and received Holy Communion, knelt in prayer at the tomb of St. Thomas à Becket.[4]

During the political troubles between Pope Julius II and the King of France, Henry VIII faithfully upheld the rights of the

---

[3] Ibidem, pp. 70 seq.

[4] Du Boys, *Catherine D'Aragon*, pp. 102, 106; Hope, *The First Divorce of Henry VIII*, p. 24; Timbs, *Abbeys ... of England and Wales*, Vol. I, p. 548.

Papacy and openly espoused the cause of the Holy League. When Martin Luther attacked the doctrine of the Church and rebelled against the authority of the Pope, the English king was among the first to raise his voice in solemn protest. In 1522, he wrote his famous *Assertio Septem Sacramentorum* in reply to Luther's heretical tenets. On being warned by Blessed Thomas More that in this work he had unduly emphasized the authority of the Pope as a temporal prince, Henry uttered the remarkable words: "We are so much bounded unto the see of Rome that we can not do too much honor unto it. Whatsoever impediment be to the contrary, we will set forth that authority to the uttermost, for we received from that see our crown imperial."[5] The book was presented to the Pope by the English ambassador in Rome, Dr. John Clarke. In grateful acknowledgment, Leo X issued a Bull in which he bestowed on Henry the honorable title of Defender of the Faith—a title which, strange to say, the English crown carries to the present day. On not less than three different occasions, the Vicar of Christ honored Henry with the golden rose as a mark of special esteem and gratitude for services rendered to the Church.[6] So deep-rooted was his allegiance to the Holy See that even when about to usurp its spiritual supremacy he compelled Cranmer to take the usual oath of obedience to the See of Rome.[7] In fine, whatever his private life may have been, certain it is that during the first years of his reign the Church and its supreme head had a firm hold on the affections of the king as well as of the English nation at large.

---

[5] Thus Blessed Thomas More publicly testified at his trial on being accused of having induced Henry to maintain in his book the authority of the Pope so as thereby "to put a sword in the Pope's hand to fight against" the king. See Roper, *Life of Sir Thomas More, Knt.*, p. 67.

[6] Annually, on the fourth Sunday of Lent, the Holy Father solemnly blesses a golden rose, which he later presents to some person or place of distinction. See *The Catholic Encyclopedia*, Vol. VI, p. 630.

[7] Dodd, *Church History of England*, Vol. I, p. 71.

To enable the reader to understand and appreciate the heroic zeal of the English Franciscans for truth and morality during the subsequent religious upheaval, it will be necessary to insert a brief account of the Observant reform in the Order of St. Francis and of its bearing on the history of the English province. Soon after the death of St. Francis, diversities of opinion and practice arose in the Order regarding the observance of the vow of poverty. While a number of brethren, supported by influential men in and out of the Order, sought to mitigate the severity of the fourth chapter of the Franciscan Rule, others advocated and observed renunciation of corporate as well as private ownership of temporalities. During the fourteenth century, these differences became more pronounced. Those who following Blessed Paul de Trinci labored for the reform of the Order were called Observants; while the others who with papal dispensations held property in common, went by the name of Conventuals.[8] In the next century, the reform movement was greatly furthered by four saintly friars known as the pillars of Observantism; viz., St. Bernardine of Siena, St. John Capistran, St. James della Marca, and Bl. Albert of Sartiano. Through their untiring efforts, the reform spread rapidly over entire Europe, so that by the eve of the Reformation the Franciscans had returned in great numbers to the original observance of the Rule. In the various provinces of the Order, there were about 1,500 Observant houses, in which, to make a rough estimate, some 30,000 friars resided. A definite separation was finally made by Pope Leo X, in 1517, so that henceforth there existed two distinct branches of the Order, the Observants and the Conventuals.[9]

According to Parkinson, it is probable that this Observant movement reached the English province early in the fifteenth

---

[8] Throughout the present narrative, we designate the former by the term Franciscans, the latter by the term Conventuals.

[9] *See Holzapfel*, Geschichte des Franziskanerordens.

century, and it was gradually adopted by most of the friars.[10] We know, for instance, that in 1454, St. John Capistran, then vicar general of the Franciscans, addressed a letter to Henry VI of England, thanking him among other things for his promise to have friaries erected for the brethren of the reform. At the chapters held in Palencia (1470) and at Bruges (1484) England was reckoned a province of the reform. The chapter held at Mechlin (1499) unanimously resolved "that the province of England having now a competent number of convents should hereafter have two votes in all general chapters, after the manner of other reformed provinces." Finally, it is known that already in 1502, the English Conventuals agreed to exchange their religious garb for the poorer and coarser habit of their reformed brethren.

Although the exact number of Franciscan friaries in England can not be ascertained, we know that in 1481 Pope Sixtus IV gave certain English nobles a grant to erect such friaries. Later, Henry VII built three convents for the Franciscans at Greenwich, Newark, and Richmond in Surrey, and caused the Conventuals to cede to them their houses at Canterbury, Newcastle, and Southampton. Parkinson thinks that after 1517, almost all the sons of St. Francis in England had accepted the reform, since after that year he finds no mention of Conventual chapters or provincials.[11] Apparently, the reform movement does not seem to have essentially marred the unity of the province. All the friars in England "were," as Parkinson puts it, "in effect true observers of their Founder's Rule, and made up one community. Furthermore, in 1498, the Franciscans held their chapter at the Grey Friars[12] in London, which was

---

[10] Parkinson, *The Antiquities of the English Franciscans,* pp. 203, 206, 207, 211, 213; *Annales Minorum,* Vol. V, p. 106; Vol. VI, pp. 112, 709; Vol. VII, pp. 176, 407.

[11] Parkinson, pp. 207, 216, 220.

[12] In England, the sons of St. Francis went by this name on account of the color of their habit.

not reckoned one of their houses.[13] And, as will be seen later, at the time of the general suppression of the province, about 1539, by far the greater number of its friaries were found to be strictly in keeping with the original severity of the Rule, depending for their daily subsistence on the charity of the people. "The truth of the thing is," Parkinson assures us, "that few of the Franciscan convents in England enjoyed any rents, and therefore it was easy enough for most of them to join in the reformation (of the Order); as in effect they did, though they continued in their own convents, by reason of the different degrees of their reformation and observance of the Rule of St. Francis." This much then is certain, that on the eve of the religious troubles, the greater number of the English friars were true followers of St. Francis, and together with the Carthusians and Brigittines formed the most zealous and most popular body of religious in England.

It was but natural for Henry VIII, so sincerely devoted to the interest and welfare of the Church, to imitate his immediate predecessors in their friendly attitude toward the Franciscans. "At the beginning of his reign," writes Stone, "he had shown them special favor, had written more than once to the Pope on their behalf, declaring that he had the most deep and devoted affection towards them, and that he found it quite impossible to describe their merits as they deserved. They presented, he said, an ideal of Christian poverty, sincerity, and charity; their lives were devoted to fasting, watching, prayer; and they were occupied in hard toil, by night and day, to win sinners back to God."[14] Their friary and church at Greenwich adjoined the royal palace, where Henry was born, and where he usually resided after his accession to the throne. Here with his saintly consort, Queen Catherine of Aragon, who was a Tertiary of St. Francis, he attended divine services. For another Tertiary, Bl. Thomas More, whose life was so intimately bound up with court affairs,

---

[13] Thaddeus, *The Franciscans in England*, p. 14.

[14] Stone, *Faithful Unto Death*, p. 1, on the authority of Ellis's *Original Letters*.

he entertained the highest regard. For almost ten years, his confessor was Fr. Stephen Baron, who was provincial in 1520, and who wrote a book for the benefit of the king, entitled *On the Government of Princes*.[15] When the Franciscans in Palestine, hard pressed by the Turkish hordes under Selim, were at last compelled to flee to Cyprus, Henry VIII personally wrote to them,[16] assuring them that since his tenderest years he had always revered the sons of St. Francis, and that henceforth he would send them an annual alms of 1,000 scudi for the maintenance of the Holy Places. Again it was a Franciscan, Fr. John Kynton, doctor of divinity at Oxford, whom the king, in 1521, engaged to write a defence of Catholic doctrine against Luther.[17]

---

[15] Mason, *Certamen Seraphicum*, p. 292; Parkinson, p. 222.

[16] For a copy of this letter, dated November 23, 1516, see *Annales Minorum*, Vol. III, p. 53.

[17] Parkinson, p. 222; Dodd, Vol. I, p. 237.

CHAPTER III
FIRST RUMBLINGS OF THE STORM

Henry seeks divorce from Catherine of Aragon—He repudiates her and marries Anne Boleyn—The Franciscans and the king's "secret affair"—Fr. William Peyto publicly rebukes the king and his court—Fr. John Elstow and Dr. Curwin—The two friars before the king—Banished.

It was not political interest but mutual affection and esteem that had joined Henry VIII and Catherine of Aragon in the bonds of wedlock. As years wore on, however, Henry's attitude toward his saintly queen underwent a sad change. Of the various causes that conspired to divert him from the path of duty, the principal one was the loose life at court. Some historians assert that it is doubtful whether he was ever a faithful husband. How far Henry in this respect shared the disgrace of other crowned heads of his time, it would be hard to determine. At all events, his frequent addresses to persons of indifferent morals were sufficient cause for alarm. The queen, no doubt, had her suspicions, but for obvious reasons remained silent; while Cardinal Wolsey, who could and should have warned the heedless king, refrained from doing so on personal as well as on political grounds.[1] Hence, in 1527, when Henry's passion for Anne Boleyn, a lady in the Queen's household, had got the better of him, he openly urged the question of a divorce from Catherine, feigning scruples of conscience regarding the validity of the dispensation he had obtained from Rome to marry her. The case was eventually brought before the Roman court, and the Pope appointed a special commission to examine it. All during the lengthy and complicated proceedings of this

---

[1] Harpsfield and two other contemporary chroniclers even assert that Wolsey and Longland, then confessor to Henry VIII, were the first to raise serious doubts in the king's mind regarding the validity of his marriage with Catherine of Aragon. See Du Boys, *Catherine D'Aragon*, pp. 149 seq.

commission, the king as well as his cringing partisans among the nobility and higher clergy knew fully well that Catherine was his lawful consort, and that his alleged fear of living in illegal wedlock with her was merely a cloak to hide the foulness of his heart.

This became clear when, seeing that the papal commission would ultimately declare against the projected divorce, he anticipated its decision, repudiated Queen Catherine, and secretly married Anne Boleyn. The sacrilegious ceremony took place on January 25, 1533, in the private chapel of the royal palace at Whitehall.[2] It was performed by Rowland Lee, but only after the lying king had assured the chaplain "that he had got a license from the Pope to marry another wife, but to avoid disturbance he wished the ceremony to take place very secretly."[3] On Saturday, May 10, Cranmer, who had just been consecrated Archbishop of Canterbury, cited Queen Catherine before his ecclesiastical court at Dunstable. When she refused to appear, he declared her "contumacious." Whereupon, to the shame and dismay of the English nation, the pliant archbishop publicly declared Henry's marriage with her null and void, and announced and confirmed his secret marriage with Anne Boleyn. The ambitious coquette was then pompously escorted from Greenwich to the Tower for coronation. The attending ceremonies bore the character of a funeral rather than of a public festivity. In a letter dated May 29, 1533, the imperial ambassador Chapuys writes to Charles V, the nephew of Queen Catherine, that the "triumph consisted entirely in the multitude of those who took part in it, but all the people showed themselves so sorry as though it had been a funeral. I am told," he continues, "their indignation grows daily, and that they live

---

[2] That this date is correct is evident from the testimony of Chapuys and of Cranmer. For obvious reasons, an earlier date, November 14, 1532, the day when Henry and Anne sailed from Calais, has been assigned for this sacrilegious ceremony. See Lingard, *History of England*, Vol. V, p. 2; Hope, *The First Divorce of Henry VIII*, p. 296.

[3] Hope, *The First Divorce*... p. 294.

in hope your majesty will interfere. On Saturday, the lady will pass all through London and go to the king's lodging, and on Sunday to Westminster, where the ceremony of coronation will take place."[4]

Henry was not slow to discern that his action against Queen Catherine had roused a spirit of discontent among the lower classes, and that the sons of St. Francis had been foremost and loudest in creating it. Indeed, from the day his "secret affair" became a topic of popular comment, the Franciscans endeavored to prevent what they clearly foresaw would lead to serious consequences. Traveling about the country in the discharge of their sacred duties, they freely and fearlessly acquainted the people with the true state of the question and thus gradually succeeded in molding public opinion against the king's ungodly design.[5] "Unspoilt by prosperity," writes Stone, "their conscience unclouded by self-interest, Henry found them far more difficult to deal with than either the Universities or the monks. They were intimidated by no threats, no promise of preferment led them astray. The most popular preachers were to be found in their ranks, and the king knew that while they were allowed to preach, the people would be told the truth, however much he tried to deceive them."[6] Accordingly, the very men who only a few years before had stood so high in his favor and esteem, were now the object of his scorn and hatred. This he showed openly for the first time in 1532, when he wrote to their minister general, Fr. Paul Pissotus, asking him to depose the provincial Blessed John Forest,[7] probably because he suspected him of having influenced the queen, his penitent, in her recent appeal to Rome. Though this made it clear to the friars that their position

---

[4] Stone, *Faithful Unto Death*, p. 14, from the Vienna Archives.

[5] Mason, *Certamen Seraphicum*, p. 6.

[6] Stone, *Faithful Unto Death*, p. 5.

[7] Parkinson, *The Antiquities of the English Franciscans*, p. 227.

was growing critical, it did not intimidate, much less silence them.

Naturally, their friary at Greenwich, under the very eyes of the king and his court, became the storm center in the coming conflict. Its inmates enjoyed the love and respect of the people, and the king realized that it was all-important to make sure of their sentiments regarding his relations with Anne Boleyn. To this end, Thomas Cromwell prevailed on one of the lay brothers of the community, Richard Lyst, by name, to serve him as spy.[8] Through secret correspondence with him, the wily minister soon learned that the friars were staunch adherents of the queen, and that they were resolved to stand by truth and justice no matter what the consequences would be.

As one of the chief agitators against the divorce the informing lay brother designated the guardian, Fr. William Peyto, a man of deep learning and sterling piety. He was born about the year 1480, at Chesterton in Warwickshire. After completing his education at Oxford, he renounced the world and joined the Franciscan Order. In view of his learning, the university conferred on him the academic degrees and elected him a fellow of Queen's College. Fr. Peyto had fully imbibed the spirit of St. Francis, and he became a zealous promoter of the reform movement in the Order. He had at one time been confessor to the queen and to Princess Mary, her only surviving child, and had since been elected guardian of the Greenwich friary.[9] In this way, he frequently came in touch with the court, saw with bitter regret how wicked flatterers and seducers had brought the king to the verge of perdition.

On Sunday, May 11, 1533, Fr. Peyto had to preach in the

---

[8] He subsequently left the Order and became a secular priest. As Judas wages for his treachery, the renegade received the vicarage of St. Dunstan's West. See Strickland, *Lives of the Queens of England*, Vol. II, p. 653, footnote. We shall hear more of Fr. Lyst, when we treat the life of Blessed John Forest.

[9] Leon, *Aureole Séraphique* (Engl. transl.), Vol. IV, p. 346; Stone, *Mary the First, Queen of England*, p. 456.

Franciscan church at Greenwich.[10] The king, whose secret

---

[10] The following account of FF. Peyto and Elstow is taken from Mason, *Certamen Seraphicum,* pp. 11-14, who drew from the *Annals* of John Stow. Gairdner's account based on the State Papers (see Hope, *The First Divorce... pp.* 274-279) differs considerably from Stow's, especially as regards the day and the year assigned for the event. According to Stow, Fr. Elstow publicly opposed Dr. Curwin on Sunday, May 8, 1533 (a later edition of his *Annals* has May 28, 1533), while Gairdner, presumably on the authority of the State Papers, says it was on Easter Sunday, 1532. Both statements present difficulties. Neither May 8 nor May 28 were Sundays in 1533; however, May 18 was a Sunday in that year. Possibly, then, May 8 is a typographical error and should read May 18; perhaps, too, the copyist for the later edition of the *Annals* misread or misunderstood the Latin *duodetricesima* (28) for duodevicesima (18). Accordingly Fr. Elstow's defence occurred on May 18, and Fr. Peyto preached on the preceding Sunday, May 11, the day after Queen Catherine was cited to Cranmer's court at Dunstable.

Cobbett, in his *History of the Protestant Reformation* (p. 51, footnote), regards this solution as probable, while the *Annales Minorum* (Vol. XIX, p. 112) declare that Stow must be read with caution (*caute legendum*), when he assigns 1533 as the year in which Fr. Peyto was banished. Therefore the editors of Volume XIX of the *Annales,* which was published in 1914, place the whole affair in the year 1532, although their reasons for doing so do not seem entirely convincing.

As to the State Papers, we find that in one case at least they make contradictory statements. On the one hand, they contain a letter written on February 4, 1533, by Fr. Richard Lyst to Thomas Cromwell, in which the lay brother mentions Fr. Peyto as one of the chief agitators against the King's divorce (see Gasquet, *Henry VIII and the English Monasteries,* p. 158). On the other hand, the same State Papers bring a letter written by Chapuys to Emperor Charles V, stating that Fr. Peyto's sermon was held on Easter Sunday, 1532 (see Camm, *Lives of the English Martyrs,* Vol. I, p. 278). Now one of these letters must be wrongly dated. We take it to be the second, for Lyst would hardly have incriminated Fr. Peyto after the latter's banishment; and he would have been banished by this time had his sermon taken place ten months before.

Other reasons which to us seem to speak for the correctness of Stow's account are the following: 1. That a provincial chapter was held at Canterbury in May, 1533, is very probable; first, because a general chapter had been held at Toulouse the preceding January, at which, as the record quoted by the *Annales Minorum* shows, Fr. Peyto was present; and second, because, as we know, during Lent, 1533, the commissary arrived to replace Blessed John Forest in the provincialship, which would naturally have called

marriage with Anne Boleyn had by this time been noised abroad, was present, surrounded by his courtiers. This then was the guardian's chance to sound a last word of rebuke and warning. Presentiments of some impending calamity were written on every countenance when the fearless friar ascended the pulpit. After relating from the Old Testament how King Achab had been misguided by the four hundred false prophets, and how he had insulted and imprisoned the true prophet Micheas and soon after died a most terrible death, the bold preacher turned to Henry and exclaimed: "Even where the dogs licked the blood of Naboth, there shall they lick also thy blood, O king. I am that Micheas," he continued, "whom thou wilt hate, because I must speak the truth and tell thee that this marriage is unlawful. And although I foresee that I shall have to eat the bread of affliction and drink the water of sorrow, yet, because the Holy Ghost has inspired and instructed me, I needs must speak." Then he inveighed most vehemently against the king's recent marriage with Anne Boleyn, and conjuring him to leave the path of crime and scandal and to hearken to the voice of conscience, he added: "I confess there are many, yea, too many preachers who for the sake of temporal preferment counsel thee otherwise and unreasonably nourish thy foolish and frail affections. And to what purpose? Forsooth, to procure fat benefices, to acquire riches, to become abbots, to obtain episcopal jurisdiction and other ecclesiastical dignities; and all the while, alas! by these and similar means they betray and ruin thy soul, thy honor, thy prosperity. These, I dare say, are the four hundred prophets whom the spirit of error and deceit has

---

for a meeting of the superiors in a chapter.—2. Again, Stow says that Fr. Peyto was "the very first (*primus omnium*) publicly to rebuke the king for the marriage contracted with Anne Boleyn," which it seems would have been premature and even highly imprudent to do fourteen months before, i.e. in the spring of 1532, when the king's "secret affair" was not yet a topic of public comment.—Finally, in his sermon Fr. Peyto speaks of the marriage as a settled fact, as indeed it was, although the public solemnities had not yet taken place.

breathed upon, and who attempt in like manner to mislead and deceive thee. But be on thy guard, O king, that having been deceived thou dost not pay the penalty of Achab whose blood the dogs licked up." Apparently, the king took this first public rebuke with good grace. His fawning courtiers, however, were stung to the quick, and henceforth they were the avowed enemies of the dauntless friars.

In the course of the following week, Fr. Peyto left for Canterbury to attend the provincial chapter, and Henry resolved to make the most of his temporary absence. To undo the effects of his sermon on the minds of the people, he engaged Dr. Curwin, a canon of Hereford, to preach a sermon on the following Sunday, May 18, in defence of his marriage. Dr. Curwin, whose pride and ambition had long since seared his conscience, hailed the opportunity of catering to his royal master and of thus securing his own emolument. Accordingly, on the following Sunday, Henry and his court again assembled in the church at Greenwich. Their eyes beamed with joy and triumph, when Dr. Curwin unscrupulously denounced Queen Catherine and in high-flown terms extolled the king for marrying Anne Boleyn and thereby ensuring the welfare of the kingdom. Feeling quite safe in the absence of Fr. Peyto, he began to heap insults on his name, calling him a dog, a slanderer, a low-minded and beggarly friar, a plotter, a rebel, a traitor, and finally shouting in boastful defiance, "I speak to thee, Peyto, who makest thyself Micheas, in order to upbraid kings; but, now thou art not to be found, being fled for fear and shame, since thou art not able to answer my arguments."

But the foolhardy speaker and his abettors had failed to reckon with another hero in the Franciscan garb. Great was their dismay and fury when, in the midst of the boaster's shameless tirade, Fr. John Elstow leaped to his feet and exclaimed from the gallery of the church: "Good sir, thou knowest that Fr. Peyto, as he was commanded, has gone to the provincial chapter assembled at Canterbury, and that he has not fled for fear of thee. Thou knowest this very well. To-morrow he will be here again. Meanwhile, I am here as another Micheas to prove from Holy Scripture, at the risk of my life, all those things as true which he hath taught. Here I stand in readiness, and thus, before God and all impartial judges, I challenge thee to this combat. Thee, thee, Curwin, I take to account, who art one of those four hundred prophets, in whom the spirit of falsehood and error is wholly entered; to thee my words are directed, who seekest to establish by adultery the royal succession; to thee, who art betraying the king into endless perdition; at thee, I say, these words of mine are aimed, at thee, who hast spoken more to satisfy thy own craving for honor and promotion, than to unburden thy clogged conscience or to guard the welfare of the king." Harpsfield, who says he heard the whole account from Elstow himself, writes: "Many other things he would have spoken, and much ado there was to stay him. At the hearing of this the king was cast into a great choler and in a great heat commanded that these friars should be conveyed thither where he should never hear more of them."[11]

On the following day, Fr. Peyto returned from Canterbury. His heart swelled with paternal pride and joy when the brethren told him how bravely one of their number had crossed swords with Dr. Curwin and had defended their guardian's good name and the rights of their lawful queen. With words of sincere gratitude and admiration, he congratulated Fr. Elstow, and at the same time exhorted the community faithfully to follow the voice of conscience in the hour of trial that he felt was now fast approaching. His presentiments proved only too true. That very day a messenger summoned FF. Peyto and Elstow before the king and his council.

We may picture to ourselves the menacing looks of hatred and vengeance that greeted the two friars on their entering the council chamber. Although their exterior bespoke meekness and humility, the fearless determination written on their

---

[11] Quoted by Gasquet, *Henry VIII ... Monasteries*, Vol. I, p. 163, footnote.

countenances made it clear that they were ready to sacrifice and suffer all for conscience's sake. On being commanded to give an explanation of their late conduct, Fr. Peyto stepped forward and again rebuked the king for his illicit relations with Anne Boleyn, at the same time predicting that, if he persisted in his iniquity, the hand of a just and avenging God would fall heavily upon him. In the course of the hearing, Henry Bourchier, Earl of Essex, exclaimed that the two friars were traitors and deserved to be put in sacks and thrown alive into the Thames. But they only smiled, and Fr. Elstow turning to the earl, said quietly: "With such things threaten those who have riches and immense possessions, who clothe themselves in gorgeous purple, and who pass their days in pleasures and amusements. For we account them as nothing; rather do we rejoice that we are driven hence for having done our duty; and," he added pleasantly, "we give a thousand thanks to God, since we know the way which leads to heaven to be open by water as well as by land; and therefore it is all the same to us whether we go by this way or by that."

Henry saw that it was useless to bandy words with these men of God. He was at a loss how to proceed against them. To send them to the block he dared not for fear of the people, who, he well knew, sympathized with his repudiated queen and revered the sons of St. Francis for their heroic zeal in her behalf. It was probably owing to this circumstance that FF. Peyto and Elstow escaped with their lives. For the present, they were imprisoned and after some time banished from the country. Both survived persecution under Henry VIII and later returned to their friary at Greenwich.

Thus FF. Peyto and Elstow were the first publicly to defy the English king, whose unbridled passions were bringing ruin and desolation on the Church and State in England. "It is impossible," the Protestant historian Cobbett declares, "to speak with sufficient admiration of these two men. Ten thousand victories by land or sea would not bespeak such heroism in the winners of these victories as was shown by these friars. If the bishops, or only one-fourth of them, had shown equal courage, the tyrant would have stopped in that mad career which was now on the eve of producing so many horrors. The stand made by these friars was the only instance of bold and open resistance, until he had actually got into his murders and robberies."[12]

---

[12] Cobbett, *History of the Protestant Reformation*, p. 52.

CHAPTER IV
OUTBREAK OF THE STORM

Henry's divorce and the question of papal supremacy—The crisis—The king usurps spiritual supremacy over the Church in England—Meets with opposition from the Franciscans—Contemplates rigorous measures against them—A favorable opportunity—Elizabeth Barton, the Holy Maid of Kent—Her revelations and the king's divorce—Two of her adherents: FF. Richard Risby and Hugh Rich—The "public penance"—The two friars defend the Pope's spiritual supremacy—Accused of high treason—The first martyrs for the faith.

HE question of the king's divorce was intimately connected with the question of papal supremacy in spiritual matters. Henry VIII had married Catherine of Aragon after Pope Julius had granted the required dispensation; and now, when the king wished to annul this marriage, he again appealed to the supreme head of the Church as the one and only competent authority to loose the bond. What he sought, however, was not an unbiased decision for the quieting of his alleged scruples, but an annulment of the marriage for the gratification of his unholy passions. "Let the Pope pronounce sentence in my favor," he declared, "and I will admit his authority, else it shall not be admitted."[1] Already in 1532, Pope Clement VII wrote to Henry threatening him with excommunication if within a month after receiving the letter he should still refuse to dismiss Anne Boleyn and take back his lawful queen, until the papal court had passed judgment.[2] But the king wantonly disregarded the Pope's admonition, so that finally his Holiness, on July 11, 1533, definitely passed sentence, declaring that the marriage with Anne Boleyn was null and

---

[1] Stone, *Faithful Unto Death*, p. 27.

[2] For a copy of this letter see Dodd, *Church History of England*, Vol. I, pp. 288 seq.

void, and that the king had incurred the greater excommunication, which would not go into effect, however, till the end of September, so as to give to the king ample time for reflection.[3]

This action of the Holy See brought matters to a crisis. During the remainder of the year 1533, negotiations between the Roman court and Henry's agents continued. The king dreaded the impending excommunication and urged his agents to do all in their power to prevent its promulgation. Great, too, was his disappointment, when it was learned that the child, which Anne Boleyn bore him on September 8, was a girl. From then on his affection for the ambitious coquette cooled perceptibly. From Chapuy's correspondence it appears that at this time the unhappy king suggested or even concluded an agreement with Charles V to reinstate Catherine in her rights. But political considerations stood in the way, while self-seeking courtiers prompted him to defy the Pope's threat and to take the divorce matter into his own hands. When, therefore, early in December, the papal Bull of excommunication was delivered to him by Thomas Cromwell, he grew desperate, and the following spring had parliament pass a bill, vesting him with powers that hitherto had been exercised solely by the Pope as spiritual head of the Church, and demanding that all priests and religious in the realm defend this new royal prerogative publicly in their sermons.[4]

As Henry and his party had expected, the Franciscans soon proved as fearless and outspoken in opposing his usurped title and authority as they had been in upholding the rights of his outraged queen. While jurists and divines debated on the nature and scope of papal supremacy, the friars, directed by their holy Rule from the start, espoused the cause of the Pope. The boldness of FF. Peyto and Elstow and the effect of their

---

[3] For the text of this papal definition see Pocock, *Records of the Reformation*, Vol. II, p. 677.

[4] Hope, *First Divorce of Henry VIII*, pp. 332, 343.

action on the people had not been forgotten. Hence, they and their confreres were mentioned in particular when orders were issued to the effect that no one was to occupy a pulpit in England unless he would undertake to defend the king's supremacy.[5] Could he but have won them over to his side, to gain the people for his cause would then be an easy matter. This thought it probably was that induced him to have the child of Anne Boleyn baptized in the Franciscan church at Greenwich with utmost splendor and solemnity. But the friars were insensible to royal blandishments when higher duties were at stake; and the king had to hear to his dismay that all over England they were publicly denouncing his rupture with Rome. Now his rage knew no bounds, and goaded on by those who had reason to hate the friars, he determined to strike terror into them and into the nation at large.

A favorable opportunity was not long in presenting itself. Near Canterbury, where the Franciscans had a friary, lived Elizabeth Barton, who seemed to be favored by Heaven with visions and ecstasies.[6] Ever since 1525, her revelations were causing a stir among the people; wherefore William Warham, the zealous and prudent Archbishop of Canterbury, appointed a commission of learned priests to investigate the matter. Of their number were two Franciscans, presumably of Canterbury.[7] The report of the commission was favorable to the Holy Maid of Kent, as Elizabeth was called, so that when she applied for admission into the Benedictine nunnery of St. Sepulcher, near by, the archbishop readily gave his consent. In the convent, her strange visions and ecstasies continued. What especially caused comment among all classes of society were

---

[5] Ibidem, p. 344.

[6] The following account regarding Elizabeth Barton is based chiefly on Gasquet, *Henry VIII and the English Monasteries*, Vol. I, chap. iv. See also Wright, *Suppression of Monasteries*, letters VI-XIII.

[7] Gasquet (p. 112) has "Father Lewis and his fellow (two observants)", on the authority of Lambard.

her bold utterances on the king's relations with Anne Boleyn.

At first, Henry gave the affair little attention. But about midsummer, 1533, shortly after his secret marriage with Anne was proclaimed to the kingdom, the Holy Maid declared it had been revealed to her to go and tell him "that if he went forward with the purpose that he intended, he would not be king of England seven months later;" and added that "this punishment would be brought about, not by any temporal or worldly power, but by God alone."[8] On hearing this, Henry became much alarmed and had the nun and those who were supposed to have advised and favored her thrown into the Tower. Among these were FF. Richard Risby and Hugh Rich, guardians of Canterbury and Richmond.

In order to delude the people and to give his proceedings the semblance of justice, it was deemed necessary to blacken the character of the Maid of Kent. Of this foul plan Cromwell and Cranmer were eager abettors. About the month of October, 1533, they subjected the nun and her adherents to a strict examination in the star chamber, and then spread the false report that the nun had signed a statement, in which she confessed her visions and ecstasies to have been a fraud to arouse popular sentiment against the king. On November 23, she and her supposed accomplices were compelled to undergo a most degrading ceremony. A high scaffold was erected at St. Paul's Cross in London, on which they were exposed as rebels and impostors to the gaze of the populace. Dr. Capon, Abbot of Hyde, occupied a pulpit opposite the scaffold. With a zeal worthy of a better cause, he publicly defended his royal master and branded his victims as lying hypocrites and dangerous plotters against the king and the country. The principal target of his strictures were the two Franciscans, whom he blamed as ringleaders of the whole affair, inasmuch as by word and deed they had influenced others in behalf of the nun. Thereupon, he read aloud the document which the king's ministers had drawn

---

[8] Hope, *Franciscan Martyrs in England,* p. 40.

up and proffered as the nun's confession.⁹ After this public humiliation, the "penitents" were conducted past a large concourse of people to the Tower. Henry was elated over the effect of this ceremony on the popular mind. To all appearances, the people's faith in the Holy Maid had been shaken; they were now more favorably disposed toward him.

Meanwhile, the question of his spiritual supremacy had become acute. The king was bent on silencing those who dared to oppose his usurped authority; and since the Franciscans had again been foremost in this respect, he decided to make an example of the two friars who were already in prison. Accordingly, FF. Risby and Rich were called on to hold a disputation with the king's men on papal supremacy. Everything short of brutal force was employed to elicit from the friars a denial of the Catholic doctrine. But, neither promises nor threats could for a moment shake their constancy. Finally, they were taken back to prison and tortured most cruelly. Here again they steadfastly professed their faith, declaring themselves ready to suffer a thousand times more, even death itself, rather than renounce him whom, as children of Mother Church and as followers of St. Francis, they held to be the only legitimate Vicar of Christ on earth.

Henry was incensed when he heard of their unflinching and intrepid constancy. The sight of Tyburn, thought he, would make their detested confreres quail, and the blood of the Holy Maid of Kent and of her adherents would quench all enthusiasm for the Pope. But, in order to condemn them to death, it was necessary to convict them of some capital offence. Therefore, on March 12, 1534, parliament was made to pass a bill of attainder, establishing it as high treason to criticize the king's marriage with Anne Boleyn or in any way to uphold the supremacy of the Pope. Now Henry could act with impunity. Without any form of trial, the holy nun and her party were

---

⁹ According to *Grey Friars Chronicle* in *Monumenta Franciscana*, Vol. II, p. 196, a similar "penance" was performed by them at Canterbury.

pronounced guilty of high treason and condemned to death.

On April 20, 1534, they were fastened on hurdles and dragged to Tyburn amid the gibes of a deluded populace.[10] Faint with suffering and bespattered with mud, the poor victims at last came in sight of the place of execution. On a scaffold stood the gallows with a caldron of boiling water; near by, on a bench, lay an axe and a huge knife. One by one the martyrs were unbound and led below the scaffold. Elizabeth Barton was the first to suffer. She was hanged and beheaded. Fr. Risby was then ordered to mount the scaffold. His gaze turned to heaven, he was praying for perseverance in the hour of trial and torture, when suddenly a courier came dashing through the crowd with a message from the king. Great was the surprise of all when it was learned that his Majesty offered life and liberty to the friars if they would renounce the Pope and acknowledge the king as supreme head of the Church in England. After reading the message aloud, the presiding officer turned to Fr. Risby and began to extol the king's mercy and long-suffering. A look of celestial peace played on the countenance of the condemned friar. This was in very deed what he had been hoping and praying for. Now he could publicly profess his faith, for which he was about to undergo torture and death. He listened in silence while the officer spoke. Then raising his eyes heavenward, he exclaimed with a loud and resolute voice, "Not only will I not rebel against the authority of the Pope, but I am ready to suffer the most cruel death for Holy Mother Church."[11]

---

[10] The details regarding the martyrdom of the two Franciscans we have drawn chiefly from Bourchier, *Hist. Eccl. de Martyrio FF. Ord. Divi Francisci* (pp. 6 seq.), whom Gasquet (Vol. I, p. 150, footnote) considers an authority, since he took the Franciscan habit in 1557 and hence had occasion to gather information from those of his brethren as well as from others who had known FF. Risby and Rich.

[11] From this declaration as well as from the king's offer to grant them full pardon, it would seem that the two friars suffered death for refusing to deny the Catholic doctrine of the spiritual supremacy of the Bishop of Rome in the Church. See Gaudentius, *Bedeutung und Verdienste des*

Hardly had he uttered this heroic profession of faith, when the executioner rushed like a madman on the holy friar, rudely flung the rope about his neck and thrust him from the ladder. Instantly he leaped toward the dangling body and cut the rope by which it was suspended. With a dismal thump, the body fell to the floor of the scaffold. Now a scene was enacted that can be better imagined than described. Seizing the huge knife, the executioner thrust it into the friar's abdomen and ripped open his body. All this while, the helpless victim, still living and conscious, moved his lips in silent prayer. Then the executioner thrust his sacrilegious hand through the gash he had made, tore out the still palpitating heart, held it up to the people and exclaimed in cold derision, "Behold the heart of a traitor." Finally, after extracting the entrails from the bleeding corpse and throwing them into the fire, he severed the head, quartered the body, and threw the limbs into the boiling caldron; later, they were exposed to public view on the gates of London, while the head was fastened to a pole and placed on London Bridge.

All eyes turned toward Fr. Rich when his name was called. With mingled emotions of pride and grief he had witnessed the horrible sufferings under which his confrere had passed to his eternal reward. Now it was his turn to die a similar death for the faith. With fearless determination, he stepped forth and mounted the ladder. While the executioner was placing the rope about his neck, the noble friar made the offering of his life to God in the words of the Royal Prophet: "I will freely sacrifice to thee, and will give praise to thy name, O God: because it is good." When the officer in the king's name offered him life and liberty if he would do the king's bidding, he smiled complacently and declared that nothing in this life could separate him from his supreme Master; that, on the contrary, he deemed it a privilege to be allowed to die in defence of Catholic truth. This was enough. Without further delay, he was thrown from the ladder, cut down, and while still living subjected to

---

Franziskanerordens im Kampfe gegen den Protestantismus, p. 28, footnote 4.

the same inhuman treatment as Fr. Risby. When the executioner seized his heart to tear it out, the martyr said with a broken voice, "That which thou hast in thy hand is consecrated to God." At this, the brutal executioner smiled disdainfully and completed his bloody work.[12]

As FF. Peyto and Elstow had been the first publicly to denounce the king's wanton policy against his lawful queen, so now again two Franciscans were among the first to suffer martyrdom in defence of papal supremacy. Although Mother Church has not yet conferred the honor of her altars on FF. Risby and Rich,[13] they are commemorated in the *Franciscan Martyrology,* on June 3, in these terms: "At London in England, the suffering of the Blessed Martyrs, Richard Risby, guardian of the friary at Canterbury, and Hugh Rich, likewise guardian of the friary at Richmond, who in defence of the Catholic faith, at the command of Henry VIII, King of England, were executed in a horrible manner."

Besides FF. Risby and Rich, two Benedictines of Canterbury and two secular priests were executed on this occasion.

That their names are not on the list of the English martyrs beatified by Pope Leo XIII in 1886, is probably owing to the fact that their martyrdom antedates the formal passing of the Act of Supremacy by seven months.

CHAPTER V
RAGING OF THE STORM, 1534-1536

Franciscans continue to oppose the king's divorce and his usurped supremacy—Fr. Pecock's sermon—First step toward the suppression of their province—Cromwell, vicegerent and vicar general—Hilsey and Browne, "grand visitors" of all mendicant friars—Their instructions—They visit the Franciscans at Richmond and Greenwich—Visitation of Southampton—Loyalty of the friars—All Franciscans arrested and imprisoned—Their friaries in the hands of the king—Subsequent lot of the ejected friars—Some released from prison and banished—Many succumb to the hardships of prison life.

ESPITE the rigorous measures which Henry VIII had taken against them, the Franciscans at home and abroad were causing the crown much trouble and anxiety. Fr. Curson, vicar of Greenwich, exhorted Fr. Robinson of Richmond to hold a sermon at St. Paul's Cross in defence of their lawful queen. Furthermore, he publicly praised the heroism which Fr. Elstow had recently manifested and supplied his needs during his imprisonment at Bedford.[1] Again, a certain Fr. John Laurence[2] informed Cromwell that two of his brethren, FF. Hugh Payn and Cornelius were providing the banished Fr. Peyto with books, and that, as he had reason to believe, they had also visited the queen at Buckden. Both friars were subsequently arrested and examined. Through no incriminating evidence could be found against them, the friars nevertheless declared themselves adherents of the queen; wherefore, Cromwell, reporting the matter to the king, asked

---

[1] Hope, The First Divorce of Henry VIII, p. 278.

[2] He was a priest and apparently an accomplice of Fr. Lyst, who commends him to Cromwell, calling him Father Larans. See infra (John Forest, note 15).

leave to have them racked.³ One of the entries which Cromwell made in his *Remembrances* about this time is very significant. "To know," he writes, "whether Vaughan shall go forward or return. Touching Fr. Risby's examination of the letter sent by Peyto to Payn the friar. To remember to send for Friar Rich to Richmond, of the letters lately come from Rome to the minister of the Friars Observants, and of the communication between Beeke and a friar, and to know the effect of those letters, which letters were directed from Elstow. To know what way the king will take with all the said malefactors." The above-mentioned Stephen Vaughan was one of the spies whom Cromwell had sent abroad to gather information. On August 3, 1533, he wrote to Cromwell that Fr. Peyto, who was staying in the Franciscan friary at Antwerp, had just published a book against the king's divorce, that he was visited every week by a friar from England, and that his friends in England were giving him pecuniary assistance. Later, on October 21, he again wrote, saying that "Peyto like his brethren is a hypocrite, a tiger clad in sheepskin, a perilous knave, and evil reporter of the king, and ought to be shamefully punished. Would to God," he adds, "I could get him by any policy. I will work what I can. Whatever Peyto does, I will find means for the king to know. I have laid a bait for him. He can not wear the cloaks and cowls sent over to him from England, they are so many."⁴

Equally bold and unyielding were the Franciscans when, early in the spring of 1534, the matter of royal supremacy came to a head. Two of their number, as we have seen, were among the first to suffer martyrdom for opposing it. "Of the whole body of the clergy," Gasquet observes, "none withstood the policy of Henry with greater fearlessness and pertinacity of purpose than the Franciscan Observants."⁵

---

³ Stone, *Faithful Unto Death*, p. 19; see also Gasquet, *Henry VIII and the English Monasteries*, Vol. I, p. 166.

⁴ Ibidem, pp. 33 seq.

⁵ Gasquet, *Henry VIII ... Monasteries*, Vol. I, p. 155.

On the very eve of Henry's rupture with Rome, on Passion Sunday, March 22, 1534, Fr. Pecock, guardian of the friary at Southampton, preached in St. Swinthin's cathedral at Winchester. Though fully realizing the terrible consequences for himself as well as for his brethren, the bold friar openly defended the rights of the Pope. He exhorted his hearers to imitate the example of St. Maurice, who suffered martyrdom rather than offend God by executing the unjust demands of the prince. "Here are many hearers," he said, "and they not all of one capacity. Some there be that understand me and some peradventure that understand me not, but otherwise do take me and shall report me, that I do speak my mind." Then, after lamenting the diversity of opinions then agitating and misleading the public, he warned his hearers against certain books that had of late been published to further the cause of the king. Taking up a volume, he read a number of authorities to prove that, according to the teaching and institution of Christ, the Pope alone, as successor of St. Peter in the see of Rome, had supreme jurisdiction in the Church. One of Cromwell's spies happened to be present in the church, and, on April 7, reported the matter to his master. In due time, the mayor of Southampton received instructions to arrest Fr. Pecock and to convey him to London. The valiant preacher was brought before Cromwell, but at the solicitation of friends he was permitted to return to his friary.[6]

That Henry VIII was determined to establish his usurped supremacy at any cost, became clear when, on April 20,1534, the Holy Maid of Kent and her adherents were barbarously executed at Tyburn. By this time, he was fully convinced that he would find in the Franciscans his most formidable and influential opponents. Hence, when relations with Rome were severed and he was declared head of the Church in England, his first acts of tyranny were naturally directed against them and their friaries. So far, he had dealt only with individual members

---

[6] Ibidem, pp. 169 seq.; see also Stone, *Faithful Unto Death*, pp. 31.

of their Order, apparently in the hope that sooner or later the others would submit. But now when he saw that neither the banishment of FF. Peyto and Elstow, nor the recent execution of FF. Risby and Rich had in any way intimidated their confreres, he became enraged and, urged on by Cromwell and his clique, decided on a campaign of general persecution against his one-time friends and favorites.

Henry's first act as head of the Church in England was to vest his zealous minister Thomas Cromwell with unlimited powers in matters spiritual. The crafty and unscrupulous politician was appointed vicegerent and vicar general of the realm with authority to preside over the meetings of the clergy. Wholly subservient to his royal master, he left nothing undone to further "the godly reformation and redress of errors, heresies and abuses in the said church."[7] To this end, John Hilsey, a Dominican, and Dr. George Browne, a prior of the Augustinian hermits, were made superiors general and "grand visitors" of all the friaries belonging to the mendicant Orders.[8] "Their instructions were precise and intended to gauge the feeling of the friars very thoroughly. The members of every convent or friary in England were to be assembled in their chapter houses and examined separately concerning their faith and obedience to Henry. The oath of allegiance to Anne Boleyn was to be administered to them, and they were bound to swear solemnly that they would preach and persuade the people to accept the royal supremacy, to confess that the Bishop of Rome had no more power than any other bishop and to call him Pope no longer. Further, the sermons of each preacher were to be carefully examined, and if not orthodox they were to be burned. Every friar was to be strictly enjoined to commend the king as

---

[7] Lingard, *History of England,* Vol. V, p. 25.

[8] Both these traitors subsequently received from the king their "thirty pieces of silver" in the shape of bishoprics. John Hilsey, after the martyrdom of Blessed John Fisher, was raised to the see of Rochester; while George Browne became Archbishop of Dublin.

head of the Church, the queen, the archbishop of Canterbury and the clergy to the prayers of the faithful. Lastly, each house was 'to be obliged to show its gold, silver, and other movable goods, and deliver an inventory of them,' and to take a common oath, sealed with the convent seal, to observe the above orders."[9]

This general visitation of all the English friaries began in the spring of 1534. The Franciscans had, indeed, little mercy to expect from these visitors, and less from the enraged king and his minister. Their two convents at Greenwich and Richmond had already shown themselves most unrelenting in their opposition to the king's lawless policy. Hence they became the first objects of his wrath and vengeance. Rowland Lee[10] and Thomas Bedyll were commissioned to visit them and to propose the prescribed articles. Shortly after the execution of the two guardians, FF. Rich and Risby, Cromwell received word from the visitors that together with the Carthusians of Sheen who had now taken the required oaths, they were employing every means to win over the neighboring Franciscans of Richmond; that so far, however, they had met with little success, although several conferences had been held with the friars. Finally, on June 13, Dr. George Browne informed Lee and Bedyll to bring the matter regarding the friaries of Richmond and Greenwich to a speedy issue. How shrewdly the royal visitors proceeded and how resolutely the friars defended the rights of the Holy See, has been handed down in a letter which Cromwell received from the two commissioners after the visitation.[11]

Saturday night, June 13, between ten and eleven o'clock, Lee and Bedyll arrived at the friary of Richmond. On the following morning, they opened legal proceedings with the

---

[9] Gasquet, *Henry VIII ... Monasteries,* Vol. I, pp. 173 seq.

[10] The same who officiated at Henry's secret marriage with Anne Boleyn.

[11] For a copy of this letter see Wright, *Suppression of the Monasteries,* pp. 41 seq. It **is** on this letter that the subsequent account is based.

superior and one of the senior friars, Sebastian by name. Thereupon, they assembled the community and tried their utmost to make them subscribe to the articles. But the friars "showed themselves very untoward in that behalf." Wherefore, the cunning visitors resorted to a trick. They proposed that the four discreets or councillors of the friary be empowered by the rest to decide and act in the name of all and to come the next morning to the Greenwich friary with the official convent seal. To this the unsuspecting brethren agreed. Elated over their success, the commissioners departed.

On the following day, visitation was held in the Greenwich friary. Here, too, the members of the community were one in their opposition to the king's demands. Accordingly, the visitors advised them "to put the whole matter in the hands of the seniors or discreets," as their brethren at Richmond had done. The royal agents later informed Cromwell that they did this "to avoid superfluous words and idle reasoning, and especially to provide that if the discreets should refuse to consent, it were better after our minds to strain a few than a multitude." But the friars saw the trap and with one voice refused to entrust the affair to the four discreets. The proposed articles, they rightly maintained, concerned each member of the community personally, and each would take the salvation of his soul into his own hands. The friars, therefore, appeared individually before the royal commissioners, who employed every means short of torture to make them submit to the king's demands. But they soon perceived that they were dealing with men who knew their duty and who were determined to fulfill it at all hazards. Neither threats nor promises could shake their constancy, especially with regard to the usurped spiritual supremacy of the king. The royal visitors were forced to admit that they "found them in one mind of contradiction and dissent from the said articles, but specially against this article: That the Bishop of Rome must be considered to possess no greater authority or jurisdiction than any other individual bishop in England or elsewhere in their respective diocese." The valiant friars argued that not only the teaching of Christ but also the Franciscan Rule which they had vowed, bound them to loyalty to the Holy See. The wily visitors on their part averred that this commandment of their Rule did not bind the English Franciscans, because there were no members of the Order in England when St. Francis wrote the Rule; that, furthermore, the clause containing this commandment had been inserted in the Rule by ambitious friars, who hoped thereby to gain the favor of the Pope, and that finally by the law of God, which stood above every religious Rule, they owed obedience and allegiance to their king. Then, to back up their sophisms, they added that both archbishops of the kingdom, as also the bishops of London, Winchester, Durham, and Bath, with many learned prelates and famous clerics had already subscribed to the articles. But the fearless friars remained firm; what others in the realm had done in this all-important question was of no concern to them. In short, all the subtle reasoning of Lee and Bedyll "could not sink into their obstinate heads, and worn in custom of obedience to the Pope." Finally, the visitors departed, greatly vexed at the "obstinacy" of these men of God. "Sorry we be," they wrote to Cromwell, "we can not bring them to no better frame of mind and order in this behalf, as our faithful mind was to do, for the accomplishment of the king's pleasure."

Of only one more friary is mention made as regards the royal visitation. When the king's agent, on July 15, came to the Franciscans at Southampton, the afore-mentioned guardian, Fr. Pecock, finding the official was not Dr. Hilsey, as he had reason to suppose, became suspicious and demanded the visitor's credentials. "Not knowing what to do," the guardian later wrote to Cromwell, "we desired him to show us his authority, and he showed us a letter to your mastership so ill-written that I could not read it plainly, under seal, as he said, of Dr. Hilsey; and knowing that he was a wise father and a good clerk we did not believe it, but begged him to show us the first writing again to see whether Dr. Hilsey had any power to substitute. This he refused, and so we would not let him proceed and he threatened us with the king's displeasure and yours."[12]

Apparently, there are no further records to show how the royal visitors fared in the remaining Franciscan friaries. Still, from the subsequent proceedings against their inmates it is quite clear that these communities, too, steadfastly refused to put their name to the articles. Indeed, the one or the other of their number seems, at least temporarily, to have declared himself willing to take the oath of allegiance. Thus, for instance, Bishop Tunstall wrote to Cromwell on November 13, commending to the king's mercy two Franciscans who had previously been expelled from the friary at Newark for adhering to the Pope and banished to Scotland, whence after suffering great hardships they had returned. These two friars were Thomas Danyell, professed at Canterbury, and Henry Bukkery, a lay brother not yet professed. "Surely," wrote Tunstall, "best it were to receive them to mercy, for other fault we cannot find in them, but their obstinacy to have cleaved heretofore to the Bishop of Rome, which now they will leave and forsake, as they say to us." Commenting on this incident, Stone says, "It was a sorry triumph for the king and Cromwell that of the whole Order, but two starved and hunted individuals could be brought, by all the machinery of persecution at their command, to falter an unwilling denial of the Pope's authority."[13] Clearly, nothing short of death and destruction could silence these formidable champions of papal authority and jurisdiction, because "secluded from the commerce and pleasures of the world, they felt fewer temptations to sacrifice their consciences to the command of their sovereign; and seemed more eager to court the crown, than to flee from the pains of martyrdom."[14]

Hence we can imagine the fury of the king and of

---

[12] Gasquet, *Henry VIII ... Monasteries*, Vol. I, p. 177.

[13] Stone, *Faithful Unto Death*, p. 43.

[14] Lingard, Vol. V, p. 18.

Cromwell, when the reports of the commissioners reached them.

Without delay, a decree was drawn up providing for the arrest of the Franciscans and the seizure of their friaries. What bitter pangs and gloomy forebodings must have preyed on the spirits of these men of God when the king's officers appeared at the various convents to carry out his orders. Their six houses were declared forfeited to the crown and were temporarily made over to the Augustinian Order. Of the friars themselves, whom the officers arrested as prisoners of the king, some were confined in other religious houses of the kingdom, while the majority were thrown into prison. On June 18, 1534, a certain Leonard Smith writing to Lord Lisle remarks incidentally, "No news but that two carts full of friars came to the Tower two days ago." And in a letter which Chapuys addressed to Emperor Charles V under date of August 11, 1534, we read: "Of seven (?) houses of Observants, five have already been emptied of friars, because they refused to swear to the statutes made against the Pope. Those in the two others expect also to be expelled."[15] By August 29, 1534, fully a year before any other religious house was molested, the agents of Cromwell had finished with the Franciscans. Far and wide the helpless friars were scattered over the kingdom, while their lowly convents, which as centers of virtue and learning enjoyed nation-wide esteem, were now in the hands of strangers.[16]

The total number of Franciscans thus turned out of their houses can not be fixed with any degree of certainty. It is estimated that two hundred were expelled. Of these a number were lodged with the Conventuals, who were forced to treat

---

[15] Stone, *Faithful Unto Death*, p. 38.

[16] Since the Franciscan friaries had little or no temporal goods, it was not greed but sheer hatred that prompted the king to suppress them.

them as prisoners.[17] "All the Observants of the kingdom," Chapuys writes, "have been driven from their monasteries for refusing the oath against the Holy See, and have been distributed in several monasteries, where they are locked up in chains, and worse treated than they could be in prison."[18] It seems, however, that in some cases their confinement was less severe, and that a number of them succeeded in making good their escape, and either remained in hiding with friends or crossed over to Scotland and Belgium. Thus, early in July, FF. Hugh Payn and Thomas Hayfield, both of the Newark friary, made an attempt to flee to the continent. Disguised in secular dress, they got as far as Cardiff. Here they obtained passage on a ship bound for Brittany. They were about to embark when the king's men discovered their identity and led them off to prison. Dr. Hilsey, who arrived shortly after, had them conveyed to London. "You shall perceive more of their crafty fashion," he wrote to Cromwell. "In all places where they come they persuade the people to hold to the bishop of Rome, calling him Pope and saying that they will die in his cause and never forsake him while they live. They rail at the books set forth *cum privilegio,* calling them heresies, and heretics that set them forth." He also accused them of ridiculing the Princess Elizabeth, by saying she had been baptized in hot water, which, however, had not been hot enough for her.[19]

A letter written by Fr. Lybert to James Becky and dated October 25, 1534, gives us a glimpse into the condition of the

---

[17] It would be wide of the mark to infer from this that the Conventuals were eager abettors of the king's lawless measures against the Franciscans. They were rather compelled to treat them as the king's prisoners and perhaps were even exhorted thereto by the Franciscans themselves as the lesser of two. evils. Furthermore, it is safe to say that the liberties which in time a number of the imprisoned friars enjoyed were to some extent owing either to the intervention of the Conventuals or to their unwillingness to do the king's full bidding.

[18] Gasquet, *Henry VIII ... Monasteries,* Vol. I, p. 189.

[19] Ibidem, pp. 180 seq.

imprisoned friars. The writer declares that he and Fr. Abraham are poorly lodged with the Grey Friars at Stamford. They are anxious to learn what their confreres at Greenwich have done or intend to do. "We hear," he writes, "that they are all sworn, and have somewhat changed their government, at which we marvel.[20] Notwithstanding, if they think that God is pleased with it, their conscience discharged, the world edified, and any profit may come of it, we desire to have a more perfect knowledge; and then we shall do as God shall inspire us, either suffer pain still, and be enclosed, or else go at liberty, as they do." Then the troubled friar asks that a number of articles be sent him, which he had forgotten on his hurried departure, and wonders that his letter, written about six weeks before, had till now remained unanswered. In conclusion, he requests that his present writing be burnt and sends greetings to his brethren and to his relatives.[21]

More deplorable, of course, was the lot of those Franciscans who had been thrown into prison. Accustomed to the peace and quiet of convent life, they were now compelled to share company with the very dregs of humanity and were loaded down with every misery and hardship that these dreadful abodes of filth and disease could offer. For the time, Henry's anger knew no bounds; and there is every reason to believe that neither insults nor torture were spared to force the friars into submission. The following fact, related by Bourchier, Mason, Wadding, and other reliable historians, shows to some extent to what frightful sufferings these men of God were subjected. In 1537, after three years of hard durance, a number of Franciscans were released from their dungeons. Four of them, however, FF. Thomas Packingham, Bonaventure Roo, John Tuit, and Richard Carter, died a few days later. "The hardships they

---

[20] Cromwell, we may readily suppose, had rumors of this kind published, in order to deceive and bewilder the other members of the province.

[21] Stone, *Faithful Unto Death*, pp. 41 seq.; Gasquet, *Henry VIII ... Monasteries*, Vol. I, pp. 191 seq.

had undergone in their confinement," Parkinson explains, "had sunk them so low that they were not able to recover."[22] The *Franciscan Martyrology* commemorates them on August 9.

The only one who ventured to intercede for the imprisoned friars was Sir Thomas Wriothesley, a member of the Privy Council. Personal contact with them had made him their friend and admirer. Being on intimate terms with Cromwell, he petitioned him to liberate the friars and give them leave to quit the country. Though the calculating minister was willing to get rid of them at any cost, the king proved less inclined to grant the request of Wriothesley. One thing alone had so far prevented him from sating his thirst for vengeance by sending the friars to the block. He knew that ever since his infamous dealings in the case of the Holy Maid of Kent, a strong feeling of dissatisfaction and indignation had taken hold of the people, which became especially noticeable when the Franciscans were suppressed and imprisoned. Even at court there were such as resented his usurping of the spiritual supremacy and thought his proceedings against the friars too severe. Therefore, when Cromwell approached him with Wriothesley's petition, he found it safer to feign mercy and had a number of friars set at liberty.

Parkinson writes under the year 1537, "The execution of many of the Franciscan Observants (in prison ever since 1534, or 1535) having been delayed by the mediation of their friend Sir Thomas Wriothesley, and not one of them coming into the king's measures, or subscribing to his supremacy, etc., it was now proposed to his majesty (as Sanders writes) that they should be some way or other disposed of, lest others by their example, might become more resolute. And now, though the king seemed inclined to have them all cut off, or hanged at once, yet being apprehensive of the infamy of such a fact, because they were numerous, and being willing to show some favor to the Privy Counsellor Wriothesley, who had pleaded

---

[22] Parkinson, *Antiquities of the English Franciscans*, p. 238.

hard for them, he spared some of them, who went into banishment, partly into the Low Countries, and others into Scotland."[23] To this action of Henry probably refers Cromwell's entry in his *Remembrances*: "Item to remember the friars of Greenwich to have license to go to Ireland."[24]

Not all Franciscans, however, were set at liberty. Many had to languish in prison often for years, until death put an end to their sufferings. From the moment they were shut up in the silence and gloom of their foul dungeon, nothing more was heard of them. It is quite probable that some were executed in secret, and that in consequence no account of their martyrdom has ever been committed to writing. From a *Contemporary Account of Bishop Fisher and Sir Thomas More* preserved in the Vatican, we learn that "an immense number of them all perished either on the scaffold or by starvation or through their sufferings in prison."[25] Parkinson informs us that "thirty-two of the same Order were removed out of the prisons of London, and being coupled two and two together with iron chains, were sent into divers other prisons of the nation, that they might perish with less murmuring and disturbance of the people; for as the author of the *Franciscan Martyrology* says, there was such an universal discontent amongst the king's subjects, and such loud outcries, even of persons of quality, on the account of the imprisonment of all the Observants, that his majesty thought fit to set some of them at liberty, and that these 32 were reserved to be made examples of. Besides these, others were starved with hunger, as an author writes,[26] and others suffocated with the intolerable stench of loathsome prisons, or perished by the inconveniences and hardships of their

---

[23] Ibidem, p. 238.

[24] Gasquet, *Henry ... Monasteries*, Vol. I, p. 190.

[25] Pocock, *Records of the Reformation*, Vol. II, pp. 553 seq.

[26] The author referred to is Fr. Francis Davenport, who flourished in the beginning of the next century and played a prominent part in the founding of the second English province.

confinement."[27] Hueber, in his *Menologium*, mentions, for September 24, thirty-four friars who died about the year 1537. And finally, on July 31, the *Franciscan Martyrology* of Arturus commemorates thirty-two friars "who, imprisoned by Henry VIII for the Catholic faith and conveyed, burdened two and two with most heavy chains, to different places, died in the Lord, after having been tortured with hunger and cold and subjected to other sufferings and hardships."

---

[27] Parkinson, p. 238.

CHAPTER VI
RAGING OF THE STORM (CONT.), 1536-1538

Disaffection among the people—The Pilgrimage of Grace—Share of the Franciscans in the northern rising—Renewed hostilities against them—Three Franciscan martyrs: Ven. Antony Brookby, Ven. Thomas Cort, Ven. Thomas Belchiam.

AFTER the suppression and expulsion of the Franciscans, a series of events in England conspired to allay for a time at least the rebellious pride of Henry VIII. "There was hardly any period of his reign," Gasquet writes, "when the king and his counsellors were more harassed than during the latter half of this year (1535). The foreign relations of the country were becoming strained. The people at home were restless and disheartened. The longest memory could not recall a summer more unfavorable to agriculture. The corn harvest was well nigh a complete failure, the yield being scarcely more than the third part of an average crop. It had rained, so said the people, ever since the execution of the Carthusians, and they looked upon this as a mark of divine anger at the misdeeds of Henry."[1] The following January when it was learned that Queen Catherine had passed away, a cry of heartfelt sympathy and regret rose from the masses; which was changed to one of triumph and gratification, however, when, four months later, Anne Boleyn, the cause of the late disturbances, mounted the scaffold to pay the penalty of her many crimes.

Meanwhile, especially in the north of England, the suppression of the lesser monasteries was creating widespread discontent, and in the autumn of 1536, the commons rose in armed protest against the encroachments of the crown on their religious and political freedom. "The suppression of the

---

[1] Gasquet, *Henry VIII ... Monasteries*, Vol. I, p. 244.

abbeys," says Gasquet, "was felt to be a blow to religion in those parts no less than a hardship to the poor, and a detriment to the country at large. The royal supremacy was looked upon as founded only on Henry's whim and as a pretension without precedent in history, while the renunciation of papal authority was held to be subversive of the principle of unity in the Christian Church, and the first step towards diversity of doctrine and practice."[2]

The insurrection, known as the Pilgrimage of Grace, broke out in Lincolnshire and in a short time spread over the whole of northern England. In October, 1536, 40,000 armed citizens headed by Robert Aske and reinforced by about 5,000 knights and gentlemen, marched to Doncaster, where the Duke of Norfolk had united his forces with the armed tenantry of the Earl of Shrewsbury. Wholly unprepared to quell this formidable array by force of arms, Henry resorted to lying and treachery. At the suggestion of Norfolk, Robert Aske had the demands of the commons drawn up in twenty-four articles. These were sent to the king for approbation, who feigning some reluctance, at last made far-reaching concessions and even offered the insurgents a general pardon. Not suspecting the king's base design, Aske prevailed on his followers to disarm and return to their homes. When, however, the king's promises were not fulfilled, the people became restless and in January rose a second time. Now Henry was prepared to meet them. What followed was a series of cruel and bloody measures against the leaders of the rebellion and of renewed hostilities against the religious houses of the kingdom. "The collapse of the movement," Gasquet maintains, "removed every restraint upon the autocratic power of the crown and opened the way for further seizure of monastic and church property."[3]

Precisely what share the Franciscans had in these northern risings is hard to determine. That many of them were still

---

[2] Ibidem, Vol. II, p. 101.

[3] Ibidem, Vol. II, p. 158.

living with the Conventuals in these parts and were again exerting their influence for the spiritual and temporal welfare of the people, seems certain from the fact that of the twenty-four articles drawn up by the insurgents the sixth one read, "To have the friars Observants restored to their houses."[4] Furthermore, during the subsequent court proceedings against the insurgents, William Stapleton testified that "one Sir Thomas Johnson, otherwise called Bonaventure, an Observant friar, who was sworn ... and assigned to the said (Grey Friars') house of Beverley ... was very busy going betwixt ... the wild people, oft laying scriptures to maintain their purpose;" and that he even "offered himself to go into the quarrel in harness to the field and so did to the first stay."[5]

Naturally, these weighty accusations, whether true or false, reenkindled the king's hatred of the friars. Hardly had the rebellion been put down when, on March 17, 1537, he wrote to the Duke of Norfolk that "from my lord of Durham's declaration and other evidences, we see that the Friars Observants are disciples of the Bishop of Rome, and sowers of sedition. You shall therefore do your best to apprehend the friars as prisoners, without liberty to speak to any man, till we shall determine our further pleasure about them."[6] What this "further pleasure about them" amounted to, became clear a few months later when three Franciscans died a martyr's death for their allegiance to the Holy See.[7]

Among the Franciscans imprisoned in 1534 was Venerable Antony Brookby (or Brorbey), a man of singular holiness and profound learning. During the early part of the reign of Henry VIII, he was engaged as lecturer in divinity in Magdalen

---

[4] Stone, *Faithful Unto Death*, p. 88.

[5] Gasquet, *Henry VIII ... Monasteries*, Vol. II, pp. 137 seq.

[6] Stone, *Faithful Unto Death*, p. 75.

[7] Our chief source of information regarding these three martyrs is Bourchier, *Hist. Eccl. de Martyrio FF. Ord. Divi Francisci*, pp. 11-28. As to the historical value of the narrative, see supra.

College, Oxford, where he had received the licentiate in theology and enjoyed the reputation of being a master of Greek and Hebrew.[8] He was, moreover, a forceful preacher, and his eloquence together with his zeal and learning made him a most formidable opponent of the king's encroachments on the rights of the Holy See. Hence, in 1534, when the religious persecution broke out, Fr. Antony was lodged with others of his Order in prison. Later, it seems, he was released and placed with the Conventuals in London. Here, having obtained license to preach, he again went about instructing and confirming the people in their holy faith.

It was apparently in the spring of 1537 that, during a sermon held in St. Lawrence Church, he boldly denounced the king for his wanton rupture with Rome and seizure of the religious houses. Suddenly, he was interrupted by a man in the audience, who leaped to his feet and threatening him with the king's vengeance demanded that he hold his peace. It was one of Cromwell's spies. But fear had no meaning for Fr. Antony; although he realized what the sequel would be, he quietly continued his sermon. Without delay, the spy reported the affair and received orders for the friar's arrest. Accordingly, when some time after, Fr. Antony was again preaching in the church of St. Lawrence, the spy accompanied by royal officers entered the sacred edifice. The preacher saw them and knew what they had come for. Having finished the sermon, he fearlessly descended from the pulpit at the foot of which the king's men were waiting for him. Gladly he suffered them to bind his hands behind his back and to lead him off to Newgate. He rejoiced in the anticipation of a martyr's crown, when the prison gates closed and he found himself among thieves, murderers, assassins, and other criminals. His cell was the darkest and filthiest in Newgate, "in which the memory of man, no one had been condemned to lie, so that the prisoners themselves were astonished at so much cruelty." Here, amid the

---

[8] See Parkinson, *Antiquities of the English Franciscans*, p. 239.

gibes and curses of his fellow prisoners, the valiant champion prayed to God for strength and perseverance in the impending struggle.[9]

Summoned before the royal commissioners, Fr. Antony maintained with unflinching boldness that the king's assumed supremacy was contrary to the ordination of Christ who, as the Scriptures taught, had built his Church solely on the Rock of Peter. He declared himself ready to suffer even the most cruel death rather than deny that faith which for centuries past had been the glory and pride of England, and which was still a treasure he cherished above all earthly things. Finally, when his tormentors saw that threats and promises availed nothing, they ordered the rack to be brought in. The friar's face was radiant with joy when the executioners led him to the instrument of torture. Rudely they thrust him beneath the wooden framework and fastened his wrists and ankles to the rollers on both ends. These were then drawn in opposite directions, till the body of the helpless friar hung suspended in the rack. Then the frightful torture began. After every refusal to admit the king's supremacy, the rollers were drawn with ever increasing force, so that finally every bone in his body was wrenched from its socket.

During this inhuman torture, the martyr fixed his gaze heavenward and prayed. A deadly pallor came over his countenance, convulsive twitchings about the eyes and lips told of his intense sufferings; there was danger that he would die on the rack. For this reason, at the command of the judge to desist for the present, he was released from the bed of pain and dragged back into the dreadful dungeon in Newgate. Lying helpless on a heap of rotten straw, the valiant friar was left to breathe his last in utter gloom and solitude. In consequence of the cruel racking, he was unable to stir hand or foot. It was, moreover, the month of July and owing to the unbearable summer heat a burning fever soon set in. Since he could not

---

[9] See Stone, *Faithful Unto Death*, p. 77, on the authority of Barezzo Barezzi.

even bring his hand to his mouth, he suffered exceedingly from thirst and hunger, and he would have died of starvation, had not a pious woman purchased leave to visit the prison and give the friar food and drink through the iron prison bars.

During the twenty-five days which Fr. Antony spent in this pitiful condition, repeated attempts were made to wrest from him a denial of papal supremacy. But in vain; the faithful friar remained true to the end. Though his sufferings were great, his loyalty was greater. Though his body lay helpless, faint with sufferings, his noble soul exulted in the freedom of the children of God and gloried in the assurance of an eternal reward awaiting him. Finally, the jailor of Newgate received orders from the king to dispatch the friar secretly. Accordingly, on July 19, 1537, one of the king's men entered the cell of Fr. Antony, and tearing the cord from the feeble body, strangled him. Later in the day, when the turnkey made his usual call, he saw the friar lying with his face on the wet stone pavement of the cell. Thinking him asleep, he tried to rouse him with a rude kick; seeing that the form did not stir, he went closer—the friar was dead. The news of Fr. Antony's death spread like wildfire through the city. And when it was noised abroad that God was testifying to the holiness of the martyr, large crowds thronged Newgate to see the miracle. With mingled emotions of joy and dread, they gazed on the dazzling light that suffused the gloomy prison and formed a halo about the lifeless body. Many who had remained untouched when Fr. Antony preached in the churches of London, were now at the sight of this miracle filled with compunction for their past weakness and they resolved then and there to cling to the old faith at any cost.

Hardly had Fr. Antony passed to his eternal reward when another Franciscan succumbed to the cruel treatment of his jailers in Newgate. Venerable Thomas Cort was of a noble and deeply religious family. Esteemed by his brethren as a true follower of St. Francis, he was known also for his profound learning and great eloquence. From the very beginning of the religious conflict in England, Fr. Thomas had been among the foremost and boldest in defending the cause of justice and truth. It seems that he was of the number of those friars who on the intervention of Wriothesley had obtained leave to quit the country. Although there are no records to show when he returned to his native land, it is certain that in the spring of 1537, he was in London publicly defending papal supremacy at the risk of liberty and life. In order to wipe out the hateful stain of excommunication and to give his action in the eyes of the people the semblance of orthodoxy, the shrewd king had appealed to a General Council.[10] The Franciscans, however, were not slow to detect the futility of such an appeal. In a sermon held in the church of St. Lawrence about this time, Fr. Thomas boldly demonstrated to his hearers that both from a theological and from a historical standpoint, the Bishop of Rome was the supreme head of the universal Church of Christ, and therefore also of the Church in England; that King Henry, by proclaiming himself head of the English Church, had arrogated to himself a title and power to which he could have no right whatever; and that, accordingly, he was to be regarded as a heretic and schismatic, as long as he continued in his opposition to the Vicar of Christ. Spies of Cromwell were present at the sermon; and, when Fr. Thomas descended from the pulpit, they arrested him in the king's name and threw him into one of the foulest dungeons of Newgate.

Despite the horrors and hardships of prison life, Fr. Thomas remained true to his convictions. He felt that his end was not far off, and he glorified God in the loathsome dungeon, which he hoped soon to leave for the mansions of eternal bliss. At the time of his imprisonment, he was in poor health, and the close confinement in the damp and filthy cell soon brought the ailing friar to death's door. After being in prison a few days, he took sick, and on July 27, 1537, just a week after the execution of Fr. Antony Brookby, his soul passed to heaven.

A miracle similar to the one that attended the death of his

---

[10] Ibidem, p. 78.

fellow friar, gave testimony also to his heroic sanctity. Fear seized the bystanders when they beheld the grim dungeon bathed in celestial light. It was the second time within a week that this singular spectacle was seen in Newgate. King Henry heard of it, and, strange to say, his better nature for a moment reasserted itself. His guilty conscience left him no peace. He feared, no doubt, that these wonderful happenings were but a final warning from Him whose sacred laws he had so wantonly trampled under foot, and who had power to hurl his black soul into the frightful abyss of pain and perdition. In this paroxysm of fear, the king gave orders that the corpse of the deceased Fr. Thomas should be decently buried. Accordingly, the martyr was laid to rest in the cemetery of the Holy Sepulcher near the large door of the church. In later years, Margaret Herbert, the wife of a glovemaker of Ghent, set a stone on the grave of Fr. Thomas; it bore the inscription:

> Hac tu qui transis Christi devote viator
> In precibus, quaeso, sis memor ipse mei.[11]

The third Franciscan who died for the faith, in the year 1537, is Venerable Thomas Belchiam. Though only twenty-eight years of age, he was known as a bold and outspoken champion of papal supremacy. Like Fr. Thomas Cort, he publicly accused the king of heresy. To prove his assertion and to confirm his fellow friars in their allegiance to the Holy See, he published a book that began with the words, "They that are clothed in soft garments, are in the houses of kings."[12] In this

---

[11] Christ-loving traveler passing this way.
Remember, I beg thee, for my soul to pray.

[12] The book was entitled *Liber Ad Fratres* (A Book to the Brethren). See Dodd, *Church History of England*, Vol. I, p. 234. "One copy of the book was left by the author to the Observants of Greenwich. It passed through the hands of the eminent Franciscan Father Thomas Bourchier, who intended to publish it, and Father Angelus Mason says it was always in the minds of the friars to print the book; but here we lose sight of it entirely, and it

work, inspired by youthful zeal and enthusiasm, he showed that by setting aside the authority of Rome and proclaiming himself spiritual head of the Church in England, the king stood in open rebellion against the Vicar of Christ on earth, and that, therefore, he ceased to belong to the fold that Christ had committed to the care of St. Peter and his successors. Thereupon, he scourged the lax morals of the royal court, calling it a haunt of sin and vice and declaring that "he that will be godly must depart the court." Finally, he upbraided the clergy of England for their cringing cowardice in those woeful days when the rights of the Church and the prerogatives of the Papacy were at stake. He criticized especially the higher clergy of whom so many were sacrificing their God and their conscience on the altar of pride and ambition, who regardless of their duties as shepherds of Christ's flock, were stooping to the whims of a ruthless and rebellious king.

Needless to say, the appearance of this book added fuel to the fury of those against whom it was directed. The youthful defender of truth and morality was seized and thrown into prison. Here he was subjected to every kind of torture. But the resolute friar bore all with heroic courage and constancy. At last, when it became clear that he would never admit the king's usurped supremacy, he was brought back to prison. Now began for him a period of untold suffering. It was his terrible lot to die, not by the halter and the knife, but of disease and starvation.

How long Fr. Thomas languished in the gloom and filth of his prison cell, is not known. Historians say that he was deprived of all necessaries of life, so that gradually his sturdy frame was reduced to a mere skeleton. Finally, on August 3, 1537, death came to his relief. The martyr passed to his reward, repeating the words of the Royal Prophet: "In thee, O, Lord, have I trusted, let me never be confounded." At the moment

---

doubtless perished, under the destroying sway of the reformers." Stone, *Faithful Unto Death*, p. 80.

when he breathed his last, an earthquake shook the prison. The jailors were terrified, and when the king heard of it, he trembled and gave orders that Fr. Thomas receive a decent burial. On searching the cell, the prison officials found a copy of the book he had written. It was brought to the king, who on reading it is said to have shed tears and lamented his utter misery. But this seeming repentance was only a passing fit of remorse and uneasiness, such as frequently came over him and embittered his last years. He soon silenced the voice of conscience and had the book thrown into the fire.

It is evident that FF. Antony Brookby, Thomas Cort, and Thomas Belchiam suffered and died in defense of the Catholic dogma of papal supremacy. Arturus's *Martyrology* and Hueber's *Menologium* commemorate them on the day on which they passed to their eternal reward. Their names also head the list of those 261 English martyrs whose cause of beatification was opened on December 9, 1886, when Pope Leo XIII approved the decision of the Sacred Congregation, providing that a Commission be appointed to introduce the cause.[13]

---

[13] See *Acta Minorum,* Vol. VI (1887), p. 49.

CHAPTER VII
St. THOMAS MORE, FRANCISCAN TERTIARY

Early youth — At Oxford — Professional studies — With the Carthusians — More's public and private life — The impending storm — He resigns the chancellorship — Poverty and distress at Chelsea — Efforts of Anne Boleyn and Cromwell to ruin the ex-chancellor—Measures of the king against him — More rejects the Acts of Succession and Supremacy — In the Tower — His loyalty put to severe tests—Brought to trial — Found guilty of high treason and sentenced to death — His last days in prison — Beheaded on Tower Hill.

OWING to the unexpected dispersion of the Franciscans and the seizure of their friaries in 1534, the extent, activity, and influence of the Third Order of St. Francis in medieval England will ever remain an unwritten chapter in the history of the English Franciscans. From the singular popularity of the friars, however, and from their characteristic zeal for the welfare of the people, we may safely assume that during the three centuries preceding the Protestant Revolution, the Third Order was widely known and fostered. That this continued down to the very eve of the religious upheaval, is sufficiently clear from the fact that, besides Queen Catherine of Aragon, also Blessed Thomas More and his second wife, Alice Middleton, were Franciscan Tertiaries. It is for this reason, too, that the noble queen of Henry VIII and his sainted chancellor have found a place in these pages.[1]

---

[1] Authorities for the statement that St. Thomas More was a Franciscan Tertiary are chiefly: Livarius Oliger, *Third Order of St. Francis* in *The Catholic Encyclopedia*, Vol. XIV, p. 642; Heimbucher, *Die Orden und Congregation der Katholischen Kirche*, Vol. II, p. 492; Holzapfel, *Geschichte des Franziskanerordens*, p. 670; *Catalogus Hagiographicus Seraphicæ Familiæ* in

St. Thomas More was born February 7, 1478, in Milk Street, Cheapside, London. His pious and accomplished father, Sir John More, Knight, served as barrister and later as judge in the Court of the King's Bench. His mother, Agnes Graunger, died a few years after the birth of Thomas. St. Antony's School in Threadneedle Street, under the direction of Nicholas Holt, was deemed the best of its kind in London. Here Thomas received his elementary training. Unusually endowed in heart and mind, he made rapid progress at school, and at the age of thirteen he was graduated with high honors. Thinking the boy too young for university life, his prudent father placed him as page in the service of Cardinal Morton, Archbishop of Canterbury and Lord Chancellor of England. This saintly and learned prelate soon detected the superior talents of the quickwitted and winsome lad. To the nobles, who frequently came to dine with him, the chancellor was wont to remark, "This child here waiting at the table, whosoever shall live to see it, will prove a marvelous man."[2] At the same time, the sanctity and learning of the Cardinal made a lasting impression on the sensitive heart of Thomas; and it was in the service of this distinguished prelate, no doubt, that the future martyr first imbibed those lofty ideals of personal holiness and that unflinching zeal for truth and

---

Acta Minorum (an. xxviii, p. 203 seq.), an official list of all the Saints, Blessed, and Venerable of the three Orders of St. Francis. It was published with ecclesiastical approbation in 1909, on the occasion of the seventh centenary of the founding of the Franciscan Order. On page 216, Blessed Thomas More is commemorated expressly as a member of the Third Order of St. Francis, a fact which we think settles the question. Despite these evidences, Father Cuthbert writes in *The Catholic Encyclopedia*, Vol. XIV, p. 645, "Blessed Thomas More is frequently spoken of as a tertiary of St. Francis, but there seems to be no historical evidence to support this statement." It is not known when he joined the Third Order; perhaps it was at the time when he was thinking of joining the first Order of St. Francis.

[2] William Roper, *Life of Sir Thomas More, Knt.*, p. 5. The author of this work was the son-in-law of the Blessed martyr, having married the latter's favorite daughter Margaret. From her he learned many details for his *Life*, which is, therefore, of special interest and value to the historian.

justice which made him so fearless an opponent of schism and heresy.

In 1492, the Cardinal prevailed on Sir John More to let the boy pursue a higher course of studies at Oxford. The Renaissance had already found its way to the university, and Thomas conceived a strong predilection for the ancient classics. "For the short time of his abode," Harpsfield relates, "being not fully two years, and for his age, he wonderfully profited in the Latin and Greek tongues; where if he had settled and fixed himself, and run his full race in the study of the liberal sciences and divinity, I trow he would have been the singular and only spectacle of this our time of learning."[3] Not only was his college life "free from all excesses of play and riot," but then already he began those practices of prayer and mortification that marked his later career. "His father ... wished that he should learn from his earliest years to be frugal and sober, and to love nothing but his studies and literature. For this reason he gave him the bare necessaries, and would not allow him a farthing to spend freely. This he carried out so strictly that he had not money to mend his worn-out shoes, without asking it from his father. More used often to relate this conduct of his father, and greatly extolled it. 'It was thus' (he would say) 'that I indulged in no vice or pleasure, and spent my time in no vain or hurtful amusements; I did not know what luxury meant, and never learnt to use money badly; in a word, I loved and thought of nothing but my studies.'"[4]

After spending about two years at Canterbury College, Oxford, Thomas answered his father's summons and repaired to London in order to prepare himself for the bar. Although the study of law was not to his liking, he applied himself very

---

[3] See Bridgett, Rev. T. E., *Life and Writings of Blessed Thomas More*, p. 9. Nicholas Harpsfield wrote in the time of Queen Mary, William Roper supplying him with material.

[4] Stapleton, quoted by Bridgett, p. 10. Stapleton's *Tres Thomæ* contains "by far the best Life of More; it was published in 1588."

conscientiously and made such rapid progress that after an unusually short period of study, he was appointed for three successive years lecturer on law at Furnival's Inn. His spare time, however, he devoted to his beloved classics and to the Latin and Greek Fathers of the Church. We may add here that, although he ever after proved an ardent advocate of the classic revival so widely fostered in his day, he never sacrificed to pagan ideals his religious convictions, but remained to the end of his life a man of strict morals and a dutiful child of the Catholic Church. About this time he was called upon to deliver a series of historical lectures on St. Augustine's *De Civitate Dei*, in the church of St. Lawrence. Many learned men attended the lectures, so that the learning and eloquence of the youthful jurist soon became the topic of public comment.

Meanwhile the time arrived for Thomas to choose a state of life. "When he was about eighteen or twenty years old," his son-in-law tells us, "finding his body, by reason of his age, most rebellious, he sought diligently to tame his unbridled concupiscence by wonderful works of mortification. He used oftentimes to wear a sharp shirt next his skin, which he never left off wholly,—no, not even when he was Lord Chancellor of England... He used also much fasting and watching, lying often either upon the bare ground or upon some bench, or laying some log under his head, allotting himself but four or five hours in a night at the most for his sleep. ... He lived for four years amongst the Carthusians, dwelling near the Charterhouse, frequenting daily their spiritual exercises, but without any vow. He had an earnest desire also to be a Franciscan friar, that he might serve God in a state of perfection."[5] Erasmus, his intimate friend and confident, likewise informs us that Thomas "applied his whole mind to exercises of piety, looking to and pondering

---

[5] Cresacre More, quoted by Bridgett, p. 31. See also Baumstark: *Thomas Morus*, p. 22; Parkinson: *Antiquities of the English Franciscans*, p. 211; Du Boys: *Catherine D'Aragon*, p. 401; G. Roger Hudleston: *Sir Thomas More* in *The Catholic Encyclopedia*, Vol. XIV, p. 690; Camm: *Lives of the English Martyrs*, Vol. I, p. 129.

on the priesthood in vigils, fasts, and prayers, and similar austerities."[6] At last, however, on the advice of his father confessor, he abandoned the idea of embracing the religious state and turned his attention to public affairs.

In 1501, More was called to the bar, and three years later, he was elected a member of parliament. About this time, an event occurred that foreshadowed the future champion of truth and justice. King Henry VII had a bill introduced demanding of the people the enormous sum of 113,000 pounds sterling as a dowry for Princess Margaret who was betrothed to James IV of Scotland. Regarding the appropriation as unjust and unreasonable, the youthful parliamentarian publicly opposed it and effected that the house voted the much smaller sum of 30,000 pounds. Unable to mulct the "beardless boy," who as yet possessed no independent state, the enraged king vented his anger on the elder More, whom, by devising "a causeless quarrel," he fined 100 pounds sterling and cast into the Tower till the sum was paid. Thomas grieved to see his father suffer on his account. But he was convinced of having done his duty, insomuch that, when Bishop Fox advised him to offer an apology to the king, he refused to do so, and he would probably have gone over sea had not the king died soon after.[7]

The accession of Henry VIII in 1509, augured well for the future welfare of the kingdom. He was already acquainted with Thomas More, having met him about ten years before in company with Erasmus of Rotterdam and received a poem from him. Since then, Henry had heard much of the promising barrister, and he cherished a high esteem for his virtue and learning. Accordingly, he summoned him to court and assured him of his royal favor and friendship. In 1510, More was appointed Under Sheriff of London. As Master of Requests he was almost constantly at court, and the youthful king, not only consulted him on political matters, but especially delighted in

---

[6] Bridgett, p. 23.

[7] Roper, p. 8.

conversing with him on scientific questions. "Because he was of a pleasant disposition, it pleased the king and queen, after the council had supped, at the time of their supper, for their pleasure commonly to call for him to be merry with them."[8]

In spite of all these royal blandishments, More preserved his independent character. In 1517, he had to defend the Pope's cause against the English realm regarding the forfeiture of a papal ship. He argued so well that the star chamber decided in favor of the Pope. Henry gladly returned the ship, and, far from being displeased with More, sought only to win his valuable service for himself. As royal speaker, More had frequently to make the Latin address; thus at the famous meeting of Henry VIII with Francis I of France in the Field of the Cloth of Gold, and again two years later, at the solemn entry of Emperor Charles V and Henry VIII in London.

Though More enjoyed the esteem and confidence of Cardinal Wolsey and in turn had great respect for the Cardinal's eminent qualities, it happened that on one occasion he found it his duty publicly to oppose him. Wolsey was peeved and exclaimed, "Are you not ashamed, Mr. More, being the last in place and dignity to dissent from so many noble and prudent men? You show yourself a foolish councillor." More calmly replied, "Thanks be to God that his royal Highness has but one fool in his Council."[9] On another occasion, the Cardinal, displeased with More's policy, said, "Would to God you had been at Rome, Master More, when I made you Speaker." "Your grace not offended," replied More, "so would I too, my Lord."[10]

In 1518, he was appointed Privy Councillor and Subtreasurer of the Exchequer. Three years later, the king created him a knight. About this time, the heretical teaching of Martin Luther was causing much comment in England. More was foremost in denouncing the heresiarch and assisted the king in writing his

---

[8] Ibidem, p. 11.

[9] Camm, p. 142.

[10] Roper, p. 20.

famous *Assertio Septem Sacramentorum*. In 1525, he became chancellor of the Duchy of Lancaster. Repeatedly, since his elevation to the throne, Henry VIII employed him on important foreign embassies. Finally, in 1529, he reached the height of his political distinction. During his absence at Cambray as English ambassador, Cardinal Wolsey had fallen into royal displeasure. Thomas More had just returned to England, when the king summoned him to court and handed him the official seal of the Lord Chancellor of the realm.

Throughout his public career, both as statesman and as writer, More's attitude toward the Church and her institutions was one of ready obedience and unswerving loyalty. Indeed, he lamented the grave abuses in the Church and joined his life-long friend Erasmus of Rotterdam in the general cry for reform; never, however, did he approve, much less share, his friend's cynical and rebellious spirit. Biased historians have sought to deduct More's religious views from his celebrated *Utopia*. That this satire is anything but an efflux of Luther's heretical teaching, is evident already from the fact that it was written in Latin before the German "reformer" raised the standard of revolt against the Church. The author "certainly had no wish," Bridgett remarks, "that it should be read by the people of England in the days of Henry VIII."[11] Furthermore, we know how readily the learned and well-minded statesman would have burned the book had he foreseen that the enemies of the Church he loved and revered would employ it as a cudgel against her. In 1523, he wrote a spirited reply to Luther and constantly urged his friend Erasmus to exert his learning and influence in the same direction.

It has been stated that Thomas More refrained from entering a religious order, because the corruption then supposed to prevail in the monasteries and friaries of England, filled him with disgust. In reply to this charge, Hutton, a Protestant historian writes: "It is absurd to assert that More was

---

[11] Bridgett, p. 101.

disgusted with monastic corruption—that he 'loathed monks as a disgrace to the Church.' He was throughout his life a warm friend of the religious orders, and a devoted admirer of the monastic ideal. He condemned the vices of individuals; he said, as his great-grandson says, 'that at that time religious men in England had somewhat degenerated from their ancient strictness and fervour of spirit;' but there is not the slightest sign that his decision to decline the monastic life was due in the smallest degree to a distrust of the system or a distaste for the theology of the Church."[12] How highly Thomas More esteemed the religious orders became clear in 1529 when he took Fish to task and by his *Supplication of Souls in Purgatory* sought to offset the evil influence of the latter's *Supplication of Beggars*, a scurrilous and slanderous diatribe on the life and habits of religious. We know, too, how, in 1533, he published his celebrated *Apology* in which he refuted the accusations made by Saint-German against the clergy in general and the religious in particular.[13]

The domestic and private life of Blessed Thomas More has never failed to win the applause and admiration of his biographers. In 1505, he married Jane Colt, the eldest daughter of a country gentleman of Essex. But the happy union was not to last long. In 1511, his wife died leaving him with four small children, Margaret, Elizabeth, Cecily, and John. From an epitaph which he wrote twenty years later, we learn how fondly he cherished her memory. He had to provide for his children, however, and for this reason married Alice Middleton, a widow. Like himself she also was a member of the Third Order of St. Francis and proved a kind mother and a dutiful,

---

[12] See Bremond, *Sir Thomas More*, tr. by Harold Child, p. 17.

[13] See Dodd: *Church History of England*, Vol. I, p. 304; Gasquet: *The Eve of the Reformation*, chap. v.

discreet housewife.[14] After living twelve years in Crosby Place, the More family moved to their new home at Chelsea, a village on the outskirts of London. Their spacious residence so famous in history stood in a beautiful garden that bordered on the Thames. Here More would resort when free from State duties to find peace and comfort in the company of his loved ones. He took special interest and delight in the education of his children, for whom he engaged able and reliable tutors. Even when not at home, he superintended their studies. Once he wrote to Margaret, his favorite daughter:

> I beg you, Margaret, tell me about the progress you are making in your studies. For, I assure you that, rather than allow my children to be idle and slothful, I would make a sacrifice of wealth, and bid adieu to other cares and business, to attend to my children and family, amongst whom none is more dear to me than yourself, my beloved daughter.

In a letter to William Gunnell their tutor he says that his children are "to put virtue in the first place, learning in the second; and in their studies to esteem most whatever may teach them piety towards God, charity to all, and modesty and Christian humility in themselves."[15]

Erasmus, a frequent visitor at the Chelsea home, says that it was a school of Christianity, where piety and virtue were in

---

[14] Bridgett (pp. 116 seq.) defends the character of Alice Middleton against such as declare that by her sharp tongue and shrewish temper she proved a termagant and greatly embittered the domestic life of More. "We have now seen," he concludes (p. 120), "all the evil that can be alleged against this lady, and it certainly does not justify our classing Blessed More amongst the ill-matched great men. To say that when his time of suffering came she did not rise to the height of his soul, is merely to class her with nearly all her contemporaries, including almost every abbess, abbot and bishop in the country."

[15] See Bridgett, pp. 135, 129.

full bloom. Daily the household would gather for evening devotion. All had to attend Mass on Sundays and holy days, and on the vigils of feasts, like Christmas and Easter, they had to be present at the midnight chanting of the office. At table, one of the girls read a passage from Holy Scripture concluded as is done in convents with: *Tu autem, Domine, miserere nobis.* Then a commentary from one of the Holy Fathers would be read or, if some learned man happened to be there, a discussion was held on the text, till finally More himself would change the topic by some well chosen jest or story.

Conformably with the Rule of the Third Order, More was greatly devoted to the poor and sick. "He used himself to go through the back lanes, and inquire into the state of poor families; and he would relieve their distress, not by scattering a few small coins as is the general custom, but when he ascertained a real need, by two, three or four gold pieces. When his official position and duties prevented this personal attention, he would send some of his family to dispense his alms, especially to the sick and the aged. ... He very often invited to his table his poorer neighbors, receiving them (not condescendingly) but familiarly and joyously; he rarely invited the rich, and scarcely ever the nobility. In his parish of Chelsea he hired a house, in which he gathered many infirm, poor and old people, and maintained them at his own expense. ... He even went so far as to receive into his family and maintain a poor gentlewoman, a widow named Paula, who had expended all she had in an unsuccessful lawsuit. To widows and orphans, when he practiced at the bar, he even gave his services gratuitously."[16]

We have seen how as a student at Oxford he practiced prayer and penance. That he continued these pious practices in later life, goes without saying. Next to his library, was a little chapel, where he spent many an hour in close communion with God. "He used to rise at two o'clock in the morning," Stapleton

---

[16] Stapleton, quoted by Bridgett, p. 143.

informs us, "and until seven to give himself to study and devotion. Every day before any other business—his very early studies alone excepted—he used to hear Mass. This duty he so strictly observed, that when summoned once by the king at a time when he was assisting at Mass, and sent for a second and third time, he would not go until the whole Mass was ended; and to those who called him and urged him to go at once to the king and leave the Mass, he replied that he was paying his court to a greater and better Lord, and must first perform that duty. Henry was then pious and God-fearing, and did not take in bad part this piety of More.

"He used daily to recite morning and evening prayers, to which he would add the seven penitential psalms and the litanies. He would often add to these the gradual psalms and the psalm *Beati Immaculati*. He also had a collection of private prayers, some in Latin, some in English, as may be seen in his English works. He had made up also, imitating in this St. Jerome and others, a small psaltery consisting of selected psalms, which he often used. He would also make pilgrimages sometimes seven miles distant, on foot, which even common people scarcely do in England."[17] Before entering on a new office, or undertaking a difficult business, he received Holy Communion. On one occasion, the Duke of Norfolk found him in church among the singers, clothed in a surplice. When the nobleman objected that the king would be displeased with such an act, the chancellor replied, "Nay, your grace may not think that the king, your master and mine, will with me for serving of God his master, be offended, or thereby account his office dishonored."[18] On another occasion, the chancellor was at table with his family. When he removed his official gown, Anne Cresacre, his daughter-in-law, noticed the hair-shirt he was wearing and began to laugh. Later when Margaret told him of it, he felt very sorry, since he wished no one but her to know of

---

[17] Stapleton, quoted by Bridgett, p. 61 seq.

[18] Roper, p. 51.

it.[19] After his martyrdom, in 1535, his confessor wrote of him, "This Thomas More was my ghostly child; in his confession (he used) to be so pure, so clean. ... I never heard many such. ... He was devout in his divine service, and ... wore a great hair (shirt) next his skin."[20]

It was with a heavy heart that Sir Thomas More yielded to the will of his monarch and, on October 25, 1529, took the required oath of office. He realized that Henry was no longer the high-minded and God-fearing prince of former years, and that he had conferred the chancellorship on him, in order to gain his support in the divorce from his lawful queen. In the fall of Cardinal Wolsey, More saw clearly what his own lot would be, when once the king's "secret affair" should involve the divine rights of the Papacy.

About a year before, while walking with William Roper along the Thames at Chelsea, he suddenly turned to his son-in-law and said, "Now would to our Lord, son Roper, upon condition that three things were well established in Christendom, I were put in a sack and here presently cast into the Thames."

"What great things be those, sir," inquired the other, "that should move you so to wish?"

"Wouldst thou know, son Roper, what they be?"

"Yea, marry, with a good will, sir, if it please you."

"In faith, son," replied More, "they be these; the first is, that whereas the most part of Christian princes be at mortal war, they were all at universal peace. The second, that where the Church of God is at this present sore afflicted with many errors and heresies, it were well settled in perfect uniformity of religion. The third, that where the matter of the king's marriage is now come in question, it were to the glory of God and quietness of all parties brought to a good conclusion."[21]

---

[19] Ibidem, p. 48.

[20] See Bremond, p. 75.

[21] Roper, p. 25.

Evidently, he foresaw what a terrible calamity the last-mentioned affair would bring upon England.

On February 11, 1531, the conflict began. Parliament wholly subservient to the king approved a royal proclamation by which the clergy were to acknowledge Henry "protector and only supreme head of the church and clergy of England, so far as the law of Christ allows." Although this new title was not clearly adverse to papal supremacy, it was at least ill-omened and dangerous. "There is no one," Chapuys wrote a few days later, "that does not blame this usurpation, except those who have promoted it. The chancellor is so mortified at it that he is anxious above all things to resign his office."[22] Pressed by the king to reconsider his resignation, More remained in office and again set himself to studying the question of papal supremacy. Finding he could not reconcile his conscience with the king's demand, he pursued a policy of silence, refusing to have anything to do with the matter. Henry was satisfied, hoping in time to win over the chancellor.

Thus a year passed by, when on May 13, the king demanded that parliament suspend the payment of the Annates to the Pope and relax the English laws against heresy. Needless to say, More again used all his eloquence and influence to crush the bills. Though the king tried to conceal his anger, the chancellor felt that the crisis had come. He would need much time now for prayer and penance, and therefore he again, on May 16, requested the king to relieve him of his office. This time Henry accepted his resignation, thanking him publicly for his long and faithful service. Indeed, by his justice, integrity, prudence, and learning, the noble statesman had gained the esteem of entire Europe. On May 22, Chapuys wrote: "The chancellor has resigned, seeing that affairs were going on badly and likely to be worse, and that if he retained his office he would be obliged to act against his conscience, or incur the king's displeasure, as he had already begun to do, for refusing to take his part against

---

[22] Bridgett, p. 234.

the clergy. His excuse was that his salary was too small, and that he was not equal to the work. Everyone is concerned, for there never was a better man in the office."[23] Though sincerely devoted to his king and country, Blessed Thomas More never lost sight of God and heaven. In fact, he was true to his king, because he was true to God, and only when Henry succumbed to his lower passions, did his noble and saintly chancellor oppose his lawless policy and fearlessly unfurl the standard of truth and justice. Shortly after his resignation, Sir Thomas Cromwell came to him at Chelsea with a message from the king. Having read the message, More said, "Master Cromwell, you are now entered into the service of a most noble, wise, and liberal prince; if you will follow my poor advice, you shall, in your counsel-giving to his grace, ever tell him what he ought to do, but never what he is able to do. So shall you show yourself a true faithful servant, and a right wise counsellor. For if a lion knew his own strength, hard were it for any man to rule him."[24] Cromwell's subsequent career showed how utterly he ignored this wholesome advice.

More's resignation meant poverty and distress for himself and his family. Deprived of his professional income, he was forced to reduce his extensive household. Having found suitable places for his servants and having disposed of all luxuries and superfluities, he told his dear ones of his plans, cheerfully adding that, if later they should have nothing to live on, "then may we yet, with bags and wallets, go a-begging together ... at every man's door to sing *Salve Regina,* and so still keep company and be merry together."[25] Although the family remained at Chelsea, More's poverty was so great that "he was not able for the maintenance of himself and such as necessarily belonged unto him, sufficiently to find meat, drink, fuel,

---

[23] Ibidem, p. 240.

[24] Roper, p. 55.

[25] Ibidem, p. 53.

apparel, and such other necessary charges."[26]

During these days of deep distress and dark forebodings, More's one thought was to arm himself by prayer and penance for the final struggle. Meanwhile, he maintained a strict neutrality on the momentous questions then agitating the country. Urged on by Anne Boleyn, who hated the ex-chancellor because he had refused to be present at her coronation, the king and his wily creature Thomas Cromwell made repeated efforts to besmirch his good name. In 1533, they put his name on the bill of attainder drawn up against the Holy Maid of Kent and her adherents. But in a letter to Cromwell, More fully established his innocence.[27] In like manner, the two Franciscans, FF. Rich and Risby, with whom he had conferred on the character of the Maid, declared him innocent of any dealings with her, prejudicial to his majesty. But his enemies, especially Cromwell, were eager for his ruin, and there is little doubt that he would have been executed with the nun and her party, had not the Lords begged the king on their knees to take his name from the bill and to await a more "just" cause for vengeance.

On March 30, 1534, the Act of Succession was passed.[28] A commission was appointed by the king before which, More was informed, he would have to appear on April 13, at Lambeth. He had previously written to Cromwell that his soul would be "in right great peril if he should follow the other side and deny the

---

[26] Harpsfield, quoted by Camm, p. 188.

[27] For a copy of this letter see Bridgett, pp. 323 seq.

[28] According to this Act, the children of Anne Boleyn were to succeed to the throne. Any English subject who refused to take the oath obliging them to observe and maintain the Act in all its effects and contents was declared guilty of high treason. The preamble which the commissioners included in the formula of the oath declared the king's marriage with Catherine of Aragon invalid and his recent marriage with Anne Boleyn valid. Now, just the contrary had been officially and solemnly proclaimed by the Holy See a week previous to the passing of the Act. The oath, therefore, necessarily implied a rejection of papal authority. This explains More's attitude.

primacy to be provided by God."[29] Whatever others might hold, to him it was now a matter of conscience, for which he was ready to suffer all. On the morning of April 13, he attended holy Mass for the last time at Chelsea and received the sacraments. Then he bade farewell to his grief-stricken family. His own heart, too, was steeped in sorrow. "I thank our Lord the field is won," he said to his son-in-law, William Roper, when the boat struck off from shore and he cast a last look on his beautiful Chelsea home.[30]

From a letter which he wrote to his daughter Margaret four days later, we learn how steadfastly he refused to take the oath which the commission presented to him, always maintaining that it would imperil his conscience. Accused of obstinacy and pride in placing his own private judgment over the decision of learned and God-fearing men who had already taken the oath, More replied, "If there were no more than myself upon my side, and the whole parliament upon the other, I would be sore afraid to lean to mine own mind only against so many. But on the other side, if it so be that in some things, for which I refuse the oath, I have (as I think I have) upon my part as great a Council and a greater too, I am not then bounden to change my conscience and conform it to the Council of one realm, against the general Council of Christendom. ... Surely as to swear to the succession I see no peril. But I thought and think it reason that to mine own oath I look well myself, and be of counsel also in the fashion, and never intended to swear for a piece, and set my hand to the whole oath. Howbeit, as help me God, as touching the whole oath I never withdrew any man from it, nor never advised any to refuse it, nor never put, nor will put, any scruple in any man's head, but leave every man to his own conscience. And me thinketh in good faith, that so were it in

---

[29] See Camm, p. 194.

[30] Roper, p. 71.

good reason that every man should leave me to mine."[31]

After the hearing, More was placed with the Abbot of Westminster and held there for four days. Not knowing how to proceed against his former friend and favorite, the king consulted the Council. Cranmer proposed a compromise that would save More and at the same time make it appear as if he had taken the oath. But Henry would not hear of this; he wanted More's full submission in set terms and finally, egged on by Anne Boleyn, he decided that the ex-chancellor would have to choose between taking the complete oath and going to prison. Of course, the man of God chose the latter, and on April 17, he was thrown into the Tower.

Though torn from those he loved, the valiant champion found the seclusion of prison quite to his liking. Convinced that he was suffering for a just and holy cause, he prepared himself for the day when he would be called upon to die in its defence. The prison was now his friary, where he could pray and study to his heart's content. Although in poor health, he continued his wonted mortifications. He never put off the hair-shirt and took the discipline regularly. The *Dialogue of Comfort Against Tribulation*, which he wrote in prison for the instruction and edification of his grief-stricken family, breathes the spirit of one living in most intimate union with God.

About a month after his imprisonment, he was visited by his favorite daughter Margaret. His enemies hoped that on her entreaties he would finally submit. In vain, however, did she

---

[31] Ibidem, p. 111. Regarding More's refusal to take the oath of succession in the proposed form Bridgett says, "By comparing the various expressions of Sir Thomas together, it seems that he was himself deterred ... by several reasons, some of which were doctrinal, and held by the doctors of the Church; but others were of a secret nature known to himself, and which he had never communicated to another, and would not reveal even to his daughter. Whether these had reference to Anne Boleyn's affinity with Henry, or her precontract of marriage with Percy, or some other impediment still more secret, we cannot now discover, any more than we know the grounds on which Cranmer pronounced that Anne's marriage with Henry had been null from the beginning" (p. 382).

plead and argue with him. "I believe, Megg," he said, "that they that have put me here ween that they have done me a high displeasure: but I assure thee on my faith, mine own good daughter, if it had not been for my wife and ye that be my children (whom I account the chief part of my charge) I would not have failed long ere this to have closed myself in as straight a room, and straighter too. But since I am come hither without mine own desert, I trust that God of His Goodness will discharge me of my care, and with His gracious help supply my lack among you. I find no cause, I thank God, Megg, to reckon myself in worse case than in mine own house, for me thinketh God maketh me a wanton, and setteth me on his lap and dandleth me."[32]

On another occasion, Margaret told her father that she had a letter, which proved how his persistence was alienating his friends. "What, Mistress Eve," More replied with a smile, "hath my daughter Alington played the serpent with you, and with a letter set you to work to come and tempt your father again, and for the favor that you bear him, labor to make him swear against his conscience and send him to the devil? Daughter Margaret," he continued, "we two have talked of this thing ofter than twice or thrice. And the same tale, in effect, that you tell me now therein, and the same fear too, have you twice told me before, and I have twice answered you too, that in this matter if it were possible for me to do the thing that might content the king's grace, and God therewith not offended, then hath no man taken this oath already more gladly than I would do."[33]

---

[32] Roper, p. 74.

[33] Ibidem, p. 119. In extenuation of Margaret's conduct Bridgett says, "The affectionate daughter had no thought of leading her father to do what was unworthy of him. When we see one so pure and wise as Margaret Roper thus deceived (she had taken the oath with the saving clause: *so far as Christ's law allows*), we can estimate the enormity of the scandal given to the laity by the prelates and clergy of England, and we can also estimate the magnificence of More's loyalty to conscience, that he should be in no ways

St. Thomas More, Franciscan Tertiary

What grieved him above all was the misery to which his family had been put on his account. This is evident from a letter which he wrote to Margaret about this time.

> If I had not been, my dearly beloved daughter, at a firm and fast point, I trust, in God's great mercy this good great while before, your lamentable letter had not a little abashed me, surely far above all other things, of which I hear divers times not a few terrible toward me. ... A deadly grief unto me, and much more deadly than to hear of mine death (for the fear thereof, I thank our Lord, the fear of hell, the hope of heaven, and the passion of Christ daily more and more assuage), is, that I perceive my good son your husband, and you my good daughter, and my good wife, and mine other good children and innocent friends, in great displeasure and danger of great harm thereby. ... Out of which (trouble) I beseech Him to bring me, when His will shall be, into His endless bliss of Heaven, and in the meanwhile, give me grace and you both, in all our agonies and troubles, devoutly to resort prostrate unto the remembrance of that bitter agony, which our Saviour suffered before His passion at the Mount. And if we diligently so do, I verily trust we shall find therein great comfort and consolation. And thus, my dear daughter, the blessed spirit of Christ, for His tender mercy, govern and guide you all, to His pleasure and to your weal and comfort, both body and souls.[34]

Lady More was also permitted to visit him. Unable to understand her husband's attitude, she used all her household eloquence to bring about his submission to the king.

"What the good-yere, Master More," she said, "I marvel that you that have been always hitherto taken for so wise a man

---

swayed by that example, thus pressed upon him by the mouth of his accomplished and beloved daughter" (p. 374).

[34] Roper, pp. 153 seq.

will now so play the fool to lie here in this close, filthy prison, and be content thus to be shut up among mice and rats, when you might be abroad at your liberty, and with the favour and good will both of the king and his council if you would but do as all the bishops and best learned of this realm have done. And seeing you have at Chelsea a right fair house, your library, your gallery, your garden, your orchard, and all other necessaries so handsome about you, where you might in the company of me your wife, your children, and household, be merry. I muse what a God's name you mean here still thus fondly to tarry."

"I pray thee, good Mistress Alice," put in More with a smile, "tell me one thing."

"What is that?" asked his wife.

"Is not this house as nigh heaven as mine own?"

"Tylle valle, Tylle valle!"

"How say you, Mistress Alice, is it not so?"

"Bone Dens, Bone Deus, man, will this gear never be left?"

"Well then, Mistress Alice, if it be so, it is very well. For I see no great cause why I should much joy in my gay house, or in any thing thereunto belonging, when if I should but seven years lie buried under the ground and then arise and come thither again, I should not fail to find some therein that would bid me get out of doors, and tell me it were none of mine. What cause have I then to like such a house as would so soon forget his master?"[35]

As time wore on without any change in More's attitude toward the required oath, his imprisonment became more severe. In November, 1534, the lands he had received from the king ten years before were confiscated. This made his family almost penniless. Repeatedly they appealed to Henry for assistance; but the cruel king and his minister only gloated over the sorrow they were thereby causing their dauntless prisoner in the Tower. Finally, all visits were prohibited, and what pained him most, he was no longer permitted to attend holy

---

[35] Ibidem, pp. 81 seq.

Mass. Despite privation and suffering, however, he was determined to persevere on the path of duty to the end. This is evident from a letter which he addressed to a priest early in January, 1535. This priest, whose name was Leader, having heard that More had relented and taken the oath, wrote to him apparently to congratulate him on his approaching deliverance from prison. "The tale that is reported," the prisoner replied in part, "albeit I cannot but thank you though ye would it were true, yet I thank God it is very vanity. And I trust in the great goodness of God that He shall never suffer it to be true. If my mind had been obstinate in deed, I would not let for any rebuke or worldly shame plainly to confess the truth; for I propose not to depend upon the fame of the world. But I thank God that the thing I do is not for obstinacy, but for the salvation of my soul, because I cannot induce mine own mind otherwise to think than I do concerning the oath. ... If ever I should mishap to receive the oath (which I trust Our Lord shall never suffer me), ye may reckon sure that it were expressed and extorted by duress and hard handling. For all the goods of this world, I thank Our Lord I set not much more by than I do by dust. ... I beseech Our Lord that all may prove as true faithful subjects to the king that have sworn, as I am in my mind sure they be which have refused to swear."[36]

On April 30, 1535, we learn from his letter to Margaret, Cromwell with other members of the Council came to the Tower to exact from him a clear and definite statement regarding the king's spiritual supremacy. Among other things they accused him of scandalizing the people by his obstinacy and threatened that the law would take its course were he to persist in his opposition to the king's demand. Declaring that he had never sought to influence any one in the matter of the oath, he continued, "I am the king's true faithful subject and daily bedesman, and pray for his highness and all the realm. I do nobody no harm, I say none harm, I think none harm, but

---

[36] Bridgett, p. 379.

wish everybody good. And if this be not enough to keep a man alive, in good faith I long not to live. And I am dying already, and have since I came here, been divers times in the case that I thought to die within one hour. And I thank our Lord that I was never sorry for it, but rather sorry when I saw the pang past. And therefore my poor body is at the king's pleasure. Would God my death might do him good."[37] A few weeks later the king's men repeated their visit. When More again shrewdly evaded an open declaration concerning royal supremacy, his enemies accused him of cowardice, alleging that for fear of death he dared not speak his mind freely. To this the holy man made the memorable reply, "I have not been a man of such holy living that I might be bold to offer myself to death, lest God, for my presumption, might suffer me to fall; and, therefore, I put not myself forward, but draw back. Howbeit, if God draw me to it Himself, then trust I in His great mercy that He shall not fail to give me grace and strength."[38]

The glorious martyrdom of the Carthusians on June 19, and that of Blessed John Fisher, three days later, made it clear to More that also his day of triumph was fast approaching. Despoiled of all his books and writing material and shut up in solitary confinement, he devoted his time exclusively to prayer and mortification. But his heart was as staunch and as cheerful as ever. Asked one day by the jailer why he always kept the blind down and sat in utter darkness, he replied with a smile of sweet composure, "What should I do? When the wares are taken away, should not the shop be closed?"[39]

On July 1, the servant of God was taken from his cell and conducted to Westminster for trial. "To make the greater impression on the people," writes Lingard, "perhaps to add to his shame and suffering, More was led on foot, in a coarse

---

[37] Roper, p. 165.

[38] Ibidem, p. 173.

[39] Sander, *De Origine ac Progressu Schismatis Anglicani,* first edition (1585), p. 81; Rishton edition (1690), p. 184.

woolen gown, through the most frequented streets, from the Tower to Westminster Hall. The color of his hair, which had lately become gray, his face, which, though cheerful, was pale and emaciated, and the staff, with which he supported his feeble steps, announced the rigor and duration of his confinement."[40] His appearance in court and his subsequent reply after the indictment had been read made a deep impression on all present. Referring to the seditious utterances which Richard Rich had falsely accused him of having made during a conversation in the Tower, the martyr said:

> "If I were a man, my lords, that did not regard an oath, I need not stand in this place at this time as an accused person. And if this oath of yours, Mr. Rich, be true, then I pray that I may never see the face of God, which I would not say were it otherwise to win the whole world." Then, having repeated the conversation as it had really taken place, he continued: "In good faith, Mr. Rich, I am sorrier for your perjury than for my own peril; but neither I, nor any other man else, to my knowledge, ever took you to be a man of such credit, as that, in any matter of importance, I, or any other, would, at any time, vouchsafe to communicate with you. And I, as you know, of no small while, have been acquainted with you and your conversation, who have known you from your youth hitherto, for we long dwelled together in one parish. I am sorry you compel me so to say, that you were esteemed very light of tongue, a great dicer, and of no commendable fame. And so in your house at the Temple, where hath been your chief bringing up, were you likewise accounted.
>
> "Can it, therefore, seem likely to your honorable lordships that I would, in so weighty a cause, so unadvisedly overshoot myself as to trust Mr. Rich, a man of me always

---

[40] Lingard, *History of England* (New York, 1879), Vol. V, p. 21.

reputed of little troth, so far above my sovereign lord the king or any of his noble councillors, that I would utter unto him the secrets of my conscience touching the king's supremacy, the special point at my hands so long sought for—a thing I never did, nor never would, after the statute made thereof, reveal unto the King's highness himself? Can this, in your judgment, my lords, seem likely to be true?"[41]

When the martyr had finished speaking, the jurymen were asked to give their verdict. After a quarter of an hour's private consultation they returned to the court room and declared the prisoner guilty of treason, whereupon the chancellor sentenced him to death by hanging, drawing, and quartering. On hearing his sentence, the holy man rose quietly from his seat. The time had now come for him to make a public profession of faith.

"Since I am condemned and God knows how," he said, "I wish to speak freely of your statute, for the discharge of my conscience. For the seven years that I have studied the matter, I have not read in any approved doctor of the Church that a temporal lord could or ought to be head of the spirituality."

"What, More," broke in the chancellor, "you wish to be considered wiser and of better conscience than all the bishops and nobles of the realm?"

"My lord," replied the martyr calmly, "for one bishop of your opinion I have a hundred saints of mine; and for one parliament of yours, and God knows of what kind, I have all the General Councils for 1,000 years; and for one kingdom I have France and all the kingdoms of Christendom."

At this, the Duke of Norfolk suggested that now the malice of the prisoner was clear. But More was nothing perturbed.

"What I say," he explained, "is necessary for the discharge of my conscience and satisfaction of my soul, and to this I call God to witness, the sole searcher of human hearts. I said further, that your statute is ill made, because you have sworn

---

[41] Roper, pp. 86 seq.

never to do anything against the Church, which, through all Christendom, is one and undivided, and you have no authority, without the common consent of all Christians, to make a law or Act of Parliament or Council against the union of Christendom. I know well that the reason why you have condemned me is because I have never been willing to consent to the king's second marriage; but I hope, in the Divine goodness and mercy, that, as St. Paul and St. Stephen, whom he persecuted, are now friends in Paradise, so we, though differing in this world, shall be united in perfect charity in the other. I pray God to protect the king, and give him good counsel."[42]

He was then brought back to prison. When Margaret waiting with other members of the family at the Tower Wharf saw her condemned father, she ran up to him, fell about his neck and kissed him. With mingled joy and sorrow he comforted and blessed her. But not satisfied, his affectionate daughter ran to him a second time; "and at last, with a full and heavy heart, was fain to depart from him: the beholding whereof was to many of them that were present thereat so lamentable, that it made them for very sorrow to weep and mourn."[43] Later, when the martyr saw that Sir William Kingston, constable of the Tower, was weeping, he said, "Good Master Kingston, trouble not yourself, but be of good cheer; for I will pray for you, and my good lady your wife, that we may meet in heaven together, where we shall be merry for ever and ever."[44]

No date had been fixed for his execution. But the martyr knew that the end was near and spent the remaining few days in closest union with God. To strengthen himself for the deadly conflict, he scourged his innocent flesh most severely. It is also said that he wrapped himself in a white sheet and like a corpse prepared for burial paced his gloomy cell meditating on death

---

[42] Bridgett, p. 422.

[43] Roper, p. 97.

[44] Ibidem, p. 96.

and eternity. On July 5, the day before his martyrdom, he sent his hair-shirt to Margaret together with a letter which was written with a charred stick and read in part:

Our Lord bless you, good daughter, and your good husband, and your little boy, and all yours, and all my children, and all my godchildren and all our friends. ... I cumber you, good Margaret, much, but I would be sorry if it should be any longer than tomorrow, for it is St. Thomas' Eve, and the Utas of St. Peter; and, therefore, to-morrow long I to go to God. It were a day very meet and convenient for me. I never liked your manner toward me better than when you kissed me last; for I love when daughterly love and dear charity hath no leisure to look to worldly courtesy. Farewell, my dear child, and pray for me, and I shall for you and all your friends that we may merrily meet in heaven.[45]

It is related on the authority of Cresacre More that when the martyr was told that the king had commuted his punishment to decapitation, he replied, "God forbid the king should use any more such mercy unto any of my friends, and God bless all my posterity from such pardons."[46] July 6, as he had desired, was the day set for his execution. Early that morning, Sir Thomas Pope, a cherished friend of his, came and told him that by the king's orders he was to die before nine o'clock. "Master Pope," was his cheerful reply, "for your good tidings I heartily thank you. I have always been much bounden to the king's highness for the benefits and honours that he had still from time to time most bountifully heaped upon me; and yet more bounden am I to his grace for putting me into this place, where I have had convenient time and space to have remembrance of my end. And so help me God, most of all, Master Pope, am I bounden to his highness that it pleaseth him so shortly to rid me out of the miseries of this wretched world, and therefore will I not fail earnestly to pray for his grace, both here, and also in the world

---

[45] Ibidem, p. 175.

[46] Bridgett, p. 431, footnote.

to come." When he noticed that his old friend was weeping, the martyr sought to comfort him. "Quiet yourself, good Master Pope," he said, "and be not discomforted, for I trust that we shall once in heaven see each other full merrily, where we shall be sure to live and love together, in joyful bliss eternally."[47]

Bodily suffering and mental anguish had not robbed him of his characteristic cheerfulness. The prospect of heavenly bliss sustained him amid the gloom of prison life and even now made his heart leap for joy when Kingston, the lieutenant of the Tower, arrived and told him that his hour had come. Gladly, almost merrily, he followed the guards to Tower Hill, the place of execution. Noticing that the scaffold shook when he placed his foot on the ladder, he turned to Kingston and said with a smile, "I pray you, Master Lieutenant, see me safely up, and for my coming down let me shift for myself." With this he mounted the scaffold, and turning to the people who had assembled in great numbers, he briefly asked them "to pray for him and to bear witness with him, that he should now suffer death in and for the faith of the Holy Catholic Church. "With profound devotion he recited the psalm *Miserere*. As was customary, the executioner begged his forgiveness; whereupon the martyr kissed him tenderly and said, "Pluck up thy spirits, man, and be not afraid to do thine office: my neck is very short, take heed, therefore, thou strike not awry, for saving of thine honesty."[48] Then having blindfolded his eyes with a cloth he had brought with him, he knelt down at the block. The executioner had already raised the ax, when the holy man, as Cresacre relates, signed for a moment's delay, and put aside his beard, saying that it had not committed treason.[49] Then he once more laid his head on the block, and while his lips moved in prayer, the fatal blow was dealt that won for him the crown of martyrdom.

---

[47] Roper, pp. 99 seq.

[48] Ibidem, p. 101.

[49] Bridgett, p. 435, footnote.

King Henry was playing at backgammon with Anne Boleyn when a messenger came and informed him that the execution had taken place. Remorse seems to have filled his black soul; for turning to his worthless paramour, he said bitterly, "Thou art the cause of this man's death."[50] Whole Europe stood aghast on learning that the former Chancellor of England had suffered death at the block. Roper relates that when Emperor Charles V heard of it, he said to the English ambassador, "Had we been master of such a servant, of whose doings ourselves have had these many years no small experience, we would rather have lost the best city of our dominions, than have lost such a worthy councillor."[51]

Thus lived and died the great Tertiary Chancellor of England, "loyal to his sovereign to the last, yet giving his life for the higher loyalty he owed to the Vicar of Christ, and bearing himself in every relation of life with the freehearted joyfulness of one for whom no earthly pleasures, cares, or trials could cloud over the blue horizon beyond which lay the vision of God."

Harpsfield informs us that the martyr's head was impaled on London Bridge. Here, according to Stapleton, it remained "for a month, when Margaret Roper bribed the man whose business it was to throw it into the river to give it to her." With the consent of the Council, she preserved it in a leaden vessel. What became of the precious relic after her death in 1544, is not known. As to the martyr's body, we are told that by order of the governor it was given to Margaret who with the assistance of her former maid, Dorothy Harris, and her adopted sister, Margaret Clements, buried it in the chapel of St. Peter ad Vincula in the Tower. "The spot pointed out at present," we learn from Bridgett, "is near the entrance to the small bell-tower; and if that was the resting-place of the holy ashes, they

---

[50] Camm, p. 237; also Strickland, *Lives of the Queens of England*, Vol. II, p. 670.

[51] Roper, p. 102.

will not have been removed to the vaults, as was the case with those in the nave, when the church was repaired in 1876."[52] By the decree of Pope Leo XIII, dated December 29, 1886, the illustrious Tertiary martyr was enrolled among the Blessed.

---

[52] Bridgett, pp. 435 seq.

CHAPTER VIII
CATHERINE OF ARAGON, FRANCISCAN TERTIARY

The Spanish princess—Departure for England—Sudden death of Prince Arthur, her consort—She marries his brother Henry—Eighteen years of marital happiness—The king's infidelity—The divorce question—Catherine and the papal commission—Before the ecclesiastical court at Blackfriars—The queen's appeal to Rome admitted—Henry retaliates—Catherine insulted and disowned—Her secluded life at the More—At Buckden—At Kimbolton Castle—Bodily and mental suffering—Royal supremacy—Within sight of the scaffold—Her last illness and violent death—An estimate of her character.

HE history of the English Franciscans during the first years of the religious persecution would be incomplete without a special chapter on Queen Catherine. Her private and public life bears a striking resemblance to that of St. Thomas More. Like him she was a Tertiary of St. Francis[1] and by unfeigned loyalty to her God and to her king made manifest how deeply the spirit of St. Francis was rooted in her noble and beautiful soul.

---

[1] Dr. Nicolas Sander is our main authority on this question. He lived from 1530 to 1581. His much-quoted work, *De Origine ac Progressu Schismatis Anglicani*, was published for the first time four years after his death. "It is now acknowledged to be an excellent popular account of the period from the Catholic point of view," says J. P. Polen in *The Catholic Enclyclopedia* (Vol. XIII, p. 436). Sander himself affirms in the preface of his work that he recounts the history of the schism "conformably with what we have gathered from public records or have drawn from both the writings and the sayings of very creditable men, or at least have known or seen ourselves." On page 5, we read: "Under the royal robe, she (Catherine) wore the habit of Blessed Francis, in whose third order she had enrolled herself." Rishton did not question this statement when he reedited Sander's work, in **1690**. It is likewise attested by Davenport, Wadding, Parkinson, Leon, Strickland, Du Boys, Guérin, Magliano, Hope, Stone, Heimbucher, and others.

Queen Catherine of Aragon was the youngest daughter of Ferdinand of Aragon and Isabella of Castile. Born at Alcalá de Henares, Spain, on December 15, 1484, she passed her infancy and early childhood in the Christian camp before the walls of Granada. In 1492, this last Moorish stronghold in Spain surrendered and henceforth became the home of Catherine. Her early education was entrusted to the Franciscans,[2] who enjoyed the favor and esteem of the Catholic Sovereigns of Spain. Under the vigilant care of her excellent mother, the gifted princess acquired those noble qualities of heart and mind which were one day to signalize her career as queen of England.

At the tender age of twelve years, Catherine was promised in marriage to Prince Arthur, the elder son of Henry VII and heir apparent to the English throne. Four years later, on September 26, she bade farewell to her cherished home and kindred and attended by a splendid retinue embarked for England. After a voyage of six days, she landed at Plymouth. Elaborate festivities marked her journey to London, where, on November 14, in St. Paul's Cathedral, the archbishop of Canterbury, attended by nineteen bishops and mitered abbots, performed the solemn marriage ceremonies.[3] Little did Arthur and Catherine, amid the rejoicings of whole England, imagine how soon grim death would shatter their bright prospects for a long and happy union. But God directs the destinies of men; they were never to live together as husband and wife. Shortly after the wedding, Prince Arthur fell dangerously ill, probably of the plague,[4] and the next spring, on April 2, he breathed his

---

[2] Guérin: *Le Palmier Séraphique*, Vol. I, p. 124.

[3] It is worthy of note that on this auspicious day Catherine was escorted from the bishop's palace to the cathedral by the Duke of York, who in after years, as Henry VIII, so cruelly embittered her life.

[4] See Strickland: *Lives of the Queens of England*, Vol. II, p. 485.

last.[5]

Catherine broken in spirit answered the summons of Queen Elizabeth, her mother-in-law, and for the present resided in the country palace of Croydon. Her parents wished her to return to Spain. The English king, however, anxious to secure the remaining half of her marriage portion which consisted of 200,000 ducats, proposed that she marry his younger son Henry. Indeed, after the death of Queen Elizabeth, he himself wished to marry Catherine. But Queen Isabella of Spain would not hear of it, and the English King did not urge the matter.[6] Finally, he succeeded in gaining the consent of the Spanish sovereigns in behalf of his son, and in 1504, Pope Julius II granted the necessary dispensation. Though Catherine had not the least misgivings as to the legality of a union with Prince Henry, she was averse to a second marriage, especially with a prince who was five years her junior. She desired to return to her native land and to join the Order of Poor Clares in the convent of Toledo.[7] Hence it was only to please her parents that she made the sacrifice, and on June 25, 1504, consented to her betrothal to Henry. A few months later, Queen Isabella died. "Thus unhappily deprived of her admirable mother, she was left a passive victim at the disposal of the two wily diplomatists, her father King Ferdinand and Henry VII."[8] The English king subjected her to every privation and indignity to extort from her father the remaining share of her dowry, while Ferdinand, greatly impoverished by the death of Queen Isabella, could not be induced to pay it. Then, actuated by rather unseemly motives,[9] Henry VII, about 1506, not only debarred his son from

---

[5] From the testament of Arthur in which he bequeathed nothing to Catherine, historians rightly infer that he never regarded her as actually his wife. See Strickland, p. 486.

[6] Du Boys: *Catherine D'Aragon*, p. 30.

[7] Guérin, p. 145.

[8] Strickland, p. 488.

[9] See Strickland, p. 497.

meeting his future consort, but even forced him to sign a written protest against his previous betrothal to her. All this combined to make Catherine's situation very embarrassing. At last a change came. Henry VII died on April 22, 1509, and he was succeeded by his son, Henry VIII.

Ever since the death of his brother Arthur, young Henry had been witness of Catherine's constancy and patience in suffering. He sympathized with the wronged princess and in time became sincerely attached to her. Catherine, too, had gradually learned to esteem the English prince whose accession to the throne was hailed as the beginning of an era of national peace and prosperity. A feeling of joy and satisfaction thrilled the English nation, when on June 3, 1509, Henry and Catherine were solemnly married at Greenwich,[10] and when on June 24, the royal pair were crowned at Westminster.[11] No one, least of all Catherine, then thought that her crown of gold would eventually become a crown of thorns.

The first years of their union proved a period of mutual love and edification, coupled with true zeal for the religious and political welfare of the kingdom. They held court chiefly in the palace at Greenwich, since Henry had a predilection for this place.[12] How highly the king esteemed his worthy spouse, we see from his letter to Ferdinand of Aragon. "Her eminent virtues," he wrote, "daily shine forth, blossom, and increase so much, that if we still were free, her we would choose for our wife before all others." Nor was this mere policy on his part. Catherine, indeed, became his adviser and confidante in all affairs of State. In 1513, during his military sojourn in Flanders, he appointed her regent, granting her powers such as no English queen had ever held. It was in great part due to her that

---

[10] Probably In the Franciscan church adjoining the royal palace.

[11] It is important to note that on this occasion Catherine appeared with flowing hair and in a white robe, which, according to custom, was permitted only to a virgin. See Strickland, p. 505; also Du Boys, p. 88.

[12] Timbs: *Abbeys ... of England and Wales*, Vol. I, p. 122.

in the same year the English army vanquished the invading Scots at Flodden Field. Catherine, indeed, was wholly devoted to Henry and to the interests of the English realm. She rejoiced at the news of Henry's victory over the French at Guinegate, and after making a pilgrimage to the Lady-shrine at Walsingham, hastened to Richmond to welcome him home.[13]

In his treatise on Christian matrimony, Erasmus cites Catherine as a model wife and mother. "What house is there," he asks incidentally, "among the subjects to their realm, that can offer an example of such united wedlock? Where can a wife be found better matched with the best of husbands."[14] In her private life, the queen was a mirror of holiness. She was wont to rise at midnight and to pray in the church while the friars chanted Matins and Lauds. At five in the morning, she dressed hurriedly, frequently averring the only time she wasted was that spent in dressing. Beneath her royal robes, she wore the Tertiary habit of St. Francis. Every Friday and Saturday she fasted, while on the vigils of the feasts of the Blessed Virgin she contented herself with bread and water. Twice a week, on Wednesday and Friday, she went to Confession and received Holy Communion every Sunday. She recited the office of the Blessed Virgin daily, and spent six hours every morning in church. At noon she would read for the space of two hours the lives of the Saints to her servants and attendants. Then she returned to church and remained there till almost supper, of which she partook very sparingly. She prayed on her knees, never using the comfort of a cushion. "Who will wonder, that so saintly a woman had to be tried in some greater fire of tribulation, in order that the odor of her virtues might be more readily diffused over the entire Christian world."[15]

Needless to say, the pious queen, as a Tertiary of St. Francis,

---

[13] Hope: *First Divorce of Henry VIII*, pp. 24 seq.

[14] Strickland, pp. 518, 531.

[15] This fair picture of Catherine's personal sanctity is taken from Sander, p. 5.

held the Franciscan friars in greatest esteem. Having spent her childhood under the wholesome influence of their brethren in Spain, she was happy now to find them equally zealous and popular in England. Their friary at Greenwich adjoined the royal palace, which naturally entailed her becoming more intimately acquainted with them. Before her marriage with Henry, she requested her father to send her a Franciscan from Spain, since she could not confess in English.[16] Later, however, when she had sufficiently mastered the language, Bl. John Forest became her confessor and adviser; and we have every reason to believe that her subsequent conduct must in great part be ascribed to the advice given her by the saintly friar.[17]

During the first years of his reign, as we have seen, Henry zealously shared in the pious practices of his queen. But alas! clouds of adversity gradually began to darken their mutual love and happiness. Of the five children with which their marriage had been blessed, all had died except Mary the youngest, who subsequently, in 1553, ascended the throne of England. These premature deaths together with the gay and loose life at court gradually estranged the heart of Henry. Catherine knew that he was no longer a true and faithful husband; she felt that her piety bored him, that her very presence was becoming irksome to him. Thus matters stood when, early in 1527, to her utter dismay she learned that Wolsey had summoned Henry to his legatine court to examine the scruples of conscience he alleged regarding his marriage.[18] The queen had only recently

---

[16] 16. Strickland, p. 495, quoting a fragmentary letter of Catherine to her father, King Ferdinand, of Aragon.

[17] This partly accounts for Henry's subsequent hatred of the Franciscans. See Stone: *Faithful Unto Death*, p. 6.

[18] Cardinal Wolsey is often accused of having first raised these doubts in Henry's mind. Dodd, in his *Church History of England*, Vol. I, pp. 72 seq., carefully examines the various theories held by historians on this question and then concludes with Cavendish, who was Wolsey's secretary, that the king's passion for Anne Boleyn "not only gave the first motion to, but carried on the whole affair."

Catherine of Aragon, Franciscan Tertiary

recovered from a severe illness, and the news of Henry's hypocritical scheming against her harassed her innermost soul. Finally, on June 22, 1527, the king himself laid the affair before Catherine.[19] The helpless queen was now convinced of the hypocrisy of her faithless consort and burst into tears when he told her to leave court, since he could no longer share her company. She argued with him and declared she would never live apart from him. Even now she treated Anne Boleyn with sweet forbearance, although she knew her to be the king's favorite and constant attendant. Only once, at a game of cards, did she tenderly reproach her rival, saying, "My lady Anne, you have the good hap ever to stop at a king; but you are like others, you will have all or none."[20]

In May and June, 1528, a plague, called the sweating sickness, carried away a number of courtiers. Anne Boleyn was the first to contract the disease. Henry stricken with fear and remorse returned to Catherine and "instead of attending to his 'secret matter,' joined the queen in her devotional exercises, confessing himself every day and receiving the Communion every Sunday and festival."[21] But no sooner had the plague abated than he recalled his favorite to court. The following October, Campeggio, the papal legate, arrived in England. The queen's ascetic habits made Henry hope that on the legate's suggestion she would readily enter the convent. But, in an interview Catherine informed Campeggio that as queen and mother she could never consent to such a thing, and boldly rebuked Wolsey for confirming the king in his shameless perfidy. "Of malice," she declared, "have you kindled this fire, especially for the great grudge you bear to my nephew the emperor, whom you hate worse than a scorpion, because he would not gratify your ambition, by making you pope by force;

---

[19] Hope, p. 50; also Stone: *Mary the First, Queen of England*, p. 38.

[20] Strickland, p. 538.

[21] Lingard: *History of England*, Vol. IV, p. 250.

and therefore have you said, more than once, you would trouble him and his friends—and you have kept him true promise, for of all his wars and vexations, he may only thank you. As for me, his poor aunt and kinswoman, what trouble you put me to by this new-found doubt God knoweth, to whom I commit my cause."[22]

On Friday, June 18, 1529, Wolsey and Campeggio opened their legatine court in the palace at Blackfriars. The king was present by proxy. Catherine, attended by her counsel of four bishops[23] and a great train of ladies, appeared in person and with due respect to the presiding Cardinals solemnly appealed to the Pope for a hearing, alleging that in England, where there was no one to take up her cause, the court would necessarily decide against her.[24] In reply, she was told to appear again on the following Monday; in the meantime, the Cardinals would consider the justice of her appeal.

Accordingly, on June 21, the king and queen appeared in person. When Henry's name was called, he arose and to delude the judges and the assembled people loudly extolled the virtues of his royal consort, at the same time professing his reluctance to part from her were it not for the scruples that panged his "tender" conscience. Disgusted at this shameless hypocrisy, Catherine asked how, if he now spoke the truth, he could have been silent these twenty years. When Henry replied that the great love he always had and still retained for her, had till now sealed his lips, the queen became indignant and in trembling

---

[22] Strickland, p. 542. Du Boys, p. 264, cites a letter of Mendoza, the Spanish ambassador, to the emperor, dated November 18, 1528. From this letter we learn how Wolsey browbeat Campeggio and in a threatening tone told him to be on his guard that what lately happened in Germany through the severity of a certain Cardinal might not also take place in England through another Cardinal. See also Hope, pp. 52-57.

[23] One of their number was a Franciscan, Fr. Henry Standish, bishop of Asaph. See Parkinson: *Antiquities of the English Franciscans*, p. 237.

[24] For the original account of these proceedings, together with a copy of the queen's appeal, see Pocock: *Records of the Reformation*, Vol. I, pp. 216-222.

accents reiterated her appeal to Rome. But the judges declared that her appeal was unjust and could not be accepted. On hearing this, Catherine went over to where the king sat and falling on her knees before him, made a heroic effort to touch his heart. "Sir," she-said, "I beseech you, for all the loves there hath been between us, and for the love of God, let me have some right and justice. Take of me some pity and compassion, for I am a poor stranger, born out of your dominions; I have here no unprejudiced counsellor, and I flee to you as to the head of justice within your realm. Alas! alas! wherein have I offended you? I take God and all the world to witness that I have been to you a true, humble, and obedient wife, even conformable to your will and pleasure. I have been pleased and contented with all things wherein you had delight and dalliance; I loved all those you loved, only for your sake, whether they were my friends or mine enemies. This twenty years have I been your true wife, and by me ye have had divers children, although it hath pleased God to call them out of the world, which has been no fault of mine. I put it to your conscience whether I came not to you as a maid? If you have since found any dishonor in my conduct, then I am content to depart, albeit to my great shame and disparagement; but if none there be, then I beseech you, thus lowlily, to let me remain in my proper state. The king your father was accounted in his day a second Solomon for wisdom; and my father, Ferdinand, was esteemed one of the wisest kings that had ever reigned in Spain; both, indeed, were excellent princes, full of wisdom and royal behavior. Also, as me-seemeth, they had in their days as learned and judicious counsellors as are at present in this realm, who then thought our marriage good and lawful; therefore it is a wonder to me to hear what new inventions are brought up against me, who never meant aught but honestly. Ye cause me to stand to the judgment of this new court, wherein ye do me much wrong if ye intend any kind of cruelty; for ye may condemn me for lack of sufficient answer, since your subjects cannot be impartial counsellors for me, as they dare not, for fear of you, disobey your will. Therefore most humbly do I require you, in the way of charity and for the love of God, who is the just Judge of all, to spare me the sentence of this new court until I be advertised what way my friends in Spain may advise me to take; and if ye will not extend to me this favor, your pleasure be fulfilled, and to God I commit my cause." Then she arose bathed in tears and bowing to the king left the court. When told that the crier at the king's bidding was calling her back, she said, "I hear it well enough; but on—on, go you on, for this is no court wherein I can have justice. Proceed, therefore."[25]

Her touching appeal had made a deep impression on all present. This the king noticed and with seeming emotion declared, "Forasmuch as the queen is gone I will in her absence declare unto you all, my lords, she hath been to me as true, as obedient, and as conformable a wife as I could in my fancy wish or desire. She hath all the virtuous qualities that a woman of her quality, or of any lower rank, ought to possess."[26] Arriving at Baynard's Castle, Catherine said to her council, "This day, for the first time, lest I hurt my cause, I have not obeyed my lord the king; but the next time I meet him, I will crave his pardon on my knees."[27] Summoned again on June 25 and 28, she refused to appear. Instead, her written appeal to the Pope was solemnly read in court.

Shortly after these occurrences, Wolsey and Campeggio visited Queen Catherine in the palace of Bridewell and begged her in the king's name to consent to a divorce. Taking the Cardinals aside, she remained for some time in earnest conversation with them. What she told them was never made

---

[25] Strickland, p. 544, quoting Cavendish; see also Hope, p. 128, and Du Boys, p. 327 (footnote 2).

[26] Hope, p. 131. For a dramatic and historically accurate version of this trial scene at Blackfriars, see Shakespeare's *King Henry the Eighth*, Act II, Scene IV.

[27] Sander, p. 37.

known. It is probable that she again reproached Wolsey for having let matters come to this pass.[28] Certain it is, both Cardinals were after this interview more favorably disposed toward her. The next October, when the legatine court resumed its sittings, Henry's council pressed the legates to give judgment. Then to the great disappointment of the king, Campeggio declared that the Pope had found Catherine's appeal justified and had already revoked her cause to Rome. With this the court was dissolved and Campeggio soon after left England.

Though incensed at this turn of affairs, Henry for a time feigned kindlier feelings toward Catherine. Indeed, when told that Rome would likely decide against him, he was even on the point of dropping the matter entirely and of reinstating the queen in her rights.[29] But he had already gone too far and egged on by Anne, again began to treat the queen with cruel contempt. Her sufferings now became wellnigh unbearable. In the autumn of 1530, Chapuys wrote to the Emperor, "The queen's ailment continues as bad or worse than ever. The king absents himself from her as much as possible, and is always here (at London) with the lady (Anne), whilst the queen is at Richmond. He has never been so long without visiting her as now, but states, in excuse, that a death from the plague has taken place near her residence. He has resumed his attempts to persuade her to become a nun; this is, however, only lost time, for the queen will never take such a step. The continual uneasiness which she endures causes her to entreat your majesty, as well in my letters as yours, that her suit be brought to a final conclusion."[30]

During the ensuing Christmas festivities which Henry attended with Catherine at Greenwich, he again asked her to revoke her appeal to Rome and to submit the affair to four

---

[28] Du Boys, 346.

[29] Ibidem, p. 410, on the authority of Cardinal Pole.

[30] Strickland, p. 549.

English prelates or secular lawyers. On her refusal, the king broke up the festive gathering and withdrew to Whitehall. Her subsequent refusal to acknowledge the king's supremacy in spiritual matters brought the affair to a crisis.[31] At Whitsuntide, 1531, a royal deputation again visited Catherine and requested her to submit the question to four English prelates and four nobles, since the king suffered great pangs of conscience. "God grant my husband," replied the queen, "a quiet conscience; but tell him I am his lawful wife, married to him by the power of Holy Church. The court of Rome has taken the matter in hand: when it speaks I will submit."[32] After the festival of Trinity, Henry and Catherine set out together for Windsor. The cruel monarch was by this time determined to take the fatal step. Accordingly, soon after their arrival, he left the royal palace and proceeded on a hunting tour with Anne Boleyn. We can readily imagine the bitter anguish that filled the soul of Catherine. But her grief knew no bounds, when about the middle of August she received a message from the king telling her that she and her daughter Mary were to leave Windsor before his return. "Go where I may," the noble queen replied, "I am his wife and for him I pray." In October, the king's envoys once more entreated Catherine on their knees to submit to a decision of English bishops. Thereupon, Catherine, too, fell on her knees and begged the envoys to use their influence with the king in her behalf. At first, she refused to go to the More in Hertfordshire, as Henry commanded, because the place was unhealthful. Finally, declining to choose a place of her own liking, she humbly obeyed his command, offering a silent prayer for him whom she was never to see again in this life.[33]

Far from allowing a sullen and vindictive demeanor to widen the breach between herself and the faithless king, Catherine rather tried to forget her injuries and to soften the

---

[31] Hope, p. 229.

[32] Du Boys, p. 420.

[33] Strickland, p. 551; see also Hope, pp. 234 seq.

heart of Henry. Shortly after her arrival at the More, on New Year's Day, 1532, she sent him a golden cup in token of her undying love and esteem; but the uncivil wretch, though praising its beauty, returned the gift, saying he could accept none from her; much less did he send her and her ladies the customary New Year's present, and he even went so far as to forbid his courtiers to do so.[34] About this time, Catherine wrote to her daughter Mary, who was residing at Greenwich. In this letter, the careworn queen does not complain of her wrongs. She merely says that the absence of the king and of her daughter troubles her; that she trusts in God, however, who will "shortly turn all to come with good effect." Then she urges her beloved child to be as assiduous in the study of Latin under her new tutor, Dr. Fetherstone, as she had been under her mother's direction.[35]

Soon after her repudiation, Catherine informed the Pope of Henry's measures against her. His Holiness, in a private letter, kindly but earnestly admonished the king to reinstate his lawful wife and to dismiss Anne, till Rome had pronounced sentence. The letter dated January 25, 1532, was sent to Catherine who, however, did not venture to forward it to Henry until the following May.[36] The latter entirely ignoring the Pope's fatherly appeal, continued to retain Anne in the queen's apartments, and, as if to defy the Holy See, had Catherine removed to Buckden (Bugden),[37] still farther distant from court. This house, where the queen lived for some months, belonged to Longland, Bishop of Lincoln, who had

---

[34] Hope, p. 237.

[35] Strickland, p. 551; the author brings the letter together with an autograph signature of the queen. Dr. Fetherstone was later martyred for the faith, and he is now numbered among the Blessed.

[36] Pocock, Vol. II, pp. 166 seq.; Hope, pp. 251 seq.

[37] According to Strickland, p. 556, Buckden was a palace four miles distant from Huntingdon. It is not noticed by Timbs in his *Abbeys... of England and Wales*, probably because it was of inferior rank.

formerly been Henry's confessor, and who was now an ardent promotor of his cause. Naturally, this circumstance nettled Catherine, while the unwholesome climate greatly impaired her health.

The next September, Anne was created Marchioness of Pembroke, and a month later she accompanied the king on a visit to the French monarch at Calais. Not satisfied with this public insult to Catherine, Henry was rude enough to send a messenger for her jewels, that Anne might wear them for the visit. The noble queen obeyed, though with reluctance, surmising, perhaps, that she would never see them again.[38]

It must have cheered the troubled heart of Catherine to know that, thanks to the activity of the Franciscans in her behalf, the people sympathized with her. If in brighter days she had had a high regard for these zealous friars, how much greater was her esteem now, when they proved the most fearless champions of her rights as wife and queen.

Equally staunch in her defense was St.. Thomas More and the Earl of Shrewsbury, who had charge of the queen's crown, and openly declared that he would never consent to have any other than Catherine wear it. Sir Henry Guildford, the Controller, and many other state officials spoke publicly in favor of the queen. The same is true of Bl. John Fisher and even of Reginald Pole, the king's cousin. Thus, in the course of time, Anne Boleyn became an object of popular contempt. In derision the people nicknamed her Nan Bullen, and on several occasions threatened to take her life. Once she would surely have met a violent death at their hands had she not received a timely warning and made good her escape.[39] According to Ludovico Falier, a Venetian visiting England at the time, general discontent with the king's unjust policy ran so high that, could they have found a leader, the people would have risen in rebellion and demanded justice for the queen they loved. On

---

[38] Hope, pp. 256, 287.

[39] Ibidem, pp. 261 seq.

December 16, 1533, Chapuys wrote to the Emperor: "You can not imagine the grief of all the people at this abominable government. They are so transported with indignation at what passes that they complain that your Majesty takes no step in it, and I am told by many respectable people, that they would be glad to see a fleet come hither in your name, to raise the people; and if they had any chief among themselves, who dared raise his head, they would require no more."[40]

Nothing, however, was farther from the mind of Catherine than violent measures against the king. But for the rights of her daughter, which she felt in conscience bound to defend, the secluded and simple life at Buckden would have been quite to her fancy. As it was, she did not lose courage, but redoubled her prayers and mortifications, and daily implored the Author of light to guide the wayward king. Her trials, however, had only begun; greater sufferings were in store for her. On April 23, 1533, she received a message from the king, informing her of his recent nuptials with Anne and forbidding her thenceforth to use the title of queen. At the same time, he commanded that all correspondence between herself and Princess Mary must cease; he knew how fond mother and daughter were of each other, and he hoped by this means to break the spirit of both.[41] On May 10, Cranmer, the newly appointed archbishop of Canterbury, convened an ecclesiastical court at Dunstable,[42] six miles from Ampthill, where Catherine was then residing. Though repeatedly summoned to appear before the tribunal, she firmly refused, and on May 23, she was declared contumacious. She lay sick on her pallet when, soon after, Lord Mountjoy and his coadjutors formally announced to her the

---

[40] Stone, pp. 47, 64.

[41] Hope, p. 307.

[42] Cranmer held this court in direct opposition to Pope Clement VII, who on January 5, 1531, issued a Bull of Inhibition, strictly forbidding all courts whatever to pronounce sentence on the question of the divorce. For a copy of this Bull see Dodd, p. 286.

court's decision in favor of the king's new marriage. Calmly, but steadfastly, Catherine objected to being styled Princess-Dowager of Wales, affirming that she was the queen and the lawful wife of the king. Bribes and threats were unavailing. The matter involved the honor and right of her daughter, which she would defend at all hazards. More than that, the salvation of her own soul was at stake, and hence "neither for her daughter, her servants, her possessions or any worldly adversity, or the king's displeasure, that might ensue, would she yield in this cause." Next day, demanding the written account of the proceedings, she took her pen and scratched the words Princess Dowager wherever they occurred.[43] On May 28, Cranmer held court at Lambeth and, to the great scandal of all England, publicly declared that the king had validly married Anne, who was, therefore, to be held and treated as queen of England. On May 29, she left for Greenwich in the queen's barge for Westminster, where on the following Sunday her coronation took place.

Though wantonly outraged in her holiest rights and tenderest sensibilities, Catherine obeyed the command of her brutal and shameless lord and returned to her miserable abode in Buckden. The people, who had witnessed the events of the preceding weeks with growing disgust and indignation, seized the occasion of her return to Buckden for public demonstrations of loyalty to her. Though they had been forbidden to style her queen, enthusiastic cries of "Long live Queen Catherine" met her at every turn. With tears the people begged her to raise the standard of revolt, declaring they would lay down their lives for her.[44] Catherine, however, though touched at this unfeigned loyalty, recoiled at the mere thought of profiting by it. Henceforth, it seems, the sole object of her anxiety was the welfare of her daughter, whom Henry was

---

[43] Strickland, p. 555, who adds that this document with the alterations made by the queen is still extant in the national archives of England.

[44] Stone, p. 56.

heaping with indignities on her account. She knew to what hardships and dangers her dear child was exposed and secretly addressed a letter to her, which read in part:

> Daughter, I heard such things to-day, that I do perceive, if it is true, the time is come that Almighty God will prove you; and I am very glad for it for I trust He doth handle you with good love. I beseech you, agree to His pleasure with a merry heart; and be sure, that without fail, He will not suffer you to perish, if you beware to offend Him. I pray you, good daughter, to offer yourself to Him. If any pangs (of conscience) come to you, shrive yourself; first make you clean, take heed of His commandments, and keep them as near as He will give you grace to do, for then are you sure armed. And if this lady do come to you, as it is spoken, if she do bring you a letter from the King, I am sure, in the selfsame letter, you shall be commanded what you shall do. Answer you with few words, obeying the King your father in everything, save that you will not offend God, and lose your own soul; and go not further with learning and disputation in the matter. And wheresoever and in whatsoever company you shall come, (obey) the King's commandments. ... But one thing especially I desire you, for the love you owe to God, and unto me, to keep your heart with a chaste mind, and your body from all ill and wanton company. ... I pray you recommend me unto my good lady Salisbury, and pray her to have a good heart, for we never come to the Kingdom of Heaven but by troubles.[45]

According to Harpsfield, who lived at the time, Catherine in some degree regained her cheerfulness and peace of mind at Buckden. She found delight in the simple manners of the country people who frequently visited her. Like a true child of St. Francis, she loved the poor and, as long as circumstances

---

[45] Ibidem, p. 60.

allowed, she assisted them in their needs. The Franciscans of the neighboring friaries likewise came to pay their respects to her[46] whose cause they had openly espoused. From them perhaps she heard that FF. Peyto and Elstow had finally been banished and were now living in exile, still true to her cause. Toward Anne she bore no resentment, but rather pitied her. One day, a gentlewoman of her household began to heap curses on the name of Anne. The queen who had been weeping, quickly dried her tears and said earnestly, "Hold your peace! Curse not—curse her not, but rather pray for her; for even now is the time fast coming when you should have reason to pity her and lament her case."[47] During the court's proceedings against Elizabeth Barton and her adherents, Catherine's prudence completely baffled the attempts of her enemies to draw her loyalty to Henry in question. "It seems," writes Chapuys, "as if God inspires the queen, on all occasions, to conduct herself well, and to avoid all inconveniences and suspicions; for the Nun had been urgent, at divers times, to speak with her, and console her in her great affliction, but the queen would never see her."[48] Gloomy forebodings must have preyed on her heart, however, when she learned that the Holy Maid and her party had been executed, and that two Franciscans, FF. Rich and Risby, had suffered inhuman torture and death in defence of papal supremacy.

Of the queen's life at Buckden we find an interesting account in Harpsfield. "Queen Catherine," he writes, "spent her solitary life in much prayer, great alms and abstinence; and when she was not this way occupied, then was she and her gentlewomen working with their own hands something wrought in needlework, costly and artificially, which she intended, to the honor of God, to bestow on some of the churches. There was in the said house of Bugden a chamber

---

[46] Camm: *Lives of the English Martyrs*, Vol. I, p. 277.

[47] Strickland, p. 556.

[48] Stone, p. 24.

with a window that had a prospect into the chapel, out of the which she might hear divine service. In this chamber she enclosed herself, sequestered from all other company, a great part of the night and day, and upon her knees used to pray at the same window, leaning upon the stones of the same. There were some of her gentlewomen who curiously marked all her doings, and reported that oftentimes they found the said stones, where her head had reclined, wet as though a shower had rained upon them. It was credibly thought that, in the time of prayer, she removed the cushions that ordinarily lay in the window, and that the said stones were imbrued with the tears of her devout eyes when she prayed for strength to subdue the agonies of wronged affections."[49]

The following spring, on March 23, 1534, Pope Clement VII officially approved the decision of the Roman court, pronouncing Catherine's marriage with Henry valid and indissoluble.[50] Meanwhile, the schism was fast maturing. Before the Pope's final decision reached the ears of the king, his pliant parliament, wholly controlled by Cromwell, had passed bills that practically severed England from Catholic unity and demanded of all English subjects under penalty of misprision of treason a solemn oath of allegiance to the spiritual supremacy of the king.[51] The fearless and outspoken opposition of the Franciscans, and especially the Pope's subsequent threat of excommunication, roused bitter hatred in Henry's heart against the queen, whom he supposed the cause of all these vexations. It is true, as Franciscan Tertiary, Catherine naturally loved the friars. In fact she was in communication with them, and she had been frequently advised by Bl. John Forest. Never, however, would she have consented to take public reprisals on the king; much less would the friars have advised such a course of action. The cross was her portion, and encouraged by the

---

[49] See Strickland, p. 556, quoting Harpsfield.

[50] For a copy of this Bull see Dodd, p. 294.

[51] See Lingard, p. 11.

words and examples of her brethren in Christ, she gloried in it. Regarding the excommunication with which the Pope threatened the refractory king, we know for certain that Catherine had done all in her power to avert the blow, so that Cardinal Pole could write, "I understand today that if the queen had not interfered, the anathema would have already gone out against the king."[52]

In May, Lee and Tunstal received orders to visit Catherine. Laying before her six articles, they tried to show why she ought to give up the title of queen. When, however, they adduced as reason the fact that Anne by the recent birth of Elizabeth had now a right to be called queen, Catherine's patience for a moment failed her, and facing her tormentors with defiant dignity she solemnly vowed never to relinquish the title of queen as long as she lived, fearlessly adding that she was the king's wife and not his subject and therefore not liable to his acts of parliament. "Henry's repudiated wife," Lingard remarks, "was the only person who could defy him with impunity: she had lost his love, but never forfeited his esteem."[53]

The uncompromising firmness with which the queen maintained her rights, gradually drove Henry and his party on to severer measures against her. Early in 1534, the Duke of Suffolk received orders for her removal to Somersham in the Isle of Ely, "a place surrounded with water and marshes, the most pestilential spot in England." At this juncture, Chapuys wrote to the Emperor:

> The Duke of Suffolk, as I am informed by his wife's mother, confessed on the Sacrament, and wished some mischief might happen to him to excuse himself from the journey. The King, at the solicitation of the Lady, whom he dares not contradict, has determined to place the Queen in the said house, either to get rid of her, or to make sure of her, as the

---

[52] Strickland, p. 559.

[53] Lingard, Vol. IV, p. 231.

Catherine of Aragon, Franciscan Tertiary

house is strong; and besides, it is seven miles from another house, situated in a lake, which one can not approach within six miles, except on one side; and the King and the Lady have agreed to seek all possible occasions to shut up the Queen within the said island, and failing all other pretexts to accuse her of being insane.

Catherine knew what was in store for her and refused to leave Buckden. She told the king's commissioners that, to remove her, they would have to break open the doors and take her by force. Not daring to do this for fear of the people, the commissioners departed.[54] When the king heard of their failure, he was furious and began to heap new insults and indignities on the helpless queen. She was robbed of her royal income and forced to content herself with what had been allowed her as Princess-Dowager. Servants and dependents, who still insisted on her royal title, were summarily dismissed and replaced by such as were willing to embitter her life, as the king ordered. Her house at Buckden practically became a prison with Sir Edmund Bedingfield as jailer, whose duty it was to observe the queen closely and to report regularly to headquarters regarding her conduct. Henry hoped to find something that would justify legal proceedings against her.[55] From Chapuys's letter we learn how anxiously the godless king was waiting for her death. In fact, it seems that he even took direct measures to hasten her end. For the imperial ambassador writes: "He (Henry) has great hope in the queen's death. He lately told the French ambassador, that she could not live long, as she was dropsical, an illness she was never subject to before. It is to be feared something has been done to bring it on." Catherine, it seems, knew all this and even feared she would be poisoned. "The queen has not been out of her room," again writes Chapuys, "since the Duke of Suffolk was with her, except to hear Mass in

---

[54] Stone, p. 66.

[55] Lingard, Vol. V, p. 7; Strickland, p. 560; Stone, p. 52.

the gallery. She will not eat or drink what the new servants provide. The little she eats, in her anguish, is prepared by her chamberwomen, and her room is used as her kitchen. She is very badly lodged; she desires me to write to you about it."[56]

To judge from Henry's inhuman proceedings against others who in days gone by had enjoyed his favor and protection, it is not unlikely that to satisfy Anne he would in the end have resorted to the murder of Catherine, had not, in the fall of 1534, another opportunity presented itself of sating his vengeance on her. The queen had spent almost two years at Buckden, and her health had suffered greatly. Probably dreading the coming winter, she asked to be removed to a milder and drier place near the Metropolis. Accordingly, the relentless king commissioned the Duke of Suffolk to convey her to Fotheringay castle on the river Nen in Northamptonshire.[57] Besides being notorious for its bad air, this place was especially disagreeable to Catherine, because it belonged to the dower settled on her by Prince Arthur. Moreover, by going there she would in some way have compromised her cause. Accordingly, she again objected, so that the duke was at a loss how to proceed, and thought there was no other remedy than to convey her by force to Somersame. She remained, therefore, at Buckden till the end of 1534; when finally she consented to take up her abode, according to the king's command, at Kimbolton castle, some ten miles distant from Buckden.[58]

Early in January, 1535, Catherine arrived there. When one remembers the precarious state of her health and the many discomforts a journey over an open country in the depth of winter entailed in those days, one may readily imagine what the outcast queen suffered, and what bitter anguish wrung her heart when at last she found herself imprisoned within the

---

[56] Stone, p. 68.

[57] In this castle, about fifty years later, another saintly queen, Mary Stuart of Scotland, spent the last months previous to her execution.

[58] Strickland, pp. 558-562.

gloomy castle walls. Kimbolton was a wet and unwholesome place; hence the queen's malady, which worry and privation had brought on at Buckden, soon became desperate.

As widow of Prince Arthur, she had a right to an annuity of 5,000 pounds sterling. But Henry maliciously deprived her of this income and allowed her barely sufficient means to maintain a scanty household. She was again placed in the custody of Sir Edmund Bedingfield, who more than once informed his royal master that Catherine's household was utterly devoid of money. How poor, in fact, she was, may be seen from her last will, in which mention is made of a new gown she had obtained on trust.[59]

The unfortunate queen had been residing at Kimbolton only a short time, when the news reached her that Princess Mary was dangerously ill.[60] Likewise informed that Henry had permitted her physician and apothecary to attend the Princess, Catherine took heart and humbly petitioned the king to allow her to nurse and comfort their ailing daughter. But the heartless tyrant, suspecting a plot to get Mary out of the country, refused the request of his loyal queen. He promised, however, to place the princess near her mother, provided the two would not meet. Catherine's subsequent letter of gratitude to Cromwell is interesting, inasmuch as it shows her mental and physical condition at this time.

My good friend, you have laid me under great obligation by the trouble you have taken in speaking to the king, my lord, about the coming of my daughter to me. I hope God will reward you, as you know it is out of my power to give you anything but my goodwill. As to the answer given you ... I beg you will give him (the king) my hearty thanks for the good he does to his daughter and mine, and for the peace of mind he has given

---

[59] Du Boys, p. 504; Strickland, pp. 570 seq.

[60] Princess Mary had been banished from court, because she persisted in the title of royalty and steadfastly refused to relinquish it in favor of Elizabeth, born to Henry by Anne Boleyn. See Lingard, Vol. V, p. 29 (footnote 2).

me. You may assure him, that if she were but a mile from me I would not see her, because the time does not permit me to go visiting, and if I wished it, I have not the means ... I have heard that he had some suspicion of her security—a thing so unreasonable that I cannot believe it entered his heart, nor do I think he has so little confidence in me. If such a thing be assumed, I beg you to tell his majesty, it is my fixed determination to die in this kingdom, and I offer my person as security that if such a thing be attempted, he may do justice upon me as the most traitorous woman that ever was born.[61]

Neither reasons nor petitions could prevail over the pride and obstinacy of Henry. He was determined once for all that mother and daughter should never meet again in this life. Even Chapuys, whom for political reasons the king was forced to treat with due deference, failed to move his heart of steel. Against all the arguments of the Spanish ambassador he objected "that there was no occasion to confide Mary to her mother's hands, for it was Catherine who had put it into her head to show such obstinacy and disobedience."[62]

Anguish and fear distracted the soul of Catherine on hearing into what confusion the king s profligacy and perverseness was plunging the country. When those of her household who sympathized with Henry's godless policy, openly accused their royal mistress of being the cause of all this misfortune, the hapless queen, weakened in mind by bodily suffering and deprived of right-minded counselors, seems, indeed, to have been troubled in conscience as to whether her mode of action could be justified before God. Many a time, no doubt, she thought of the faithful Franciscan friars, from whom in days gone by she had so often obtained advice and consolation. How fearlessly they had defended her cause and the rights of the Pope; how terribly they had already been visited by the king's anger and vengeance. Surely, their attitude

---

[61] Stone, pp. 78 seq.

[62] Ibidem, p. 80.

toward the king's policy was a model on which she might safely fashion her own. These reflections accompanied by ceaseless prayer, reassured her and buoyed up her drooping spirits.

About this time, the unfortunate queen learned to her dismay that Fr. John Forest, her former confessor and spiritual adviser, had been imprisoned in Newgate, and that he would soon be led to execution. Despite the danger of having her letter intercepted and thus bringing new sufferings on herself as well as on her aged father and friend, she nevertheless wrote to him, knowing how much a word of cheer from her would gladden his last hours.[63]

> My Honoured Father—You who have had so long experience in directing others in doubtful matters, can have no difficulty in directing yourself, for not only will your religion, but your learning also convince you, that you ought to be prepared, if it be necessary, to suffer death for the name of Christ, and under such circumstances not to shrink from so doing. Go onwards, then, and be of good courage, for if in these torments you endure a small amount of pain, you are well assured that you will receive an eternal reward. To relinquish such a reward as this for the dread of the suffering, might well be accounted the act of a confirmed madman.
>
> But alas for me, your daughter! one born to you in the wounds of Christ, whom for a season you leave here in her solitude; leave, I repeat, in the depth of her distress and affliction. And this I may venture to say because I am losing him whom alone I followed in the things of God, because I

---

[63] This letter and Bl. John Forest's reply are taken from Stone: *Faithful Unto Death*, pp. 54 seq. The author translates them from Fr. Thomas Bourchier: *Hist. Eccl. de Martyrio FF. Ord. Min.*, remarking that this edition of the friar's valuable history contains the only perfectly correct version of the letters. The Parisian edition of 1586 brings (pp. 53 seq.) a slightly different version of them. Parkinson and Du Boys transcribe the letters from Sander.

knew him to be deeply instructed in human and divine knowledge. And of a truth, if I may freely express to you what I wish, I would rather go before you through a thousand torments than follow after you. And even were it possible to obtain what one most earnestly desires, who is there, I ask, who would be content to live upon nothing but hope?

Casting aside therefore my own individual wishes, I would prefer that the whole of these matters should remain in the hands of Him who gave us Himself for our example. This He did when He said, "Thy will be done," thereby giving up His own will, rather than gratify His own inclinations. You will go before me, yes, you will precede me, but your prayers will obtain for me, that I should follow you along the same pathway, advancing, as I trust, with an ever braver and steadier footstep. Onwards, then; be assured that albeit the pangs that you suffer be grievous, yet I share them along with you. Without doubt, they shall earn for you a crown which never withers, a crown prepared for those who endure for the name of Christ, provided that with unflinching and unwavering courage you suffer the agonies which are awaiting you. Remember your ancient and noble family, and this thought will assuredly animate you to bear with a brave spirit the death which awaits you for the name of Christ. You who are illustrious by the title of your family, will not basely defile its nobility by yielding to the impious demands of the King. I do not forget that you esteem the dignity of your Order in so far, and no farther, as it is correspondent with virtue. Surrender, then, and with all joy, that body of yours to its Creator, that body which for so long a period has led a holy life under the garb of the poor Institute of St. Francis.

And yet, when I, your obedient daughter, remember how great will be the sorrow which I shall endure for your sake, I know not what to say. This arises chiefly from the thought that you are leaving me without comfort of any kind. My abode in this world, and my anticipations, can be nothing else than misery; a real death in a living life. Nevertheless, I trust in the Lord, to whom I have said, "Thou art my lot in the land of the living," that land in which I hope to meet you shortly, when the storms of this world shall have ended, and I shall have passed into the peaceful life of the blessed.

Farewell, my honoured Father, and always remember me in your prayers while on earth, and I trust they will be my chiefest consolation when you shall have obtained an entrance into the Kingdom of Heaven.

Your daughter Catherine, with a heart full of sorrow.

As is evident from the tone of the letter, the queen thought that the blessed martyr had only a short time to live.[64] Her fears were confirmed on the receipt of the following beautiful letter from the saintly friar.

> My most serene Lady Queen and my very dear daughter in the heart of Christ Jesus.
>
> I have received your letters from Thomas, your young servant, and having read them, I experienced an incredible joy by reason of your great steadfastness in the truth which I perceive in you—I mean your faith in the Holy Church your Mother. Standing firm in this, you will assuredly obtain salvation. Nor have you any reason to be doubtful on my account, as if I could submit to disgrace my grey hairs by any such fickleness. In the meantime, I earnestly entreat you to be unwearied in your prayers to God for me (for whose spouse the Church we are suffering so many and so severe torments), that He would receive me into His glory, for which I have striven so frequently as a member of the Order of St. Francis, namely for forty-four years, and am now in the sixty-fourth year of my age. At such a period of

---

[64] The martyrdom of Bl. John Forest, as we shall see, did not take place till May 22, 1538.

life as this a man easily perceives that people can do without him; consequently I am most earnest in my prayer that I may be dissolved to be with Christ.

In the mean season, do you be careful to shun that pestilential teaching of the heretics so thoroughly that, even if an angel were to come down from heaven bringing with him a doctrine different from that which I brought you, on no account ought you to give any credence to his message, but to reject it. Should he advance any revelation which dissents from that which I taught you long ago, give no ear to it, for it does not come from God. Take these few words as if in place of the consolation which you may expect chiefly from our Lord Jesus Christ, to whom I chiefly recommend you, as also to my father St. Francis and St. Catherine, to whom I most earnestly entreat you to pray for me, when you shall hear that I am in the midst of my sufferings.

And now I bid you farewell. I have sent my rosary to you, for only three days of my life remain to me.

From a letter which Elizabeth Lady Hammond, one of the queen's faithful gentlewomen addressed to Bl. John Forest we learn how Henry ever anxious to detect some flaw in the queen's conduct had Kimbolton castle closely searched for secret letters and for persons previously expelled from her service; and further, how the king's agents by their threatening attitude terrified the queen and her ladies.[65] Thus the dreary year 1535 dragged on, bringing Catherine ever nearer to death's door. "The fury of her enemies," writes Guérin, "increased in proportion as her sufferings grew more intense. She was almost constantly sick in bed."[66]

It was probably in the fall of 1535 that Cranmer visited her and in the king's name commanded her to sign the act

---

[65] Stone: *Faithful Unto Death*, p. 58; Strickland, p. 564; Du Boys, p. 508.

[66] Guérin, Vol. I, p. 142.

recognizing Henry's spiritual supremacy over the Church in England. At this, the queen became indignant; but being unable longer to bear up under her hardships, she fainted.[67] Hatred and revenge possessed Henry's rebellious mind, when he was told of Catherine's refusal to take the oath of supremacy. On November 6 and 21, Chapuys informed the emperor of the danger that threatened the queen and her daughter. He claimed to have it on reliable authority that the king "would no longer remain in the trouble, fear, and suspense he had so long endured, on account of the queen and princess ... and that he meant to have them despatched at the next parliament. ... These are things," he continues, "too monstrous to be believed; but considering what has passed, and goes on daily—the long continuance of these menaces—and, moreover, that the C... (Anne), who long ago conspired the death of the said ladies, and thinks of nothing but getting rid of them, is the person who governs everything, and whom the king is unable to contradict, the matter is very dangerous."[68] What the faithful ambassador feared never came to pass. The sudden demise of Catherine before the opening of parliament prevented Henry from taking these last terrible measures against his faithful and saintly queen.

About this time, an incident occurred which shows how even to the very end the queen enjoyed the love and favor of the lower classes. A workman of Grantham near Kimbolton, while working in his field, accidentally unearthed a huge brass pot that contained besides some silver chains and ancient rolls of parchment, a large helmet of pure gold set with precious stones. Thinking of the queen in her poverty, he brought the treasures to the castle, with the request that they be given to her. But Catherine was already at death's door.[69]

In the latter part of December, Catherine realized that her

---

[67] Ibidem, Vol. I, p. 143.

[68] Stone: *Mary the First, Queen of England*, p. 90.

[69] Du Boys, p. 504, on the authority of Harpsfield.

end was near. When Chapuys, whom she had summoned for a last interview, arrived at the castle, he found her in a pitiable condition. Seeing at a glance that it was now only a question of a few days till death would come to her relief, he decided to stay with her to the end.[70] On New Year's day, Lady Willoughby who thirty years before had attended Catherine as maid of honor, by sheer strategy gained access to her.[71] We are told that frequently in a state of delirium the dying queen imagining her daughter near would stretch forth her arms and exclaim, "Mary, my child!"[72] Humbly she begged the king for a last interview with the princess for whose sake she had borne her heavy cross these many years. But even now the cruel despot remained cold and obdurate. At last, only a few days before her death, Catherine called one of her maids to her bedside and dictated the following pathetic letter to her unworthy consort:[73]

> My Lord and dear Husband:—
> I commend me unto you. The hour of my death draweth fast on, and, my case being such, the tender love I owe you forceth me, with a few words, to put you in remembrance of the health and safeguard of your soul, which you ought to prefer before all worldly matters and before the care and tendering of your own body, for the which you have cast me into many miseries and yourself into many cares. For my part I do pardon you all; yet, I do wish and devoutly pray God that He will also pardon you.
> For the rest I commend unto you Mary, our daughter, beseeching you to be a good father unto her, as I heretofore desired. I entreat you also, on behalf of my maids, to give

---

[70] Stone, *Mary ... of England*, p. 92.

[71] Strickland, p. 567.

[72] Guérin, p. 143.

[73] Strickland, pp. 564 seq.

them marriage-portions, which is not much, they being but three. For all my other servants I solicit a year's pay more than their due, lest they should be unprovided for.

Lastly do I vow that mine eyes desire you above all things.

It is said that Henry wept when he read this touching avowal of his rejected queen's undying love and loyalty.[74] But alas! his better self was wholly enfettered by one whose only hope of complete triumph lay in the death of the noble queen.

During the visit of Chapuys and Lady Willoughby, Catherine rallied somewhat. There was still hope for a temporary recovery, so that on January 5, the ambassador deemed it safe and advisable to leave Kimbolton. He promised, however, to return at the first intimation of danger. On January 9, he asked Cromwell for an audience with the king. How shocked he was when in reply he received the sad news that forty-eight hours after his departure from Kimbolton Catherine had suddenly passed away. Sir Edmund Bedingfield announced her demise in these words: "January 7th, about ten o'clock the lady-dowager was *aneled* with the holy ointment, Master Chamberlayne and I being called to the same, and before two in the afternoon she departed to God."[75]

"The suddenness of her end, and the circumstances immediately following it, caused so much suspicion, that at the time there was hardly any one who did not firmly believe that she had been poisoned."[76] According to the ambassador's

---

[74] Sander, p. 85.

[75] Strickland, p. 508, on the authority of the State Papers.

[76] Stone: *Mary ... of England,* p. 92. Whether the king was in any way implicated in this heinous crime is not known. As we have seen, he certainly longed for Catherine's end, and he probably would have had her condemned to death and executed by the next parliament. As to Anne Boleyn's share in the murder of the queen, Gasquet, in his *Henry VIII and the English Monasteries* (Vol. I, p. 285), declares on the authority of Friedmann that the crime was perpetrated "if not at the instigation, at least with the connivance

subsequent letter to the emperor, Catherine died two hours after midday, and eight hours later an autopsy was held in the greatest secrecy. Neither the bishop of Llandaff, confessor of the queen, nor her physician were allowed to be present. Immediately after, one of the three men who at the king's command had performed the examination confided the results to the queen's confessor, "but in great secrecy, as a thing which would cost his life. ... On my man," continues the ambassador, "asking the physician if she had died of poison, he replied that the thing was too evident, by what has been said to the bishop, her confessor, and if that had not been disclosed, the thing was sufficiently clear from the report and circumstances of the illness."

In the same letter of Chapuys we are informed how the king and his court party rejoiced when the news arrived that Catherine was dead. The next day, on Sunday, Henry "was clad all over in yellow, from top to toe." After dinner, he proceeded to the hall where the ladies were dancing and acted "like one transported with joy." Having sent for the infant Elizabeth, he took her in his arms and presented her to his fawning courtiers. No less exultant was Anne Boleyn. "Now," she exclaimed, "I am indeed a queen!" Hastening to her parents, she bade them be glad with her, for now her triumph was complete. On the day of the queen's funeral, Anne out of contempt for Catherine appeared in yellow and made her ladies do the same, although the king had commanded black to be worn on that day.[77] Mary was heartbroken when she heard of her mother's sudden demise. "Of the princess, my cousin," the emperor wrote, "I hear only that she is inconsolable at the loss she has sustained,

---

of Anne Boleyn."

[77] Strickland, p. 678. Could the wretched woman have only foreseen what was in store for her. Henry's aversion to her gradually became more pronounced. On May 9, four months after the death of Queen Catherine, he had her tried and condemned to death for high treason, and that by the very parliament that would probably have passed the same sentence on the rightful queen.

especially when she thinks of her father's past behaviour towards her, and the little favour she can expect for the future."[78]

The last will of Catherine bears eloquent testimony to the eminent virtues that marked her sad but glorious career.[79] The first provision she made was that her body "be buried in a convent of Observant friars."[80] In life the royal Tertiary had ever cherished the highest regard for the sons of St. Francis, and hoping perhaps that in time they would be allowed to return to their convents, the saintly queen could find no more suitable resting place after death than in the midst of those who like her had suffered for justice sake. But alas! her dying wish was entirely disregarded. Writing to Lady Bedingfield[81] on arranging for the funeral of his "dearest sister lady Catherine," the king ordered that, on January 26, the corpse should be escorted by the principal gentry of Kimbolton to Peterborough, about four miles north, and interred in the abbey church. At the subsequent suppression and spoliation of the religious houses in the kingdom, Henry made some show of regard for the queen he had wronged, and spared the beautiful abbey church, where as late as 1847, the old verger still pointed out to travelers the little brass plate that marked the last resting place of the glorious Tertiary Queen Catherine of Aragon.[82]

Concerning Kimbolton Castle, Timbs informs us that "the room in which she (Catherine) died remains. The chest, in

---

[78] Stone: *Mary ... of England*, p. 98.

[79] Strickland, p. 569, quotes the will from Strype's Memorials.

[80] Stone: *Faithful Unto Death*, p. 62, quotes a letter of Chapuys to the emperor, dated January 21, 1536. In this letter, the ambassador writes: "The Lady Catherine, in her memorandum of last wishes, desired to be buried in a convent of Observant friars. Cromwell replied that as to the burial it could not be done as she had desired, for there remained no convent of the Observants in England."

[81] Strickland, p. 571, quotes the letter.

[82] Ibidem, p. 573.

which she kept her clothes and jewels, her own cipher on the lid, still lies at the foot of the grand staircase."[83] From a letter of Horace Walpole, dated June 22, 1772, we learn that at Ampthill "nothing remains of the castle, nor any marks of residence but a small garden." At his suggestion, a cross was erected to Catherine's memory, on which he had engraved the following verses:

> In days of old, here Ampthill's towers were seen,
> The mournful refuge of an injured queen.[84]

Every student of this period of English history is acquainted with Shakespeare's drama, *King Henry the Eighth.* The poet's sympathetic treatment of Queen Catherine of Aragon mirrors the sentiments of the English nation in the beginning of the seventeenth century. To show how correct historically is Shakespeare's delineation of her character we take the liberty, even at the risk of wearying the reader, to quote at some length from H. N. Hudson's commentary on the play. His remarks will serve at the same time as a summary of the queen's many beautiful traits.

"She maintains the same simple, austere, and solid sweetness of mind and manners through all the changes of fortune. Yet she, too, rises by her humiliation, and is made perfect by suffering, if not in herself, at least to us: for it gives her full sway over those deeper sympathies which are necessary to a just appreciation of the profound and venerable beauty of her character. She is mild, meek, and discreet; and the harmonious blending of these qualities with her high Castillian pride gives her a very peculiar charm. Therewithal she is plain in mind and person; has neither great nor brilliant parts; and of this she is fully aware, for she knows herself thoroughly: but she is nevertheless truly great,—and this is the one truth about

---

[83] Timbs, p. 497.

[84] Strickland, p. 574.

her which she does not know,—from the symmetry and composure wherein all the elements of her being stand and move together: so that she presents a remarkable instance of greatness in the whole, with the absence of it in the parts. How clear and exact her judgment and discrimination! Yet we scarce know whence it comes, or how.

From the first broaching of the divorce, she knows the thing is all a foregone conclusion with the king; she is also in full possession of the secret why it is so: she feels her utter helplessness, being, as she is, in a land of strangers, with a capricious tyrant for the party against her, so that no man will dare to befriend her cause with honest heartiness: that no trial there to be had can be anything but a mockery of justice, for the sole purpose will be to find arguments in support of what is predetermined, and to set a face of truth on a body of falsehood; she has no way therefore but to take care of her own cause; her only help lies in being true to herself; and indeed the modest, gentle, dignified wisdom with which she schools herself to meet the crisis is worth a thousand-fold more than all the defences that any learning and ingenuity and eloquence could frame in her behalf.

"Her power over our better feelings is in no small degree owing to the impression we take, that she sees through her husband perfectly, yet never in the least betrays to him, and hardly owns to herself, what mean and hateful qualities she knows or feels to be in him. It is not possible to overstate her simple artlessness of mind; while nevertheless her simplicity is of such a texture as to be an overmatch for all the unscrupulous wiles by which she is beset. Her betrayers, with all their mazy craft, can neither keep from her the secret of their thoughts nor turn her knowledge of it into any blemish of her innocence; nor is she less brave to face their purpose than penetrating to discover it. And when her resolution is fixed, that "nothing but death shall e'er divorce her dignities," it is not, and we feel it is not, that she holds the accidents of her position for one iota more than they are worth; but that these are to her the necessary symbols of her honor as a wife, and the inseparable garments of her delicacy as a woman; and as such they have so grown in with her life, that she can not survive the parting with them; to say nothing of how they are bound up with her sentiments of duty, of ancestral reverence, and of self-respect. Moreover many hard, hard trials have made her conscious of her sterling virtue: she has borne too much, and borne it too well, to be ignorant of what she is and how much better things she has deserved; she knows, as she alone can know, that patience has had its perfect work with her: and this knowledge of her solid and true worth, so sorely tried, so fully proved, enhances to her sense the insult and wrong that are put upon her, making them eat like rust into her soul. ...

"Catherine in her seclusion, and discrowned of all but her honor and her sorrow, is one of the author's noblest and sweetest deliverances. She there leads a life of homely simplicity. Always beautiful on the throne, in her humiliation she is more beautiful still. She carries to the place no grudge or resentment or bitterness towards any; nothing but faith, hope, and charity; a touching example of womanly virtue and gentleness; hourly in heaven for her enemies; her heart garrisoned with 'the peace that passeth all understanding.' Candid and plain to herself, she loves and honours plainness and candour in others; and it seems a positive relief to her to hear the best spoken that can be of the fallen great man who did more than all the rest to work her fall. Her calling the messenger 'saucy fellow,' who breaks in so abruptly upon her, discloses just enough of human weakness to make us feel that she is not quite an angel yet; and in her death scene we have the divinest notes of a 'soul by resignation sanctified.'"[85]

---

[85] Hudson: *Shakespeare: His Life, Art, and Character*, Vol II, pp. 196 seq.

CHAPTER IX
BLESSED JOHN FOREST, O.F.M.

Birth and parentage—Enters the Franciscan Order—Doctor of Oxford—Provincial of England—Espouses the queen's cause—Fr. Richard Lyst, traitor and spy—Blessed Forest and the king—Attempt to remove Forest from the provincialship—Staunch defender of papal supremacy—Imprisoned, tried, condemned to death—Martyrdom delayed—With the Conventuals in London Entrapped in the confessional—Before the Privy Council—Once more in Newgate—Tried for heresy—Sentenced to die at the stake—His alleged submission—Drawn on a hurdle to Smithfield—The friars and the bishop—Dreadful torture and death.

E have seen in the course of our narrative how fearlessly the English Franciscans championed the rights of Queen Catherine, and how bravely they suffered banishment, imprisonment, torture, and death in defence of papal supremacy. We have contemplated the life and martyrdom of the illustrious Tertiary Chancellor Bl. Thomas More, and have seen the saintly Tertiary Queen Catherine of Aragon, insulted, discrowned, and repudiated by a faithless and cruel king. Before continuing our sad but edifying story, we must direct our attention to a man whose glorious example of unswerving loyalty to truth guided and encouraged the friars at the outbreak of the storm and finally won for him the martyr's crown.

Bl. John Forest was born in 1471. It is probable that the place of his birth was Oxford, where according to Wood there resided about the middle of the fifteenth century a family by the name of Forest.[1] William Forest, the poet priest, is supposed to have been related to the martyr.[2] As appears from the letter of Queen

---

[1] Thaddeus, *Life of Blessed John Forest*, p. 2.

[2] *The Catholic Encyclopedia*, Vol. VI, p. 144. Among his writings is a long poem on Queen Catherine of Aragon.

Catherine,[3] he was of an ancient and noble family. Of his early years nothing is known beyond the fact that, as Wood observes, "he was from his childhood educated in piety and learning."[4] During the last two decades of the fifteenth century, the reform movement in the Order of St. Francis was fast gaining ground in the English Province, while the friars by their zeal and sanctity were attracting nation-wide attention. Hence we can readily imagine how the parents of Forest rejoiced when he told them of his desire to forgo the promises and pleasures of the world and to embrace the secluded and holy life of the Franciscans. Gladly they consented, and in 1491, the young man of twenty summers[5] received the gray habit in the friary at Greenwich.

The year of novitiate and the subsequent years of study were spent in seclusion and prayer. Shut off from worldly cares and distractions, the youthful friar was laying the foundation of that magnificent structure of Franciscan ideals which was destined to stand unshaken amid the fury of warring elements. Little did he surmise, kneeling in prayer before the image of his heavenly Queen, what great things were in store for him, and what a noble part he was one day to play for the spiritual welfare of his country.

In 1500, at the age of twenty-nine, we find Forest residing in the friary without Watergate, a suburb south of Oxford, where he devoted himself to the study of theology. Later, he pursued a higher course in the sacred sciences, presumably at the university of Oxford. Here, as Wood informs us, he supplicated

---

[3] See the foregoing chapter.

[4] Parkinson, *Antiquities of the English Franciscans*, p. 241.

[5] The year of Forest's birth (1471) and that of his entrance into the Franciscan Order (1491) are based on his letter to Queen Catherine, which was most probably written in 1535. (See the foregoing chapter.) In this letter, he says expressly that he is in his sixty-fourth year, and that he has passed four and forty years in the Order of St. Francis. Other historians affirm that he was seventeen years of age when he entered the Order. See Parkinson, p. 241.

the venerable regents for permission to take the degree of doctor of divinity. Whether he was admitted, is not known. Although Wood thinks that Forest received the degree neither at Oxford nor at Cambridge, still he says that, especially about the year 1517, the registers of Oxford were badly kept. This, Parkinson urges, may account for the absence of Forest's name from the roster of Oxford doctors, "or perhaps," as he suggests, "he was a doctor of Paris."[6] At all events, it is certain that he held the title; for, besides Wood, also Stow, Godwyn, How, Holinshed, Pits, Wadding, Davenport, Bourchier, Mason, and most later historians, like Dodd, apply it to him; while the fact that Hugh Latimer, on the morning of Forest's martyrdom, repeatedly addressed him as Doctor, seems to remove all doubt in the matter.

As years went on, Fr. John Forest became known far and wide as a man of eminent learning and sterling sanctity. Wholly imbued with the spirit of St. Francis, he labored zealously in establishing and spreading the Observant reform among the friars in England. It was quite natural, therefore, that, probably on the death of the provincial Fr. Stephen Baron, about the year 1520, he was elected by the friars to succeed him.[7] It must have been in virtue of his authority as provincial superior that, on January 22, 1525, he received orders from Cardinal Wolsey to preach at St. Paul's Cross and publicly to

---

[6] See Parkinson, p. 241.

[7] That Forest was provincial is asserted by Wood, Parkinson, Dodd, Magliano, Leon, Gasquet, Holzapfel (on the authority of Wadding), and by the *Breviarium Romano-Seraphicum.* Thaddeus and Hope accept it as at least probable, while Stone thinks "there can be little doubt" that he held the office. That, as Wood and Dodd say, he succeeded Fr. Stephen Baron in this office, is denied by Parkinson. The latter (p. 222) places Forest after a certain Fr. William, who had succeeded Baron, but on being elected definitor general was constrained to resign the provincialship. We may add that several incidents in the life of Forest and the prominent part he played at the outbreak of the religious troubles show that he was provincial superior, whom the other friars were obliged to obey, and whom above all the king sought to win over to his cause.

pronounce the censures of the Church on nineteen friars of the Greenwich community. They had left the friary without permission as a protest against Cardinal Wolsey, who wished to make a canonical visitation of their convent, to which act he claimed his legatine jurisdiction empowered him. Though the friars had evidently failed by thus transgressing the enclosure rule, and by the very act had incurred papal censures, still the justice of their protest can not be denied, since Pope Leo X, on the request of Henry VIII, had exempted them from the jurisdiction of his legate.[8] "But," as Stone remarks, "in the manner of their repulse, they were undoubtedly wrong and Forest saw in it a flaw in their loyal attitude towards the See of Peter, of which he was so jealous a watchman."[9]

This remarkable incident in the life of Forest shows how by his sanctity and learning he had secured the confidence of the highest civil and ecclesiastical authorities in England. He was subsequently appointed regular preacher at St. Paul's Cross. This was at the time the most popular pulpit in England. Hence it gave the zealous friar an opportunity to exert a vast influence on the public mind.

As a fervent Tertiary of St. Francis, Queen Catherine had learned to esteem the worthy provincial of the Franciscans, to whom, we know, she was singularly devoted. Besides appointing Forest her chaplain at Greenwich, she chose him as her confessor and spiritual adviser. To him she confided the innermost secrets of her soul, especially when the dark clouds of domestic tribulation began to gather over her. We have every reason to suppose that her noble and heroic forebearance with her faithless consort must be in great part ascribed to the wise counsel of the Franciscan provincial, in whose prudence she placed absolute trust. The beautiful letter she wrote to him shortly before her demise, breathes the spirit of a loving and

---

[8] See Parkinson, p. 224; also *Grey Friars Chronicle* critically edited in *Monumenta Franciscana* (Vol. II) by Richard Howlett (p. 190).

[9] Stone, *Faithful Unto Death*, p. 48.

confiding child, grateful to the last for the many benefits received at the hands of her spiritual father. Him alone, she remarks in this letter, she followed in the things of God, because she knew him to be deeply instructed in human and divine knowledge.[10]

Needless to say, Forest was wholly in sympathy with the wronged queen. Well versed in the sacred sciences, he was from the start convinced that her marriage with Henry was valid and indissoluble. Hence, when the question of the king's "secret affair" became a matter of public comment, he had already put aside all doubt and hesitation, and was among the first openly to defend Catherine's rights whenever occasion offered. After 1531, when the queen by order of Henry was residing at the More in Hertfordshire, her former confessor frequently visited her. This is plain from a letter which a spy addressed to the king. "As concerning the Friars Observants," he says, "they came at divers times to confess the ladies and gentlewomen, and sometimes they said it was their way from one of their houses to another. As many names as I did know I shall declare Riche, Peto, Sabastyan, Curson, Robynson, Fforest and Neswick, with divers others."[11]

The king was well aware, not only of the provincial's mind on the divorce question, but of the great influence the dauntless friar was exerting on those with whom he came in touch. Accordingly, he summoned him one day to the royal palace and conferred alone with him for more than half an hour. It has never been learned what passed between the king and the friar during this private interview. But we may take it for granted that the man of God, like another John the Baptist, bravely showed his royal master the utter untenability of his position and warned him against the dangerous path he was pursuing. If the wayward king was displeased with the friar's unfavorable decision, he could not but admire his frankness and sincerity.

---

[10] See the foregoing chapter.

[11] *Camm*, Lives of the English Martyrs, *p. 277.*

He subsequently ordered some beef from the royal table to be brought to the Greenwich friary.[12] Perhaps he hoped in this way to make him and the community more favorably disposed toward his projected divorce. We know how poorly he succeeded with the Franciscans at large. It remains to be seen how the provincial met the advances of the king, and how much he had to suffer in defence of truth and justice.

Cromwell, Henry's pliant tool, and Anne Boleyn, his worthless bauble, were keeping the Greenwich community under close surveillance. They were determined to know the sentiments of each friar regarding the much mooted question, and to this end they succeeded in winning the services of Richard Lyst,[13] a lay brother of that friary. The letters[14] of this renegade to his royal patrons are still extant. They show that the writer was no longer true to his vows, and that he was discontented with his station as lay brother and with the strict Franciscan mode of life. Blinded by promises of royal preferments, he so far lost sight of the duties he owed to God and to his Order as to play the base role of rebel and traitor.

In one of his letters to Anne Boleyn, the unhappy friar tells "his friend" that for his fidelity to her and to the king, he has much to suffer, and has often been called in derision Anne's chaplain. He is not yet a priest, he avers, but he has ambition to become one and to say one hundred Masses for her welfare.

---

[12] See Gasquet, *Henry VIII and the English Monasteries*, Vol. I, p. 158.

[13] "This Richard Lyst," Gasquet notes, "says in another letter that he was 'of old lord cardinal's servant.' He 'has dreadful dreams three or four nights each week,' and thinks 'he could serve God better in another state than' as he is, and 'get rid of' his trouble. He adds, 'The information I sent you about friar Forest deserves support.' A few months after he writes as a student in 'first orders' from Clare Hall, Cambridge, saying he intends to be a 'secular priest.' " (p. 159.)

[14] They are quoted in part by Stone, pp. 7 seq., as found among the Cottonian MMS. and in Ellis's *Original Letters*. Though they bear no date, it is most probable that they were written in the interval between the summer of 1532 and the following spring.

Bl. John Forest, OFM

Such a thing is possible now, he adds, because the young woman to whom he was "made sure in the way of marriage, before his coming into religion, is departed to the mercy of God." He concludes with a petition for money; he had purchased clothes and other things for his mother and is now forty shillings in debt.

How bitterly he hated Fr. Forest and sought to cripple his influence, we learn from a letter which he addressed to Cromwell.

> Sir, your Mastership shall understand that Father Forest, which doth neither love nor favour you, hath laboured divers ways to supplant and bring Father Larans,[15] which is the King's faithful, true subject, out of favour, both with the King's Grace and with all our fathers and brothers, and also, as much as in him is, to expulse him out of our convent of Greenwich; and his original and chief cause is, because he knoweth that Father Larans is provided, and will also preach the King's matter, whensoever it shall please his Grace to command him, and so the very truth is, that Father Forest will not preach the King's matter himself, nor yet suffer Father Larans by his will to do so. Also I think, it were very convenient and necessary that the Chancellor of London were spoken unto, no more to assign Father Forest to preach at Paul's Cross. Our fathers have oftentimes assigned me to associate Father Forest when he hath gone forth in preaching, because they have supposed in me some intelligence and learning; and many a time when he hath preached, I have sitten

---

[15] Stone (p. 8) observes that " 'Father Larans' was probably a certain Friar Laurence, whom Father Forest apparently succeeded in turning out. There is a letter among the Cotton manuscripts from John Laurence to Cromwell, relative to his return to his cloister, the King having seemingly ordered the Greenwich Franciscans to take him back. In this letter, he begs Cromwell to insist on his being lodged in a certain room, in which he will have access to the outside world, be comparatively uncontrolled, and have freedom to correspond about the 'King's matter.' He entreats him not to allow him to be sent back to his old quarters." Later, as Camm notes (p. 181), this Laurence gave evidence against FF. Rich and Risby in the affair of the Holy Maid of Kent.

under the pulpit with a pair of red ears, because I have heard him so often break Master Priscian's head; therefore, in my judgment, it is more convenient for him to sit at home with his beads than to go forth and preach. Also, I pray your Mastership, have me meekly recommended unto my Lady Marquess of Pembroke (Anne Boleyn), unto whom I am much bound unto, and also that poor mother of mine, by the reason of her charitable benefits.

On another occasion, the unworthy friar has weighty accusations to make against FF. Peyto, Elstow, Forest, and others. He is anxious to tell Cromwell all he knows, in order to ease his "heart sore to see, perceive, and know the unkindness and duplicity of Father Forest against the King's Grace," who has bestowed so many benefits on the provincial and on the whole community. "The word 'duplicity,' " Stone remarks, "is characteristic of the writer's confused state of mind; he apparently estimates the value of a conscience at the price of 'a great piece of beef,' which Father Forest had received as a present, 'from the king's table.' "

During the year 1532, rumors of Henry's proposed marriage with Anne Boleyn were sweeping like threatening clouds over the country. Gloomy presentiments weighed on the hearts of the people who knew the strong will of their sovereign. Catherine no longer resided with him in the palace at Greenwich. Anne Boleyn already occupied the apartments of the rejected queen, and it was felt throughout the length and breadth of England that Henry would eventually espouse her and have her crowned queen, no matter what the ecclesiastical court at Rome would decide regarding his former marriage with Catherine.

Owing to the proximity of their convent to the royal palace, it was but natural that the Greenwich friars should frequently converse among themselves on the king's matter. Little did they suspect that in their very midst was one who stood in secret correspondence with the queen's enemies, and who was constantly reporting their utterances to headquarters.

Cromwell, anxious to establish himself in the royal favor, was not slow to acquaint the king with Lyst's venomous depositions. This explains why Henry, once so well disposed toward the friars, now began to hate them, especially those of Greenwich, who were loudest of all in condemning his policy. Though he still feigned friendly feelings toward the provincial, in his heart he was determined to let him feel his displeasure. As confessor of Queen Catherine, he thought, Forest might have induced her to submit to the royal will. Instead, he had all along favored her cause, had exhorted his brethren to do likewise, and had even forbidden Fr. Laurence to preach the opposite. He must thwart the influence of this obstinate and loudmouthed friar. Accordingly, in the summer of 1532, the minister general of the Order received a letter from the English king, demanding that he depose the Franciscan provincial and appoint in his stead Fr. John de la Haye, of Flanders, who would be unbiased in his view on the important question. The minister general prudently evaded the difficulty by replying that he had no power to depose a provincial, but would send the desired friar as commissary general to England.[16]

The commissary general did not arrive till the following spring. In the meantime, Lyst continued his vile depositions, and Forest, it seems, was repeatedly summoned before the king to answer for the conduct of his subjects. At a chapter of the province,[17] held in August, 1532, the provincial informed the assembled friars that the king was greatly displeased with them; that he had even been thinking of suppressing their Order in England; that he would desist for the present, however, being satisfied with his (Forest's) readiness to have the minister general replace him by a friar of Henry's choice. "All this," observes Camm, "reflects no little credit on Forest, who, it is clear, played a considerable part in these conciliatory

---

[16] Parkinson, p. 227.

[17] This was perhaps the chapter at which all the members of the Order in England were assembled.

measures, without in any way compromising his own high principles."[18]

On September 26, 1532, the Franciscan friars held chapter at Richmond. This we learn from a "warrant under the sign manual to Cromwell as master of the jewels, to deliver to the Friars Observants, now at their chapter at Richmond, to be employed as alms, L6, 13s, 4d."[19] Whatever may have been transacted at this chapter, we are not inclined to believe that the friars consented to the election of a new minister provincial. They were too much in sympathy with Forest to accede to the wishes of the king for his removal from office.[20] The following February, shortly after Henry's marriage with Anne Boleyn, the provincial was again at court. But Lyst had previously apprised Cromwell of Forest's coming, and had supplied him with serious accusations against the friars. It was, therefore, with mingled feelings of sorrow and alarm that, on returning to the convent, the man of God called his brethren together and told them how coldly he had been received at

---

[18] Compare this statement with the author's assumption regarding Forest's supposed temporary submission.

[19] Thaddeus, p. 15.

[20] Here, it is true, one of Cromwell's letters, dated September 13, 1532 (see Thaddeus, p. 14), confronts us with a difficulty. On the reverse of this letter is found a brief note in which Cromwell lists the six Franciscan friaries with the names of their respective wardens or guardians and places, Fr. Peyto (Peyton) at the head of the list as minister. Although this note does seem to have some connection with the chapter held on September 26, 1532, at Richmond, still it is by no means certain that Cromwell was correctly informed as to the results of the chapter. What was more natural under the circumstances than that the friars should for the present at least keep the name of their minister provincial secret from royal officials? Moreover, this note is perhaps merely a plan of Cromwell's, showing what he would wish when once Fr. Forest should be removed from his office as provincial. In fact, this theory becomes quite probable when we remember how willing Forest was to have the minister general send one to rule the province in his stead.

court, and how enraged the king was at the entire community.[21] But he was none the less determined to continue on his course of action; and we may take it for granted that, in his zeal for the spiritual welfare of his brethren, he exhorted them faithfully to pursue the path of duty and to bear up like true sons of St. Francis under the trials and afflictions that were sure to overwhelm them in the near future.

It must have been early in 1533 that Forest with deep sorrow became aware of Lyst's treachery. The informing lay brother, on his part, was racked with fear and remorse when he learned that his misdeeds were laid bare. In April, he wrote to Cromwell, requesting that his previous letters be burned, lest their contents be turned against him. At the same time, he pleaded for the minister's and the king's protection. Forest, he complained, would have nothing more to do with him and refused to answer him, when he offered "to make some amends unto God and to the religion whom he hath offended." Little faith, however, must be placed in this accusation against the saintly friar. If he really did treat the informer harshly, it was only to try him. How insincere Lyst was, we can judge from a letter he addressed to Cromwell soon after the arrival of the commissary general. He writes:

> There is a good father of our religion, a Frenchman, come from beyond sea unto us, which is chosen and assigned to be our minister, head, and ruler, here in this province, and I trust he shall do much good among us, if he will be indifferent *secundum veritatem*, as I trust he will, and help to reform Father Forest especially, and also some other things to be reformed among us. And so, if it were the King's pleasure and yours, good it were and also convenient, the King's Grace and also your Mastership to speak with our foresaid new minister, and to inform him under what manner he should use himself among us concerning the King's gracious honour. Also if it were your pleasure to help to reform Father Forest, and to get him removed out of this house,

---

[21] Camm, pp. 279 seq.

either to Newark or to Newcastle, I think you should do a meritorious deed, and have great reward of good therefor, and many thanks and prayers of many in our religion. And as for my part, I have done, and yet will do as much as is in me possible, to the furtherance and accomplishment of the same, with the grace of Jesu, who have you in His blessed keeping. Amen.

During Lent, the commissary general arrived, and at a chapter held soon after he was recognized as provincial.[22] To ensure the removal of Forest from the vicinity of Greenwich and of the royal court, Lyst had resorted to base trickery. He drew up a lengthy statement containing all the calumnies his black heart could fabricate against his worthy fellow friar. Having sent this statement to Cromwell, he laid a copy of it before the new provincial. Thus the latter, no longer free to act as justice demanded, was in some way forced to sacrifice Forest, in order to avoid greater difficulties. "Indeed," says Camm, "so wrongly were things now ordered, that it would seem as though the destiny of the noblest father in the province were decided by the whim of the basest brother."[23] In May, Lyst informed Cromwell that "Father Forest, your little friend and less lover, and mine also, for all his great cracks" had been removed from Greenwich. The worthless renegade added that his letter incriminating Forest had been duly considered by the new minister and by all the fathers of the house, who in consequence had removed Forest to a convent in the North. "This," Stone observes, "is so obviously the testimony of a false witness that we need be at no great pains to refute it. There is absolutely no evidence to show that Father Forest was ever out of favour with his brethren, but that, on the contrary, if we except the conduct of a few renegades such as Lyst and Laurence, we find the greatest unanimity among them with

---

[22] Camm, Vol. I, p. 250.

[23] Perhaps this was the chapter which Fr. Peyto attended as warden of Greenwich on the day after his sermon against the king's proposed marriage with Anne Boleyn.

regard to Henry's marriage with Catherine."[24]

Bitter anguish rent the soul of Forest when he beheld to what a pass the king's "secret affair" had come. The storm of persecution, he felt, was inevitable. Soon it would spell death and destruction for the Order he loved so tenderly and for the Church for whose welfare he had labored so long. What pained him most was the thought that one of his own brethren had wantonly severed the ties that bound him to the law of God and to the Rule of St. Francis, and that he was bartering his immortal soul to gain the favor of a corrupt and godless court. As to his own removal from office, he looked upon it as a special favor from Heaven. Now he was free from weighty cares and responsibilities, and had ample time to devote himself entirely to prayer and penance. Many an hour he knelt before his hidden God in the tabernacle, wrapt in fervent prayer for the king, that he might leave the path of iniquity; for the queen, that she might carry her cross with patience and perseverance; for the unfortunate lay brother, that he might see his mistake and repent in time; for his other brethren and for himself, that they might remain firm in the hour of trial when they should be called upon to choose between the holy law of God and the wicked demand of the king. What joy and pride must have thrilled his loyal heart on learning that FF. Peyto and Elstow had boldly upbraided the king for his lawless policy, and rather than deny their sacred trust, had gladly gone into exile.

It is not known for certain to which convent in the North Forest was transferred, nor how long he remained there. Perhaps it was at this time that he undertook to write his book in defence of the Church and of the Pope. Beginning with the words, "Let no man take the honor to himself, but he that is called by God, as Aaron was," the book is a strong invective against the king's usurping of the spiritual supremacy, which belonged to the Pope alone. Whether this had anything to do

---

[24] Stone, p. 12.

with the friar's imprisonment in 1534, is not clear.[25] There is little doubt, however, that Henry was enraged when he heard of it,[26] so that, when late in the spring of that year, he determined to imprison the Franciscans and confiscate their convents, Forest was among the first to suffer. That he was in prison in 1534, seems quite certain from an official report in which the man of God is mentioned as being "there (London) in prison." To this Gasquet remarks, "Perhaps the most conclusive proof that he was probably in prison at this time is that we hear no more about him. Cromwell's 'remembrances' are silent about this formidable opponent."[27] Neither is it certain whether he was in an ecclesiastical or a civil prison. Possibly, he was at first detained in the convent of the Grey Friars on the North Side of Newgate Street in London, and late in 1534 was cast into Newgate prison for again refusing to take the oath of supremacy, which, we know, became law on November 18 of that year.

Slanderous tongues did not scruple at the time to besmirch the name of Forest, so widely known for sanctity and learning. Hall's Chronicle was especially influential in spreading these libels and leading later historians into error.[28] Thus Wood avers that Forest had taken the oath of royal supremacy, while Stow contends that the friar himself later admitted he had taken the oath only with the outer man, but never consented thereto in conscience.[29] "If this were true," declares Stone, "it would be in such direct opposition to all that we know of Father Forest's firmness under trial, of his strength of character, his sincerity and fearlessness, that his life would be a hopeless tangle of

---

[25] Bourchier, *Hist. Eccle. de Mart. FF. Ord. D. Francisci*, pp. 31 seq. Though later historians say that Forest wrote this book in Newgate, Bourchier speaks of it rather as one of the causes that led to the martyr's imprisonment.

[26] Stone, p. 56, on the authority of Wood.

[27] Gasquet, Vol. I, p. 167.

[28] Stone, pp. 49 seq.

[29] See Parkinson, p. 243; Gasquet, Vol. I, p. 195, footnote.

contradictions. It would have been so poor a preparation for a martyr's death, that instead of the cry of jubilation with which he greeted the fire and gallows, we should expect to hear him bartering for his life at the stake. But one who had stood up and publicly denounced his brethren, for their resistance to the representative of the Pope, one who, in the face of the king's ruthless passion, had persisted in an attitude which said as plainly as words could say, 'It is not lawful for thee to have this woman to wife,' was not the man to condescend to a mean subterfuge, in order to save a life which he had repeatedly exposed with greatest indifference. He was by his position, by his acknowledged virtue, and by his talents, a leader of men. Through his influence, the friars of Greenwich had been guided safely through the shoals and quicksands of the divorce and the royal supremacy, and if he had succumbed with his 'outer man,' he would have been the only member of his community to take the oath."[30]

We may take it for granted that the king's agents repeatedly visited Forest in prison and did all in their power to win him over to Henry's cause. The faithful and fearless friar was as staunch in his allegiance to God and to his Order as the royal commissioners were zealous in the service of Henry and of their own interests. He gloried in the thought of dying for the faith, as FF. Rich and Risby had done but a twelvemonth before.[31] Never, with the help of God, would he prove disloyal in a cause for which they had laid down their life. Cromwell fully realized this; he gave orders that the friar's durance be made more severe and at last had him condemned to death. Though for some reason the sentence was not immediately carried out, the fact that it had been passed on him, is sufficiently attested by the letter he wrote to Queen Catherine three days before his martyrdom was to take place.[32]

---

[30] Stone, p. 48, citing Canon Dixon's History of the Church of England.

[31] See chapter IV.

[32] See the foregoing chapter.

During his confinement in Newgate, he received a letter from Lady Elizabeth Hammond, at one time his penitent and now lady in waiting on the queen. In his letter, he is told how the queen is grieved and alarmed over his impending doom; that he should try to escape from prison, if possible, lest the queen fall into an illness that would prove fatal. To this the holy man replied:

> My Daughter, Elizabeth Hammond:—
> I am, indeed, sorely grieved at the sorrow which you and your mistress feel about the pains I am enduring, just as if there were no resurrection unto glory. These are certainly not principles which among other lessons of piety I have frequently impressed upon you; if they are, however, then know that at the time I was erring wide of the true road. Were I willing to barter my faith and deliver myself to the devil, from fear of suffering or from a desire for the riches of this world, I could without doubt easily escape; do thou, however, not entertain such thoughts. Learn, therefore, to suffer for the true teaching of Christ and for his spouse and thy mother, the Church, and do not attempt to turn me from those torments by which I hope to obtain eternal happiness.
> Follow, I beseech you, in the footsteps of the Queen, your mistress, imitating the glorious example you see in her, and pray for me, that they may increase the severity of the torments which they intend to inflict on me, since they are but small when compared with the glory of God which they are to further.[33]

About 1536, as we have already heard, a number of events combined to cool for a time at least Henry's rage against the first opponents of his tyrannical and bloody measures. Possibly at this juncture, Fr. Forest, like other members of the province, was permitted to leave Newgate and to take up his abode with the Grey Friars in London.[34] Mental and bodily sufferings had

---

[33] Bourchier, pp. 61 seq.

[34] This, we think, accounts for Forest's liberation from Newgate and for his subsequent sojourn in the London friary as satisfactorily as the supposition, made by some historians, that he took the oath with the saving clause, *as far*

Bl. John Forest, OFM

greatly enfeebled him, and the king perhaps was still in hopes that clemency on his part and the influence of others less faithful would in the end triumph over the aged friar. How Forest lived in the London convent we learn from the memorandum of Lord Mordaunt who, in 1537, made his Easter confession to him.[35] Subject to the Conventual warden, a nominee of the king, Forest led a life of seclusion and prayer. Most conscientiously he observed the vow of poverty. He refused to take any remuneration from Lord Mordaunt, referring him to the porter, who had charge of all money matters. He was not allowed to preach, but said the Lady's Mass every day and was much engaged in the confessional. On the question of the king's usurped supremacy, he was silent except where duty forced him to speak.

Though the friar's outward conduct gave his enemies little chance for accusations, at heart he was as loyal and zealous as ever. Cromwell was anything but satisfied with Forest's condition in the London friary. Wholly bent on bringing him to the scaffold, he not only engaged spies to watch him, but even went so far as to abuse the Sacrament of Confession. The aforementioned memorandum of Lord Mordaunt is nothing less than a deposition regarding Forest's procedure in the sacred tribunal of Penance.[36] Previous to the spring of 1538, however, nothing but vague and incoherent rumors could be gathered, until finally Cromwell struck upon a diabolical plan. One day, while Forest was hearing confessions, a certain Waferer entered the sacred tribunal. After making some sort of confession, the vile wretch complained that his conscience was troubling him ever

---

as Christ's law allows, a supposition entirely irreconcilable with the friar's previous and subsequent conduct regarding the oath.

[35] The memorandum is quoted in full by Camm, Vol. I, pp. 293 seq. It is dated February 23, 1538. This date, however, "must not be taken as that on which the incident happened, but as that on which the memorandum was written." Thaddeus, p. 15.

[36] Camm, Vol. I, p. 295.

since he had taken the oath of supremacy. Exhorted by the man of God to repent of his sin and to trust in the mercy of God, the hypocrite asked the unsuspecting friar whether he, too, had taken the oath. "No," came the ready reply, "I would rather burn than swear such a thing." This was enough. "Thank you," replied Waferer, "I do not wish to know more." With this he rose from his knees and reputed the matter to headquarters.[37]

Now Cromwell and his clique had positive proof that Forest was dissuading penitents from taking the oath. Without delay, the priest was summoned before the Privy Council, over which Cromwell presided. With great courage and skill he again defended the papal supremacy, at the same time maintaining strict silence on all matters that pertained to the seal of confession, lest he unwittingly implicate his penitents. "He succeeded in saving others," remarks Camm, "though his bold confession of the Faith, the boldest perhaps that we have of any martyr of this period, cost him his life."[38] Cromwell in his blind fury was not satisfied with having him die the death of a traitor; he would have him convicted of heresy and burned at the stake.[39]

For the present, the helpless victim of base deceit was lodged in a solitary dungeon in Newgate. Here he underwent all the horrors and hardships that hatred and cruelty could devise. His hands and feet were bound with iron chains, and for several days he was left there suffering the greatest misery.[40] His condition must have been most pitiable. He was now sixty-seven years of age, and his health was much impaired by the

---

[37] Stone, p. 52.

[38] Camm, Vol. I, p. 297.

[39] This is evident from the *Excerpts* of Forest's so-called *Confessions,* i.e., the examination he was subjected to before the Privy Council. Cromwell's mind in this regard is further clear from Cranmer's letter written to him on April 6, 1538. See Camm, Vol. I, p. 301.

[40] See Bourchier, p. 39.

sorrow and worry of the last few years. He greeted his solitude, however, as a special favor from above and employed his time preparing for the final struggle.

On May 8, after a month of woeful durance in Newgate, Forest was arraigned before Cranmer's court at Lambeth. He realized that this was the beginning of the "greater combat," as he chose to call it in a letter to Bl. Thomas Abel,[41] one of his former penitents. Raising his eyes to heaven he prayed with all the ardor of his soul, "I give thee thanks, Lord God, who hast deigned to call me, a most miserable sinner, to the singular privilege of professing to-day, here in the presence of all, the true faith that I cherish, and of freely declaring what I hold regarding thy pure, unsullied, and only spouse, the Roman Catholic Church. For the threats of the king, I fear not, nor consider the torments that, no doubt, are awaiting me on account of my faith; and so far am I from seeking and striving after earthly honors that I will not accept them, but will gladly suffer death."[42]

After the usual court preliminaries, Forest was ordered to abjure as "most abominable heresies" four articles which on Cranmer's suggestion had been drawn up with a view to indicting him for heresy. The four articles read:

That the Holy Catholic Church was the Church of Rome, and that we ought to believe out of the same;
That we should believe in the Pope's pardon for the remission of sins;
That we ought to believe and do as our fathers have done

---

[41] He was a secular priest, a man of eminent sanctity and learning, and from the start a staunch advocate of Queen Catherine's rights, who had appointed him her chaplain and director of music. In 1533, when the case of the Holy Maid of Kent came up, he was imprisoned, but later set free. He openly defended the papal supremacy, for which he was again cast into prison and finally, on July 30, 1540, martyred at Smithfield. His name was on the list of those whom Pope Leo XIII enrolled among the Blessed on December 9, 1886.

[42] Bourchier, p. 45.

aforetime fourteen years past;

That a priest may turn and change the pains of hell of a sinner, truly penitent, contrite of his sins, by certain penance enjoined him in(to) the pains of purgatory.—Which said articles be most abominable heresies, blasphemy against God, and contrary to Scripture and the teaching of Christ and His Apostles, and to abhor any true Christian heart to think.[43]

Although he clearly foresaw what the sequel would be, the fearless friar declined to make the required abjuration. He was convinced that the first three articles embody Catholic doctrine; and as to the fourth, he readily detected its insidious character and firmly refused to forswear it in its proposed form. Accordingly he was remanded to Newgate. His confinement now became less severe, if Latimer's suspicions are correct. Latimer writing to Cromwell, on May 18,[44] claimed he had heard that Forest was permitted to confer with others imprisoned for the faith and even to hear holy Mass and receive the sacraments. Probably, the jailer admired and felt for the feeble old friar bearing his sufferings so patiently, and allowed him such liberties as were compatible with his own safety. Perhaps, too, it was only a last attempt on the part of Forest's enemies to cajole him into submission. Be this as it may, prayer and meditation strengthened the man of God in his determination bravely to fight the good fight to the end. In vain, therefore, the royal officials came to him in prison and demanded that he sign the abjuration of the four articles. Neither threats nor promises could shake his constancy. With equal intrepidity he turned a deaf ear to Cromwell directing that he attend Latimer's sermon at St. Paul's Cross, on May 12, and do public penance for his heresies.[45] Needless to say, this uncompromising attitude of the loyal friar infuriated his

---

[43] Camm, Vol. I, p. 302, quoting from Wriothesley's *Chronicle*.

[44] For a copy of this letter see Camm, Vol. I, p. 312.

[45] See Camm, Vol. I, pp. 310 seq.

enemies. He was forthwith pronounced a confirmed heretic and sentenced to die at the stake. In his afore-mentioned letter to Cromwell Latimer consented "to play the fool" and preach the sermon at Forest's burning.

Before relating the details of the glorious martyrdom that crowned the beautiful life of Bl. John Forest, we must examine whether he verbally abjured the four articles and declared his willingness to do public penance at St. Paul's cross, as Camm seems inclined to believe.[46] The only authorities for this story are Hall and Wriothesley. Hall writes: "He was after sundry examinations, convinced and confuted, and gladly submitted himself to abide the punishment of the Church." Wriothesley's testimony reads: "John Forest, Friar Observant, Doctor of Divinity (was) adjured for heresie on the eighth day of the month of May, at Lambeth, before the most reverend father in God, Thomas Cranmer, Archbishop of Canterburie, with other. ... The articles (were) subscribed with his own hand (and he) sworn and abjured on the same, and after sworn again to abide such injunction and penance as he should be enjoined by the said court."

This twofold testimony, so derogatory to the fair name of Forest exerts such a pressure on Camm that he is unable to believe the affair a "mere fabrication," since "all other chroniclers support it."

In the first place, it is not true that *all* other chroniclers support it. "Not only," says Stone, "are Sander and Bourchier silent as to the charge, but Foxe, always so ready to make much of any tale to the discredit of Catholics, makes no mention of any projected penance at St. Paul's Cross."[47] Neither does Collier seem to know anything of the affair. He simply says,

---

[46] "Though the articles," Camm remarks, "were signed in writing, the 'abjuration' or 'submission' was by word of mouth only. If it (the written abjuration)," he adds, "could have been produced (by Latimer on the morning of Forest's martyrdom), it certainly would have been" (p. 310, footnote).

[47] Stone, p. 64.

"By what law they could stretch his (Forest's) crime to heresy is hard to discover, for he was tried only for dissuading his penitents in confession from owning the King's Supremacy."[48] Of more modern historians whose works we have been able to consult, Leon, Guérin, Hope, Gasquet, Thaddeus, Domenichelli simply ignore the story, Parkinson and Spillmann discard it as incredible, while Dodd and Stone take it up and refute it.

But, who are Hall and Wriothesley whose testimony Camm dares not discard as a "mere fabrication"? Hall was a contemporary of Henry VIII; up till 1533, he wrote on passing events. When he ceased to write, Richard Grafton, a bitter Protestant, indiscriminately published what Hall had collected, whether authenticated or not.[49] "The part relative to Forest," as Camm himself remarks, "may have been based upon some political pamphlet of the time."[50] Hall, therefore, as Stone contends, "is not responsible for the statement referring to Forest," and since Grafton declares he "added nothing of his own," the supposed account of Hall "and the story told by Wriothesley four years later, have one and the same origin, the real author remaining incognito."[51] Why Wriothesley repeated the libel is obvious. For he "had no leaning towards the religious orders, but went entirely with Henry in his ruthless nationalism and greed."[52] Thus the extrinsic evidence supporting the story of Forest's verbal abjuration is extremely weak. It is solely based on the assertion of men whose testimony is, to say the least, questionable for the very reason that they were contemporaries of the friar whom they basely maligned and of the king whose cause they sought to further. Hence we fail to understand why Camm finds it so very hard

---

[48] Gasquet, Vol. I, p. 197.

[49] See Stone, p. 50.

[50] Camm, Vol. I, p. 325.

[51] Stone, p. 50.

[52] Stone, p. 63, footnote 5.

to "escape the conclusion that, whatever Forest may have done or said on May the 8, he did not 'confess the faith' with credit to himself."[53]

From intrinsic reasons it becomes still more evident that the story is in very deed "a mere fabrication," hatched in the biased mind of some obscure political agitator, then published as Hall's statement by a malicious bigot, and finally repeated by one who was anything but fair in matters that concerned the persecuted friars. How, we ask, can this supposed momentary weakness of the heroic martyr be reconciled with his characteristic constancy and attested learning? If four years before he steadfastly refused to admit the king's supremacy in matters spiritual, is it credible that he would have acted less firmly now when he saw that clear and express tenets of his holy faith were at stake, and when he realized what terrible consequences the least weakness on his part would necessarily entail on himself, on his brethren, and on the whole Church in England? Had he not been among the first openly to oppose the king in his beastly passion and towering pride? Had he not seen FF. Peyto and Elstow go into exile, and FF. Rich and Risby mount the scaffold for the sake of truth and justice? Had he not, like a solicitous father, warned Queen Catherine against "that pestilential teaching of the heretics?" Was not his intrepid zeal in her cause the ever-recurring refrain of Lyst's letters to Cromwell? And now we should believe that either puzzled by difficulties or baffled by fear he wavered and at last submitted, and that in a cause for which he himself had already suffered untold hardships. Indeed, he was advanced in years and broken in health, but none the less prudent and fearless. Even granting that, as Camm thinks, he was "puzzled by the difficulty of a problem before him," only a gross misconception of the friar's character can lead one to believe that because he was puzzled he gave in. No, in that case, he would evidently have demanded a written statement of the four articles together with sufficient

---

[53] Camm, Vol. I, p. 309.

leisure to study and weigh the fourth one, which on account of its studied ambiguity at first sight presented difficulties. Never, at least, would he have abjured them either singly or collectively in their proposed form.

That his imprisonment after May 8 was less severe than before, is by no means certain. In his letter to Cromwell, Latimer says only that he has heard this to be the case, and does not know "whether through the fault of the sheriff or the gaoler, or both."[54] Then, if he did adjure, why did not his enemies make capital out of it for the purpose of discrediting him in the eyes of the people? Moreover, why was he sent back to Newgate at all? Would not the convent of the Grey Friars, quite subservient to the will of the king, have been a far more suitable place to bring him to a full submission? Finally, why did not Latimer on the morning of the martyrdom when Forest publicly branded him as an apostate, retaliate by adducing this supposed verbal abjuration of his fearless opponent? Such an exposure would certainly have gone far toward rehabilitating the confused bishop, and would have dealt the fair reputation of the heroic friar a telling blow in the eyes of the vast concourse of people. But Latimer made no mention of it whatever. In fact, as we shall see, the manner of his procedure during the disputation was entirely that of a man straining every nerve to wean his opponent from principles which he had never denied, and which he was not likely to deny now though the most dreadful tortures and death stared him in the face.

Confronted by this overwhelming evidence, we do not hesitate to maintain that the story of Forest's verbal abjuration of the four articles is wholly "a mere fabrication" of his enemies, a base libel on his name and on the Order to which he belonged. Dodd must have had chroniclers like Hall and Wriothesley in mind when he wrote, "Now laying all circumstances together, what several (not *all*) historians have

---

[54] The letter is quoted by Camm, Vol. I, p. 312; also by Stone, p. 65.

reported, concerning this religious man's behaviour, will, I presume, be judged rather calumnies than real fact."[55]

Like one whose most cherished desire was about to be fulfilled, the valiant champion of truth and justice rejoiced on learning that in a few days he would be led forth to die for the faith. Early Wednesday morning, May 22, Cromwell's minions entered the martyr's dungeon. Binding his hands and feet, Fr. Marcos tells us, they fastened the aged friar to a hurdle and dragged him from Newgate through the streets of the city to the suburb Smithfield. What tortures must have racked his feeble and emaciated frame on this last painful journey. How he must have prayed for strength when arriving at the place of martyrdom he beheld from his bed of pain the singular spectacle before him and heard the murmurings of the surging multitude. From Garcias we learn that a proclamation had been issued in the city, inviting the people to attend Latimer's sermon, which would begin at eight o'clock. Wriothesley, an eyewitness of the scene, tells us that above ten thousand citizens had assembled to see the final struggle of one whose fearless opposition to the king had attracted nation-wide attention.[56]

Within sight of the convent and church of the Grey Friars, on a plot of ground closed in by a railing, stood two platforms; one of these was supplied with a chair for the martyr, while the other had a sort of pulpit, from which Latimer was to preach. Near the martyr's platform was seen a huge wooden statue of St. Dervel Gadarn (Darvell Gatheren). It was so large that eight men could scarcely carry it. The people of Llanderfel, in Wales, had held it in great veneration on account of the miracles said to have been wrought through the intercession of the Saint. An old prophecy had it that one day the statue would set fire to a forest. Hence, when Ellis Price after confiscating it wrote to

---

[55] Dodd, *Church History of England* (Brussels, 1737), Vol. I, p. 237.

[56] See Stone, p. 66, on the authority of Garcias, a Spanish chronicler and "undoubtedly an eye-witness of the martyrdom."

Cromwell on April 6, 1538, for further instructions, the spiteful minister, anxious to ridicule the Catholic veneration of images, ordered the statue to be brought to London and to be used at the burning of Bl. John Forest. "It is a singular fact," Thaddeus observes, "that those who laughed at the prophecy, ridiculed miracles, and denied the truth of the Catholic religion, now became, as it were, instruments in the hands of God to bring about at least the apparent, if not the true, fulfillment of the old prediction."[57] From the gibbet erected in another corner of the enclosure, dangled a heavy chain, while a store of fagots and straw lay beneath it. Above it was fastened a placard bearing in large letters the following blasphemous doggerel:

> David Darvell Gatheren,
> As saith the Welshman,
> Fetched outlaws out of Hell;
> Now he is come with spere and shilde,
> In harness to burn in Smithfielde,
> For in Wales he may not dwell.
>
> And Forest the Friar,
> That obstinate liar,
> That willfullie shall be dead,
> In his contumacie
> The gospel doth denie,
> The King to be supreme head.

Near the gate of St. Bartholomew's Hospital, stood another long platform. This was intended for the Lords of the Privy Council and for the city mayor and other men of civil authority and influence.

On reaching Smithfield, the executioners immediately loosened their victim from the hurdle and led him to the platform, which he was ordered to mount. A solemn hush fell on the vast multitude when at a given signal Latimer ascended

---

[57] Thaddeus, p. 67.

the pulpit and began his defence of royal supremacy. No doubt, he had prepared his sermon well and left no argument untouched that might draw the friar from the faith for which he was ready to die. The martyr was aware that he would not get a fair hearing; hence during the faithless bishop's tirade against the Pope, he prudently kept silence.[58] At last, after preaching over an hour, Latimer turned to him and asked in what state he would die. At this Forest arose and with a loud, clear voice replied "that if an angel should come down from Heaven and show him any other thing than he had believed all his life time past he would not believe him, and that if his body should be cut joint after joint, or member after member, brent, hanged, or what pain soever might be done to his body, he would never turn from his old sect of this Bishop of Rome." Then facing Latimer he chid him saying, "that seven years agone he durst not have made such a sermon for his life."[59]

But Latimer had long since learned to stifle the voice of conscience. Hence he coldly disregarded the well-meaning rebuke of his former friend.

"Dr. Forest," he urged, "above all I am astonished that thou, whom I hold for one of the most learned men in the realm, should be accused of being a Papist, and I refuse to believe it till I hear it from thine own mouth."

"Thou has known me for many years, Latimer," the friar calmly retorted, "and I am still more astonished at thee, that for the pomps of the world thou hast endangered thine own soul. Dost thou not recollect what thou didst write me against the emperor, when he was against Rome and the Pope, and how thou with all thy voice didst denounce them all as heretics? Recollect how we, the doctors of the Church, considered the act and condemned it, and decided that those who did it should be excommunicated. What wert thou then, Latimer, a Papist or a

---

[58] According to Fr. Marcos, Forest tried to speak, but the heretics made so much noise that he could not be heard. See Camm, Vol. I, p. 316.

[59] Wriothesley, quoted by Camm, Vol. I, p. 316.

heretic?"[60]

"I am no heretic," shouted the bishop, quite discomfited, "but rather was I then deceived, and am now enlightened with the Holy Spirit, and if thou wilt call upon thy better self, thou also wilt receive the light, for thou art now blind." This duplicity and perversion deeply pained the man of God. How he longed to reclaim this erring fellow priest, who in his mad pursuit after royal preferments had wantonly strayed from the path of duty.

"Oh, Latimer," he pleaded, "I think thou hast other things in thy heart! But since the king has made thee from a poor student into a bishop, thou art constrained to say this. Open thou thine eyes; take example by that holy Bishop of Rochester and the blessed Thomas More, who renounced the goods of this world, and chose rather to die than to lose their immortal souls."

"O God," cried Latimer, at a loss what to say, "how great are the snares of the Bishop of Rome, who has kept men in darkness for so many years."

Evidently, he was engaged in a losing game with his doughty adversary. To save himself and his cause in the eyes of the people, he must play a different card.

"And look thou, Dr. Forest," he hastily continued, "that thou mayest see the snares and the falsity of his saints, they shall bring hither one of the idols of the Bishop of Rome."

At these words, the statue of St. Dervel was brought and placed on the platform occupied by the friar.

"Look, Dr. Forest," repeated Latimer, pointing to the image, "this is one of the idols of the Bishop of Rome, and for my own part," he added contemptuously, "I think the priests ought to have given the Bishop of Rome half of his profits."

The blessed martyr could not refrain from laughing.

"I am not surprised," he said, "that what thou sayest should

---

[60] Here was Latimer's chance to make a count in his own favor by referring to the martyr's recent abjuration, had such an abjuration actually been made.

have happened, for the priests are so greedy, that they well might invent that, and much more; but do not think that the Pope sanctions any such thing."

Sorely vexed at the obvious discomfiture of Latimer and anxious to see Forest in his torments, Cromwell abruptly terminated the disputation.

"My Lord Bishop," he exclaimed, "I think you strive in vain with this stubborn man. It would be better to burn him."

Far from intimidating the intrepid friar, the minister's words rather served to embolden him.

"Gentlemen," he said defiantly, "if I were willing to sacrifice my soul, it would not have been necessary to come to this place."

"Take him off at once," commanded Cromwell, pale with rage.

Unspeakable joy thrilled the brave soul of Forest when he realized that at last the long looked for moment had come. Turning toward the three men still supporting the statue, he smiled and said playfully:

"Brethren, I pray ye, do not drop it on me, for my hour is not yet come."

Wholly intent on overcoming the constancy of the valiant friar, Latimer once more addressed him. There was a suspicion of sadness and sympathy in his voice that showed how his own soul was racked with remorse.

"Brother Forest," he pleaded, "I beseech thee to turn. The king will give thee a good living, for I know full well that if thou wishest thou art well able to give doctrine to great numbers."

But compared with the promise of eternal life, this world with all its goods had no value in the eyes of the blessed martyr.

"All the treasures of the world, Latimer," he replied, "will not move me from my will; but I much desire to speak with one of the gentlemen here."

Thereupon, the Duke of Norfolk arose to go over to where

Forest stood. Cromwell, however, intercepted him.

"My Lord Duke," he commanded, "take your seat again; if he wants to say anything, let him say it out that we can all hear."

Though mortified at this public indignity, the Duke was constrained to obey. He well knew that Cromwell was all-powerful with the king. When Forest perceived that no one would be permitted to speak with him in private, he turned quietly toward his enemies and making the sign of the cross, exclaimed:

"Gentlemen, with this body of mine deal as you wish."[61]

Provoked beyond measure, Cromwell gives the sign. The throng of spectators gaze in breathless silence at the venerable friar, who offers no resistance when the executioners drag him down from the scaffold and lead him to the gibbet. Heedless of the torments he knows are in store for him, the dauntless champion raises his eyes to heaven and declares, "Neither fire, nor fagot, nor scaffold shall separate me from Thee, O Lord."[62] The executioners tear off his outer habit, gird him about the waist and under the arms with the iron chain[63] that dangles from the gibbet, and draw him upwards, so that he hangs suspended over the straw and fagots. These they now ignite, a dense volume of smoke ascends, and soon the inhuman torture begins. Tongues of fire lick the martyr's feet. Racked with pain, he involuntarily raises them and clutches the scaffold; but only for a moment; and as if repenting of the act, he willingly lets go his hold and suffers the flames to do their work. Fed with chips hewn from the statue of St. Dervel, the heat becomes well-nigh

---

[61] The above dialog and details are taken from Garcias's narrative as quoted by Stone, pp. 66 seq., and by Camm, Vol. I, pp. 317 seq.

[62] Bourchier, p. 48.

[63] Thaddeus, p. 69. Sander (ed. 1585, p. 90—ed. 1690, p. 243) says that two chains were fastened round the martyr's arms. Bourchier (p. 49) speaks only of one chain, which was secured round his waist (circa ventrem). "One would like to think," remarks Camm (p. 320), "that the martyr was hung by the middle, in order that he might be the sooner suffocated, but it is to be feared that the motive was to make him look ridiculous."

unbearable, while the heartless executioners grasp their halberts and with their aid bring the martyr into a swinging motion. A strong wind sweeps over Smithfield and fans the flames to one side, so that they reach only his lower extremities. Though untold agony convulses the martyr's body, his soul is rapt in sweet communion with Him who died on the cross to save mankind. Above the crackling of the fire and the low murmurs of the bystanders, he is heard praying for strength and perseverance; beating his breast with his hands, he cries, "In the shadow of thy wings I will trust, until iniquity pass away."

Two hours have now elapsed. Still dangling from the gibbet, oppressed by the scorching heat and smoke, the man of God is patiently waiting for death to end his fearful sufferings. The spectators are filled, some with disgust at the obstinate friar, many with sympathy for him. At last, the executioners approach the gibbet and loosen its supports, so that it crashes with its burden into the greedy flames. At this, the heroic martyr prays aloud, "In thee, O Lord, have I hoped, let me never be confounded: deliver me in thy justice. Bow down thy ear to me: make haste to deliver me." Amid the crackling of the flames, his prayers grow fainter and fainter. Then a last, "Into thy hands I commend my spirit"—the martyr's voice is heard no more[64]—his beautiful soul freed from its prison of clay has ascended to the mansions of unending bliss to receive the martyr's crown and to join the triumphant ranks of those "who have despised the life of the world, and have arrived at the reward of the kingdom, and have washed their garments in the blood of the Lamb."

It is related that while Bl. John Forest was in the midst of his torments, a snow white dove was seen fluttering about the gibbet and settling at last on the head of the martyr. Furthermore, we are told, the Saint's right hand, mouth and tongue remained untouched by the fire, "as if God," remarks

---

[64] Thaddeus, p. 70.

Thaddeus, "would thus show his approval of all he had written and spoken in defence of the Faith."[65] Nothing certain is known regarding the whereabouts of the martyr's relics. Father Thaddeus thinks it is "most probable that the mortal remains of Father Forest still lie hidden at Smithfield, near the corner of St. Bartholomew's Hospital opposite the gate of the ancient priory,"[66] where, according to Garcias, they were interred on the day of his glorious martyrdom. Already in 1638, Fr. Arturus a Monasterio thus commemorated him in his *Franciscan Martyrology:* "At London, in England, memory of Blessed John Forest, an apostolic man and martyr, who, by order of Henry VIII, King of England, was cast into prison for the defence of the Catholic Faith, and after a cruel imprisonment, sentenced to death; being suspended on a gibbet, a slow fire was lighted at his feet and he was inhumanly roasted, until at length, being all consumed by the fire, he went up to heaven victorious." On December 9, 1886, Pope Leo XIII declared him blessed together with the Tertiary Martyr Thomas More and fifty-two others, who between the years 1535 and 1583 shed their blood in England in defence of the faith. The feast of Bl. John Forest is celebrated annually on May 22, throughout the Franciscan Order.

---

[65] Thaddeus, p. 71. See also Guérin, *Le Palmier Séraphique,* Vol. V, p. 470.

[66] *The Catholic Encyclopedia,* Vol. VIII, p. 464.

CHAPTER X
DEATH AND DESTRUCTION, 1538-1547

Renewed measures against the Franciscans—Three martyrs: FF. Antony Brown, John Waire, and Hemmysley—The Conventual friars—Their poverty—During the first years of the religious upheaval—The royal visitors—Wholesale robbery and vandalism—Subsequent lot of the Conventual houses and of the ejected friars.

Like Blessed John Forest, a number of his fellow friars, whose detention in the Conventual houses had also become less severe, were again using their influence in behalf of papal supremacy. Hence the spies of Cromwell found much to report against them, so that the hatred of their enemies was enkindled anew, and Henry determined to wreak fearful vengeance on these obstinate "sowers of sedition." We have already seen how, in consequence, three Franciscans were thrown into prison in 1537 and died there as martyrs of the faith. Little, however, is known regarding the subsequent fate of the other members of the suppressed province. From the scanty records available, we may safely conclude that they were again hunted down like criminals and subjected to every sort of indignity. While some succeeded in either remaining concealed or in leaving the country, others fell into the hands of their pursuers and were thrown into loathsome dungeons, where shut off from the outer world they spent months and years amid untold sufferings, until death at last came to their relief. Between 1538 and 1547, the year of Henry's tragic end, the martyrdom of only three Franciscans has been recorded.

On August 4, 1538, four months after the glorious death of Bl. John Forest, the Duke of Norfolk informed Cromwell that the justices of assize at Norwich had examined Fr. Antony Brown, who once belonged to the Greenwich community and who was now living as a hermit. The valiant friar, we learn, wrote out his own confession, and refusing to alter his views on papal supremacy, he was found guilty of high treason and condemned to death. His execution, however, was delayed for ten days, because it was thought "convenient that a sermon should be made by the bishop of Norwich, as was by the bishop of Worcester at the execution of Forest." In the interval, nothing was left undone to shake the constancy of Fr. Antony. "This afternoon," writes the duke, "we so handled the said friar that we brought him to this point, that he would not stick upon the authority of the bishop of Rome to be supreme head of the Church,[1] but in no wise could we bring him from the opinion that the king ought not to be supreme head of the Church, saying that no temporal prince was *capax* of that name and authority." In vain did the bishop of Norwich and Dr. Call, a Conventual friar, argue with him. Accordingly, "we have delivered him," continues Norfolk, "to the sheriff to be carried to the gaol and there to suffer according to his foolish doings upon Friday next. Before his death the said bishop shall make such a sermon as we trust shall be to the king's highness contentation and apparent to the people (who, we think, will be there in great number) that this unhappy foolish friar is well worthy to suffer and that his opinions be false and untrue. My Lord," he adds, "the cause of the sending of this man in so great haste unto you is because that if the king's majesty and you shall think it convenient to have him to be brought to the Tower, there to be more straightly examined and to be put to torture, you may despatch this bearer or some other with command to the sheriff accordingly, so that the same may be with him at Norwich by Friday at ten o'clock." Again the bishop sought to win Fr. Antony over to the king's side. But his efforts proved fruitless. The servant of God remained firm to the end. Particulars regarding his martyrdom have not come

---

[1] This is probably to signify, as Spillmann remarks, that he did not successfully defend the doctrine of papal supremacy. See *Katholikenverfolgung in England*, Part I, p. 204.

down to us, but "there can be little doubt," says Gasquet, "that the sentence of death was carried out on Friday, August 9, 1538.[2]

A year later, on July 8, another Franciscan, Fr. John Waire (Maire) suffered martyrdom at St. Thomas Waterings in Southwark. With him were executed Griffith Clark, a secular priest and vicar of Wandsworth, also the latter's curate and his servant. Details of their martyrdom, however, have not been recorded. "John Stow says, he had not seen the indictment; but Catholic writers, who are particularly inquisitive concerning such matters, all agree they suffered for denying the king's supremacy; this year and the next being remarkable for that sort of executions."[3]

The last Observant friar who is known to have died for the faith before the demise of Henry VIII we find commemorated in Grey Friars Chronicle under the year 1546; viz., "And the xvi. day of Julii was burned in Smythfelde for grett herrysy ... Hemmysley a priest, wyche was an Obesruand freere of Richmond."[4]

It is time that we recount the history of the Conventual friars during these first years of the conflict. Approximately, they were at the time about 800 in number,[5] distributed over some 70 houses.[6] Although they had not formally joined the

---

[2] Gasquet, *Henry VIII and the English Monasteries,* Vol. II, pp 251 seq.

[3] Dodd, *Church History of England,* Vol. I, p. 214; Hope, *Franciscan Martyrs in England,* p. 16; Stone, *Faithful Unto Death,* p. 81; Thaddeus, *The Franciscans in England,* p. 17. Fr. Waire's name is on the list of English martyrs whose cause of beatification has been introduced. See *Acta Minorum,* Vol. VI (1887), pp. 49 seq.

[4] *Grey Friars Chronicle* in *Monumenta Franciscana,* Vol. II, p. 211.

[5] This estimate is based on Gasquet (*Henry VIII ... Monasteries,* Vol. II, p. 241), who reckons eleven friars for each convent.

[6] It is very probable that, as Thaddeus states (*The Franciscans in England,* p. 15), the English Province numbered 73 friaries at the time of the Dissolution. Gasquet, however, in his *English Monastic Life* (pp. 251-318), accounts for

Observant reform, still it is quite safe to assert that they were favorably disposed toward it. We know, for instance, that already in 1502 they had changed their habit for the one adopted by their reformed brethren.[7] As to the vow of poverty, which constituted the essential difference between the Observantine and the Conventual body in the Order, they practically belonged to the former; for, as Little says, "from the smallness of the lands held by the friars and from the smallness of their regular incomes from other sources, it may be inferred that they depended for their livelihood mainly on voluntary and casual alms (including legacies), and this inference is supported by the evidence of the straits to which the friars were reduced whenever for any reason the supply of alms was cut off or diminished."[8] Again the same author writes, "The reply of the guardian of the Grey Friars of Coventry to the royal commissioners in 1535 might truthfully have been said by most of his fellow guardians: 'Friar John Stafford, guardian of the same house, being examined on oath, says that they have no lands nor tenements nor other possessions, nor revenues spiritual or temporal of any yearly value, but only "limitations" in the country and uncertain charitable gifts of the people.'"[9]

That the Conventuals, in the beginning of the religious

---

only 64 houses. Whence this discrepancy? In the first place, Gasquet mentions only those houses that were situated in England proper, omitting, therefore, the four in Scotland; to wit, Dumfries, Dundee, Haddington, Roxburgh. Furthermore, he fails to mention six others; namely, Berwick, Brougham, Ludlow, Penrith, Stoke, Walsingham, which were located in England proper and, according to Parkinson (*Antiquities of the English Franciscans,* Part II, passim), are accounted for by such historians as Wadding, Leland, Mason and Davenport. This fact, it seems, induced Thaddeus to take them up in his list of the friaries. Finally, Gasquet adds one house, Haverford East, which Thaddeus does not mention.

[7] Little, *Studies in English Franciscan History,* p. 61, quoting a London Chronicle edited by Kingsford.

[8] Little, ibidem, p. 27.

[9] Little, ibidem, p. 46.

upheaval, were less conspicuous than their brethren of the Observance in opposing the policy of Henry VIII, must not pass for a sign that they were less devoted to the cause of truth and justice. There is every reason to believe that when the question of papal supremacy came to a head, they as a body were staunch in their allegiance to the Holy See. A few of their number, indeed, are known to have sympathized to some extent with the rebellious king's measures.

Thus Fr. Thomas Chapman, guardian of the London convent, assured Cromwell that some of his community were willing to change their habits as soon as ordered to do so, and at the same time he gave the minister the names of such as had of late supported Fr. John Forest with alms.[10] Again, as stated above, Dr. Call defended the king's supremacy at the trial of Fr. Antony Brown. As to Fr. Alexander Barklay, it was perhaps this same policy of submission to the royal will that safeguarded his remaining in England till his death in 1552, although previously he had been denounced by the king's men as doing "much hurt in Cornwall and Devonshire both with open preaching and private communications." It was probably in the summer of 1538, after the dissolution of the friaries, that Cromwell one day met him near St. Paul's cemetery. "Yea," he said, on seeing the friar in his habit, "will not that cowl of yours be left off yet? And, if I hear by one o'clock that this apparel be not changed, thou shalt be hanged immediately for example of all others."[11] How many more of the Conventuals in this way at last succumbed under the pressure of threat and promise, it is impossible to determine.

On the other hand, we know of some who, like the Observants, refused to submit and underwent great hardships for conscience sake. This was owing perhaps to the fact that in the summer of 1534, as we have heard, they were compelled to

---

[10] Camm, *Lives of the English Martyrs*, Vol. —, p. 297.

[11] Gasquet, *Henry VIII... Monasteries* (popular edition, 1906), p. 144, footnote. See also *Encyclopedia Britannica*, Vol. III, p. 317.

receive many of the expelled Observants into their houses, and thus had occasion to become more intimately acquainted with their reformed brethren. Many, no doubt, admired them for their virtues and gradually imbibed their principles and ideals, so that in time they, too, became unflinching supporters of papal supremacy. Parkinson tells us that the Conventual community at Ware strenuously denounced the king's attitude toward the Pope, and that for this reason it was dissolved as early as 1534.[12]

Others, we find, were cast into prison for being too outspoken in their defence of the Holy See. When FF. John Hunt and Robert Ellis had to leave their convent, they were asked whether they would again wear the habit; whereupon "they both said they would not for a year or two and by that time perchance there would be another change." For this reply they were imprisoned.[13] Again, Fr. William Petty, who belonged to the Jersey community, was found guilty of high treason and condemned to death for maintaining the spiritual supremacy of the Pope. Writing to Cromwell for instructions regarding this friar's execution, Southwell declares, "Petty is subtly witted as he is ingenious, and hath as pleasant instrument for the utterance of his cankered heart as I have heard."[14] At Reading, the members of the community were mostly men of advanced age. The guardian, Fr. Peter Lawrence, was a personal friend of Dr. London, the royal commissioner, who in September, 1538, confiscated the convent, but allowed the friars to remain provided they would not wear the habit. For a time, it seems, they complied, trusting perhaps, like so many others at the time, that after a few years the king would relent or die. A year later, however, in November, the guardian together with Fr. Giles Coventry, one of the community, are found on the list of

---

[12] Parkinson, Part II, p. 12.

[13] Gasquet, *Henry VIII ... Monasteries*, Vol. II, p. 261, footnote.

[14] Gasquet, Ibidem, p. 264.

prisoners in the Tower.[15]

During the suppression of the lesser monasteries, in 1535 and 1536, the Conventual houses had not been molested, since, as Parkinson says regarding the one at Coventry, "there was nothing to be got by their ruin, forasmuch as they had no endowment of lands, etc."[16] After the northern rising, however, when motives of revenge were added to those of avarice, the Conventual houses with all that belonged to them were appropriated by the crown. Now it became manifest how the friars were practicing the vow of poverty. Parkinson's account which is based on Speed, Leland, and Weever, and Wright's *Suppression of the Monasteries,* which contains 142 letters[17] written by the king's officials immediately after their visit to the religious houses, show clearly that the great majority of the Conventual friaries had little or no valuation. Indeed, many are not even mentioned, while others are recorded as having "no rents"—"no lands"—"no value." Regarding landed endowments apart from the sites of the friaries, Little contends that they were "small in amount, of recent origin, confined to a few houses, and devoted to special services."[18] "The friars had nothing in propriety, nor in common," writes Fuller, "but being mendicants, begged all their subsistence from the charity of others. True it is they had cells or houses to dwell in, or rather to hide themselves in. So the foxes have holes and the birds of

---

[15] Gasquet, Ibidem, pp. 265, 336.

[16] Parkinson, Part II, p. 34.

[17] The greater portion of these letters, Wright assures his readers, are reprints from a volume in the Cottonian Library in the British Museum. The author's purpose in publishing these letters was to show, as he himself says, "the facility with which the inmates of the monasteries, at the time of their dissolution, confessed to vices from the very name of which our imagination recoils." Whatever truth there may have been in the charges proffered by the royal visitors against the religious, it is a striking fact that in all the letters not a single instance occurs where the sons of St. Francis are accused of leading lives unworthy of their sacred calling.

[18] Little, p. 23.

the air have nests; but all this went for nothing, seeing that they had no means belonging thereunto. It will be objected that many convents of friars had large and ample revenues, as it will appear by perusing the Catalogue in Speed's tables. I have nothing to return in answer hereunto, save only that ... these additions of lands unto them are of a later date, and, believe it, not of their seeking, but their benefactors casting upon them."[19]

A few figures will show how well these words apply to the Conventual friars. At the time of the suppression, their annual revenues at Walsingham, Bedford, and Aylesbury were a little over £3. After visiting the friars at Aylesbury, John London wrote to Cromwell, "I found them very poor and in debt, their ornaments very coarse, and very little stuff of household." The largest of their friaries, according to Leland, was the one at Northampton; and yet the yearly income here was only £6 17s. 5d. The house at Bridgenorth was rated at £4 per annum. On surrendering it, the friars declared "that they were not able to live; for the charity of the people was so small that in three years they had not received in alms in ready money the sum of ten shillings a year, and they lived only by a service that they had in the town in a chapel on the bridge."[20] At Coventry, according to Dugdale, "they had no lands, nor other possessions, spiritual or temporal, but only liberty in the country to receive the charity of good people."[21] At Boston, the royal agent found the four houses of friars, one of which belonged to the Conventuals, very poor and the inmates in great need. In the Conventual friary at Lincoln, he found nothing worth mentioning save the conduit which the mayor and the aldermen asked to have turned into public use. Regarding their house at Gloucester, the commissioner

---

[19] Parkinson, preface to Part II, p. iv.

[20] Hope, *Franciscan Martyrs in England*, pp. 65 seq.

[21] Parkinson, Part II, p. 34. From this it would seem that the Conventuals, in strict keeping of the Rule of St. Francis, were wont to go on quest for their daily subsistence.

reported, "The Gray Friars is a goodly house, much of it newly built, especially the church, choir, and dormitory; the rest small lodgings; divers leases out for years of lodgings and gardens; no lead but a conduit and small gutters." At Stafford, they had "the choir leaded and a chapel, small implements, no plate but a chalice and six sponys (spoons?), in rents 6s. 4d.," while at Shrewsbury were found "a proper house, small implements, no jewels but a plate cross (of) silver, and a little chalice of little value; no rents but their house and about three or four acres of arable land lying to it."[22]

Parkinson brings the copy of an instrument to which, in October, 1539, friars of Coventry and Stamford affixed their names, thereby surrendering the convent to the crown.[23] The document is interesting inasfar as it shows what a comedy of legal formalities were gone through to give the proceedings the semblance of justice.

> For as much as we the warden and friars of the house of St. Francis in Coventry, in the county of Warwick, commonly called the Grey Friars in Coventry, do profoundly consider, that the perfection of Christian living does not consist in dumb ceremonies, wearing of a grey coat,[24] disguising ourselves after strange fashions, "doking, nodding, and becking," in girding ourselves with a girdle full of knots, and other like papistical ceremonies, wherein we had been most principally practiced and misled in times past; but the very true way to please God, and to live a true Christian man, without all hypocrisy and feigned dissimulation, is sincerely declared unto us by our Master Christ, his Evangelists, and Apostles: being minded hereafter to follow the same, conforming ourselves unto the will and pleasure of our supreme head under God on earth, the King's majesty, and not to

---

[22] Wright, *Suppression of the Monasteries,* pp. 192, 199, 204, 205.

[23] Parkinson, Part II, pp. 35, 27.

[24] Here Parkinson remarks, "The friars were not such fools as to have, at any time, believed that Christian perfection consists in dumb ceremonies, or in any outward dress; but this was said for them."

follow henceforth the superstitious traditions of any foreign potentate or peer; with mutual assent and consent,[25] do surrender and yield up into the hands of the same all our said house of Saint Francis, Grey Friars, in Coventry, with all the lands,[26] tenements, gardens, meadows, waters, pondiards, feedings, pastures, commens, rents, reversions, and all other our interest, rights, or titles, appertaining unto the same. Most humbly beseeching his most noble grace to dispose of us, and of the same, as best shall stand with his most gracious pleasure: and further freely to grant unto every one of us his license under writing and seal to change our habits into secular fashion and to receive such manner of livings as other secular priests commonly be preferred unto. And we all faithfully shall pray unto almighty God long to preserve his most noble grace with increase of much felicity and honor. And, in witness of all and singular the premises, we the said warden and convent of the Grey Friars in Coventry to these presences have put our convent seal, the fifth day of October, in the thirtieth year of the reign of our most sovereign lord King Henry the Eighth, or anno 1539.

Such were the instruments which the commissioners laid before the friars. Referring to the one just adduced, Gasquet observes, "Although the document has often been pointed to as proof that the religious themselves confessed the iniquity of their lives, no reasonable man can doubt that, like other so-called 'confessions,' this was a readymade document."[27] To throw dust in the eyes of the people, they were made to read as if the friars surrendered voluntarily. The fact is, however, they were morally forced to sign, being told that, whether they did so or not, their possessions by an act of parliament already

---

[25] Parkinson observes that Dugdale suggested the term *forced* in place of *mutual assent and consent*.

[26] "This is for form's sake," comments Parkinson; "for it was well known that the friars there had no lands, tenements, etc., whatever is said in the form." The instruments had been formulated by the commissioners to suit all emergencies.

[27] Gasquet, *Henry VIII ... Monasteries,* Vol. II, p. 268.

belonged to the king; that non-compliance would serve only to make matters worse; and that it would, therefore, be wisest for them to make a virtue of necessity and do the king's bidding.[28]

So radical and thoroughgoing was the procedure of Richard Ingworth and his fellows that within a twelvemonth all the friaries of the Conventuals were in the hands of the king. After turning out the helpless friars, the commissioners forthwith set about dismantling the buildings of whatever might realize a few shillings for the royal coffers. Thereupon, the sites were either sold or leased for a mere pittance. It is touching to read how wantonly they despoiled the friaries at Stafford and Litchfield.[29] The missals, linens, and sacred vestments in the sacristy, the crucifixes, candlesticks, statues, pews in the church and choir, the furniture in the friary, yes even the cooking utensils in the kitchen and buttery—everything that was not thought worth while forwarding to headquarters, was offered for sale, the friars themselves in some instances becoming the purchasers. Thus we find, for instance, that the guardian of Stafford bought two brass pots and Fr. Wood one of the sacred vestments.

Only meager accounts have come down to us as to the eventual fate of the buildings. The friary at Yarmouth with other lands was given to Cromwell.[30] As a rule, their new owners either let them fall to ruin, or had them wantonly defaced and torn down, or had them converted to profane uses. Thus, when Parkinson wrote, the belfry of the friars' church at Coventry was used as a barn. The author says that he himself had seen a tasker threshing in it.[31] In some instances, the houses were obtained by the city for public use. Thus, as we have heard, the mayor and aldermen bartered for the conduit

---

[28] See Parkinson, Part II, p. 27, quoting Fuller.

[29] See Wright, pp. 266-278, where he brings the accounts of John Scudamore regarding the sale of certain friaries.

[30] Little, p. 225.

[31] Parkinson, Part II, p. 36.

of the Lincoln friary. At Grimsby, the city officials desired half of the house "to make of it a common house of ordnance and other necessaries for the defence of the king's enemies if need be," because it stood "very well for the purpose, near the water and open to the sea." At Worcester, the friary was sold to the city, after the superfluous buildings had been demolished. At Reading, the church was successively used by the city as a town-hall, a workhouse, and a jail.[32]

Only of the houses at London and Oxford have interesting details been transmitted to posterity. The beautiful church of St. Francis in London, on the north side of Newgate Street, that harbored the tombs of more than six hundred persons of royalty and distinction, was at first used as a wine store. Seven years later, on January 3, the king had the church reopened, wishing to found a new parish to be known as Christ Church. But the value of the property was so small that to support the parish he was constrained to add to it St. Bartholomew's Hospital in Smithfield, the churches of St. Nicholas and St. Evin and as much of St. Pulcher's as lay within Newgate, together with an annual grant of five hundred marks in land. During the great London Fire, in 1666, the church was destroyed. It was subsequently rebuilt on the site where the choir of the old church stood.[33] In 1552, Edward VI had the convent buildings repaired and turned over to the city to be used as an orphanage and school, which for many years after was known as Christ Hospital or Blue Coat School. A part of the wall belonging at one time to the library is thought to be the only fragment left of the ancient friary.[34]

At Oxford, the stately buildings with their spacious garden and orchard were leased for a paltry sum, which was paid to

---

[32] Gasquet, *Henry VIII ... Monasteries*, Vol. II, pp. 273 seq.

[33] *Grey Friars Chronicle*, pp. 213, 216; Parkinson, Part II, p. 2; Camm, p. 290, footnote.

[34] Parkinson, Part II, p. 7; Staunton, *The Great Schools of England*, pp. 442-462; *Encyclopedia Britannica*, Vol. XIV, p. 844.

the king till the year 1545, when he sold the premises. "Then down went the trees," writes Wood, "and the grass plots were everywhere trodden out of all form; nay, the church itself was entirely pulled down, and the stones and statues, and the very monuments of the dead escaped not, but were wholly demolished, taken away, and disposed of, for any use that could make the sale of them bring a penny." The same historian informs us that when he was a student at Oxford, about the middle of the seventeenth century, a little old building could still be seen, which it was said had once been the study of FF. Roger Bacon and Thomas Bungey.[35]

More deplorable was the subsequent lot of the ejected friars. The only ones known to have obtained pensions were Fr. Thomas Chapman, guardian of London, and his fellow guardian of York. "The rest," Gasquet writes, "were dismissed from their houses with some small gratuity, generally only a few shillings, and left to provide for themselves."[36] They wandered about from place to place, homeless and penniless, entirely dependent on the charity of the people. But these were poor themselves, owing to frequent taxations, and moreover dared not show too much favor and openly offer protection to those on whom the hand of the king had fallen so heavily. Of the ejected friars, none suffered greater hardships than the priests. "Only one or two individuals," says Gasquet, "were granted any pension for their support. As a rule a few shillings (on an average apparently about five shillings) was delivered to each one on being turned out into the world to find their own living as best they might. Even when they secured what is known as a 'capacity'—that is, permission to act as one of the secular clergy—employment was by no means easy to be obtained. The bishops were no lovers of the wandering friars, and the destruction of so many churches diminished the possibility of

---

[35] Parkinson, Part II, pp. 25 seq.; Leon, *Aureole Séraphique,* Engl. transl., Vol. IV, p. 352, footnote.—Anthony Wood was born in 1632 and died in 1695.

[36] Gasquet, *Henry VIII ... Monasteries,* Vol. II, p. 454.

obtaining any cure of souls, even had they been willing to present them to any."[37] Hence we hear Richard Ingworth pleading on their behalf with Cromwell. "They are very poor," he writes to the minister, "and can have little service without their capacities. The bishops and curates are very hard to them, without they have their capacities."[38] On another occasion, the same commissioner informs Cromwell, "I have written to divers of the bishops and with divers I have spoken to license them (the friars) till after Michaelmas, and at that time I have promised to send their license to certain places where they shall have them free, for the most part of them have no penny to pay for the charge of them."[39]

To what measures individuals would resort in their extreme need, we learn from the case of Fr. Richard Sharpe. Unable to procure an instrument that would commend him to some bishop and legalize his acting as priest, he borrowed the one which his confrere, Fr. John Young, had obtained. Of this he made a copy in his own name and, as may be supposed, presented it to some bishop. But the forgery was discovered and, in April, 1539, Fr. Sharpe was arraigned for treason and condemned to be hanged, drawn, and quartered. For some reason or other, the sentence was not carried out and later the friar was set at liberty.[40]

Another circumstance that caused the ejected friars great anguish of soul was the fact that government spies were closely watching their every movement. Any word or act of theirs that could be interpreted as a sign of dissatisfaction with the late proceedings against them, was immediately reported to headquarters. In consequence, the poor friars knew not whom to trust nor whither to turn for comfort and relief. Thus, in the

---

[37] Gasquet, Ibidem, p. 273.
[38] Wright, p. 193.
[39] Wright, p. 210.
[40] Gasquet, Ibidem, p. 471.

course of time, their condition grew from bad to worse. That in the end some of the number gave way under the pressure of want and distress and went over to the king's side, is not to be wondered at. On the other hand, it is safe to say that the great majority remained true to their faith and calling and gradually succeeded in leaving their native land for Ireland, Scotland, and Flanders, where, since 1534, many of their reformed brethren of the Observance had found a hearty welcome.

CHAPTER XI
DIVINE RETRIBUTION, 1547-1558

Last days of Henry VIII—Remorse and despair—His death—The prophecy of Fr. Peyto fulfilled—Reign of Edward VI—Efforts to introduce Lutheranism—Further confiscation and spoliation of religious houses—The "Funus Scoti et Scotistarum" at Oxford—Reign of Mary the Catholic—England reunited with the Church of Rome—Franciscans again at Greenwich, London, and Southampton—Their activity and influence—Death of the queen.

F ever an English monarch had to taste the bitter fruits of a life spent in sin and crime and was made to realize in his own person how "heavy lies the head that wears a crown," it was Henry VIII, during the last years of his inglorious reign. Widespread dissatisfaction, pauperism, immorality, and religious indifferentism among the lower classes, who menacingly clamored for the charitable ministrations of the ousted monks and friars; bitter discord and senseless wrangling on matters of doctrine among the clergy,[1] who railed at one another and chafed under the yoke of the Six Articles; rivalries and intrigues among the courtiers,[2] who were only waiting for the death of their royal patron to satisfy their own greed and ambitious designs; strained relations and open hostilities with foreign powers, who while resenting Henry's

---

[1] In his last speech in parliament on religion, Henry VIII deeply lamented the dissensions among the clergy. See Lingard, *History of England*, Vol. V, pp. 99 seq. In his *Church History of England*, Vol. I, pp. 315 seq., Dodd brings a copy of this speech.

[2] Cromwell had betrayed his trust both as minister and as vicar general. On June 10, 1540, he was arrested for embezzling and misapplying royal funds and subjected to the bill of attainder, "a most iniquitous measure, but of which he had no right to complain, as he had been the first to employ it against others." In vain he appealed to the King for mercy. No one dared to raise a voice in his defence, and on July 28, he was beheaded. Lingard, pp. 70 seq.

religious and political despotism, sought to profit by his present helplessness; marital troubles within the royal household, aggravated by the bodily ailments of the royal voluptuary:—such was the gloom and desolation that followed in the wake of that dreadful storm which Henry's unbridled passions had conjured up against the Church in England.

What made his declining years most miserable were the pangs of remorse that harrowed his guilty soul. Realizing that he was at variance with Protestants as well as Catholics and convinced in his heart that the latter alone possessed the true and saving faith, the unhappy king was anxious to become reconciled to the Church. Accordingly, as early as 1541, he sent Stephen Gardiner, Bishop of Winchester, to the diet of Ratisbon, which Charles V had summoned with the Pope's sanction for the purpose of restoring religious unity in Europe. Though the English bishop and the German Emperor did all in their power to realize the wish of Henry VIII, nothing in the end came of it, "because," as Sander puts it, "he (Henry) prized the glory of men higher than the glory of God." In the autumn of 1546, six months before his death, the English king took another step in this direction. Pressed by serious illness from which he had little hope of recovering, and harassed by qualms of conscience for having severed the bond of Church unity, he began to consult privately with some bishops as to how he might be reconciled to the Apostolic See and thereby also with the Christian nations. For obvious reasons, however, the selfish dignitaries flattered him declaring that by divine inspiration he had renounced the primacy of the Pope, and that he had nothing to fear since his action had been fully sanctioned by parliament. Bishop Gardiner alone was sincere; he suggested that Henry lay the affair before parliament; or, should time not allow this, that he at least commit his wishes to writing, assuring him that God would take his good will for the deed. But Gardiner's efforts proved unavailing against the flattery and deceit of the royal sycophants.[3]

Finally, after months of bodily suffering and mental anguish, the woeful end came. Black despair, like a hideous specter, haunted the last hours of the refractory king. Lying helpless on his bed of pain, and staring wildly into the darker recesses of the room, he would groan, "Monks! monks!"[4] On January 28, 1547, when told that his last moment had come, he became frantic with fear and despair. Calling for a cup of wine, he turned feebly to one of the attendants and exclaimed, "All is lost!" then he sank back on his pillow and expired.[5]

On February 14, the corpse was conveyed from Westminster to Windsor castle for burial. On this occasion, the prophecy of Fr. William Peyto, made fourteen years before in the friary church of Greenwich, was literally fulfilled. The cortege halted for the night at the monastery of Syon. During the journey, owing perhaps to the jogging of the chariot, the coffin was damaged and the corpse injured. The next morning, a pool of blood was found on the pavement of the church where the remains had been placed. To repair the damage, embalmers and plumbers were summoned. They were about to begin their work, when "suddenly was there found among their legs a dog, lapping and licking up the king's blood, as chanced to King Achab, before specified. This chance one William Consell reported, saying he was there present, and with much ado drove away the said dog."[6] Such was the horrible end of Henry VIII, whom Stubbs, the Anglican bishop and historian, characterizes as a "strong, high-spirited, ruthless, disappointed,

---

[3] Sander, *De Origine ac Progressu Schismatis Anglicani*, ed. 1585, pp. 97 seq., 102 seq.; ed. 1690, pp. 287 seq., 312 seq.

[4] Strickland, *Lives of the Queens of England*, Vol. III, p. 256, on the authority of Harpsfield.

[5] Sander, ed. 1585, p. 105; ed. 1690, p. 323.

[6] Harpsfield, quoted by Hope, *Franciscan Martyrs in England*, p. 68. See also Strickland, p. 260, quoting a contemporary document. According to Hall, this incident occurred in the room where Henry died. See Hope, p. 67.

solitary creature; a thing to hate or to pity or to smile at, or to shudder at or to wonder at, but not to judge."

Edward VI, the son of Henry VIII and Jane Seymour, was only nine years old when he ascended the throne.[7] During his brief reign (1547 to 1553), schismatical England was hurled into the more dismal abyss of heresy. Eager to safeguard Catholic dogma and practices, the late king had published the *Book of Articles* and the *King's Book* and had compelled parliament to enact the Statute of the Six Articles. But now the mighty monarch was dead, and the very men who had been most obsequious to him in life, were the first to ignore his wishes. They made common cause with the foreign heretics and by degrees swept away the last vestiges of Catholic belief and discipline. Headed by Cranmer, they hailed the accession of young Edward whom they knew to be thoroughly imbued with heretical tenets. What encouraged them most, however, was the fact that the Duke of Somerset, appointed protector of the realm during his nephew's minority, was a zealous adherent of the new teaching. According to Lingard, eleven-twelfths of the English population were still strongly attached to the old faith.[8] But Cranmer and Somerset were determined to establish Protestantism, and they left nothing undone to carry out their design. Where persuasion and deception failed, unmasked tyranny succeeded. "They key-stone of the arch had been taken away when Henry broke with the Head of the Church, and the Sacraments, followed in more or less rapid succession, till by a gradual and natural sequence nothing was left but a heap of

---

[7] Shortly before his death, Henry ordained that Edward, his son by Jane Seymour, was to inherit the crown, and that, should he die without an heir, Mary, Henry's daughter by Catherine of Aragon, was to succeed him in preference to Elizabeth, born to him by Anne Boleyn. "From this it is most certain," Sander infers, "that he repudiated Catherine out of malice and in bad faith, actuated solely by a desire to possess himself of Anne Boleyn." Sander, ed. 1585, p. 105; ed. 1690, p. 318.

[8] Lingard, p. 151.

ruins."[9]

One of the saddest results of the spoliation of religious houses which continued during Edward's reign, was the wholesale destruction of libraries. Invaluable manuscripts, costly books, important records and documents were either committed to the flames or sold to shopkeepers for a few shillings. Great, indeed, must have been the havoc, if a contemporary like Bale did not hesitate to declare, "Our posterity may well curse this wicked fact of our age, this unreasonable spoil of England's most noble antiquities."[10] Already during the preceding reign, the royal visitors had laid hands on the valuable library of Oxford university. Layton informed Cromwell that they had bound Duns Scotus in Bocardo, a prison in Oxford, and that they had banished him and all his obscure glosses from the university; he "is nowe," the wretch boasted, "made a comon servant to evere man, faste nailede up upon postes in all comon howses of easment."[11] During Edward's reign, in 1550, carloads of books were publicly burned in the marketplace at Oxford. Here again, the writings of Fr. Duns Scotus were the principal object of the "reformers'" rage and vandalism. His doctrine, strictly in keeping with Catholic dogma, was as popular among the scholars of the past centuries, as it was sacred to the Order to which he belonged. This explains why his works were above all conspicuous during that senseless demonstration of hostility toward Catholic teaching. And further, to deal his fair reputation a telling blow, the base proceedings were styled *Funus Scoti et Scotistarum,* "as if," Parkinson remarks, "the preeminence among Scholastics, and the right of preference in the schools had been due to the

---

[9] Stone, *Faithful Unto Death*, p. 91.

[10] Parkinson, *Antiquities of the English Franciscans*, p. 246. Bale, an ex-Carmelite, was a bitter and outspoken enemy of papal supremacy and of the religious Orders.

[11] *Wright*, Suppression of the Monasteries, *p. 71.*

Subtle Doctor Duns Scotus and his followers."[12]

Great was the dismay of the reforming party, when, on July 6, 1553, King Edward died and Princess Mary, the daughter of Henry VIII and Catherine of Aragon, at last entered London amid the acclamations of the populace. The noble queen, whom long years of suffering had taught the value of Catholic faith and worship, was determined to undo the work of her father and of her brother. During her first parliament, in 1553, she had the Catholic liturgy and disciplinary laws of the Church reestablished. On November 23, 1554, Cardinal Reginald Pole, her kinsman, was joyfully welcomed in London as papal legate a latere. A week later, in full session of parliament and in the presence of the queen and her royal consort Philip II, of Spain, he presided at the solemn ceremony of reconciliation, and absolved them and the entire nation "from all heresy and schism and all judgments, censures, and penalties therefor incurred." How the heart of the Queen Mary must have leaped for joy when the hall reechoed with a fervent "Amen" and all the members rising from their knees proceeded to the chapel, where they chanted the *Te Deum* in thanksgiving.[13] Little did she imagine that within a few years this joy would again be turned into sorrow.

Queen Mary had hardly ascended the throne, when the Franciscans reappeared on the scene. Before the end of 1553, though not yet officially recognized, they resided in their old friary at Greenwich. Naturally, they enjoyed the favor and esteem of their sovereign. How much had they not suffered in defence of her mother and of the Holy See? Would they be less faithful and zealous now in her own cause? Gratitude, therefore, as well as prudence and justice prompted her to rebuild and enlarge their friary at Greenwich and to recall those of their Order who were still living in exile.[14] In the

---

[12] Parkinson, p. 247.

[13] Lingard, p. 223. See also *Annales Minorum*, Vol. XIX, pp. 1 seq.

[14] Parkinson, p. 251.

spring of 1555, the work of restoration at Greenwich was completed, and, on April 7, the sons of St. Francis were solemnly reinstated by the Bishop of Rochester.[15]

We can easily imagine the joy of the friars when they returned to the familiar scenes of their former labors. Many a time they must have recalled the trials of the past years and spoken with the deepest reverence of those who had since won the crown of martyrdom for the faith. What emotions of gratitude to God and to their queen thrilled their hearts, when they assembled for choir and meditation in the very church where twenty years before Fr. Peyto had so boldly defied the king and his court. How warmly, too, they welcomed their brethren returning from exile. Besides FF. Peyto and Elstow, there were FF. John Standish, John Richel, and John Gray, all men of singular virtue and learning, and the Spanish Franciscans who had accompanied their royal master Philip II to England.[16]

Gradually the number of friars increased, much to the satisfaction of the queen, who had two more houses, at London and Southampton, erected for them.[17] In November, 1555, twenty-five friars were residing in their convent at Greenwich,[18] of which Fr. Elstow was appointed guardian. Queen Mary chose Fr. Peyto as her confessor and spiritual adviser,[19] while Fr. Stephen Fox apparently held the office of custos.[20] A few names of such as were received into the Order during Mary's reign have come down to us. Fr. Richard Britan, an Oxford scholar, had already suffered a long imprisonment

---

[15] Stone, *Faithful Unto Death*, p. 95.

[16] Parkinson, pp. 251, 254, 260.

[17] Ibidem, p. 251.

[18] Pastor, *Geschichte der Paepste* (Freiburg, 1913), Vol. VI, p. 604.

[19] Parkinson, p. 251.

[20] Mason, *Certamen Seraphicum Provinciae Angliae*, p. 15. See also Parkinson, p. 257.

under Henry VIII for openly defending the Pope's supremacy. Sander, who knew him at Oxford, tells us that he was a man of great mortification. He died shortly after his reception at the Greenwich friary.[21] The other novices, FF. George Dennis, Thomas Bourchier and NN. Nelson,[22] lived to witness the renewed persecution that began with the accession of Queen Elizabeth.

Needless to say, the Franciscans were awake to the pressing needs of the times, and with their customary zeal began to minister to the spiritual wants of the people. "The spirit of St. Francis," writes Stone, "was once more alive in the land. The friars taught and preached and exhorted as before; and if they were spurned and treated with insolence, as sometimes happened now, they taught and preached and exhorted all the more. It was the business of the shepherds to chase the wolf from the fold; it was the business of the friars to repair the damages which the wolf had done, to bind up the broken and confirm the weak."[23] A copious source of many evils were the abuses to which Sacred Scripture had been subjected by the heretics. Fr. John Standish "observed, with great grief of mind, the intolerable abuses which arose from the rash and false interpretations of the Holy Scriptures, made by women and illiterate men, who were then indifferently permitted to read those sacred books in their mother language; and he used his utmost endeavors to have this weighty affair laid before the parliament, to obviate for the future all such abominable irreverences being done to the word of God, to hinder such profanations of the sacred text, and to prevent the erroneous and dangerous impressions apt to be made on the minds of the ignorant people by the ridiculous explications of taylors, weavers, coblers, silly women, and all sorts of mechanicks, who filled the thoughts of their unwary hearers with such remarks

---

[21] Parkinson, p. 249.

[22] Ibidem, pp. 256 seq., 261.

[23] Stone, *Faithful Unto Death*, p. 100.

as were unworthy the holy mysteries of the Christian faith. On these important considerations Standish writ and published a book upon this subject, and entitled his work, *Of not publishing the Bible in vulgar Languages.*[24] In a sermon held before court, Fr. Alfonso Castro, a Spanish Franciscan, denounced the Council for taking measures against the heretics, that were not in keeping with the Christian law of charity.[25] This same friar held his famous controversy with Cranmer in Bocardo prison at Oxford and finally induced him to sign a recantation of his heretical tenets.[26]

How the heretics were disposed toward the friars, and how they even resorted to open violence against them, may be seen from the following incident. One day, FF. Peyto and Elstow were returning home from London, when suddenly a mob gathered to assault them. Seeing the danger to which they were exposed, the friars made good their escape by leaping into a boat. They, indeed, saved their lives, but someone in the crowd hurled a stone, which struck Fr. Peyto and broke one of his

---

[24] Parkinson, p. 251.

[25] Ibidem, p. 250; Stone, *Mary the First, Queen of England*, p. 264; Pastor, p. 585; Lingard, p. 231. For these rigorous proceedings of the Council against obstinate heretics, Protestant historians lay the blame on Queen Mary and consequently style her "Bloody Mary." For a critical and lucid refutation of this groundless charge, we refer the reader to Stone's *Mary the First, Queen of England*, chapter xiii. "It is as great an historical absurdity," the author of this best work on Queen Mary maintains, "to apply to Mary the epithet 'bloody,' as it is to attach that of 'good' to Queen Elizabeth" (p. 371).

[26] Parkinson, p. 150; Stone, *Faithful Unto Death*, p. 101. Cranmer, who had done so much harm to the Church and State in England during the reign of Henry VIII and Edward VI, is without doubt one of the most despicable figures in English history. When, after a life of crime and scandal, he was finally convicted of heresy and handed over to the secular arm, he basely feigned repentance, hoping thereby to save his life. Queen Mary, only too eager to believe the hypocrite, although he had wronged her so greatly, would have used all her influence in his behalf. But public justice demanded retribution. On the day of his execution, the wretched man publicly recanted all the previous recantations he had made and died an apostate and a heretic.

ribs.[27] Queen Mary, on the contrary, repeatedly showed that she favored the friars. As we have heard, she provided them with three convents. On Saturday, March 21, 1555, Cardinal Pole was ordained priest at Lambeth, and on the following day, he said his first Mass and received the episcopal consecration in the Franciscan church at Greenwich, in the presence of the queen and the entire court.[28] In August of the same year, shortly before King Philip's departure for the continent, their majesties went in solemn procession to the friary church at Greenwich.[29] Subsequently, while her royal consort was abroad, the queen resided in the Greenwich palace, and we may suppose that she was in frequent consultation with Fr. Peyto, her confessor and spiritual adviser. A year later, however, the relation between the queen and Fr. Peyto was perhaps less cordial. In view of his learning and virtue and in reward for his unswerving loyalty to the Church, Pope Paul IV, with the unanimous approval of the Cardinals, created him Cardinal and appointed him to succeed Cardinal Pole as legate a latere in England.[30] Prior to 1547, while yet in exile, the distinguished friar had been named Bishop of Salisbury; but in his humility he gladly relinquished his claim, when Bishop Salcot (Capon), a nominee of Henry VIII, returned to the old faith.[31] Little then need we be surprised if now he used every lawful means to escape the new dignity thrust upon him, the more so because this appointment was to the prejudice of Cardinal Pole, whom he loved as a friend and esteemed as a man of eminent qualities. "No one," says Stone, "felt his incompetency for the dignity and office conferred upon him more than Fr. Peyto himself, and he entreated the Pontiff

---

[27] Parkinson, pp. 249, 253.

[28] Stone, *Mary ... of England*, p. 408, footnote, on the authority of Wriothesley.

[29] Stone, *Faithful Unto Death*, p. 97; Strickland, p. 567.

[30] *Annales Minorum*, Vol. XIX, pp. 110, 113.

[31] Ibidem, Vol. XIX, pp. 109, 113. See also Stone, *Faithful Unto Death*, p. 90, footnote.

to be allowed to decline them, as too great a burden for the old shoulders."[32] In a letter to the Pope, he stated that he could not show himself in the streets of London without being insulted.[33] But the Pope insisted and demanded that he come to Rome; whereupon, it seems, Fr. Peyto departed for the continent. He remained in France, where in April, 1558, he departed this life.[34] How little this affair estranged the queen from the friars may be seen from the fact that in her last will, dated April 30, 1558, she bequeathed five hundred pounds to the guardian and convent of the Franciscan friars at Greenwich and two hundred pounds to those at Southampton.[35]

Worry over the coldness and neglect of Philip II, her royal consort, and anxiety regarding the succession to the throne, had gradually undermined the health of Queen Mary. To this came the fall of Calais, on January 8, 1558, a disaster which made the public mind restive and distrustful, and which was a severe blow not only to the queen but also to the cause of the Catholic Church so dear to her heart. During the following spring and autumn, her health sank rapidly so that with the advent of autumn she felt her end fast approaching. Anxious that the work of restoration be continued after her death, and at the same time justly doubting the orthodoxy of Princess Elizabeth, who would succeed her as queen, she sent commissioners to examine her on the matter of religion. The unscrupulous Princess swore that she was a Catholic; and accordingly, on November 6, the queen sent her jewels to Elizabeth, again requesting her to further the old religion, when once the reins of government would be in her hands. Finally, on the morning of November 17, the end came. A priest was celebrating holy Mass in her room; and when he "took the

---

[32] Stone, *Mary ... of England,* p. 457.

[33] Pastor, Vol. VI, p. 608.

[34] *Annales Minorum,* Vol. XIX, p. 113. See also Leon, *Aureole Séraphique,* Engl. tr., p. 357, footnote.

[35] Stone, *Mary ... of England,* pp. 507 seq.

Sacred Host to consume it, she adored it with her voice and countenance, presently closed her eyes and rendered her blessed soul to God."[36] She was laid to rest on December 14, in Westminster Abbey on the north side of Henry VII's chapel. It was the last royal funeral conducted in England according to the rites of the Catholic Church.

---

[36] Ibidem, pp. 466 seq. That same day, at seven in the evening, Cardinal Pole breathed his last.

CHAPTER XII
UNDER THE LAST TUDOR, 1558-1603

Queen Elizabeth's perfidy—Excommunicated by the Pope—The persecution against Catholics revived—Queen Elizabeth and the Franciscans—The friars expelled and banished—One of the exiles, a martyr—Franciscans in England during Elizabeth's reign—Fr. John Storrens martyred in 1572—Venerable Godfrey Buckley, O.F.M.—At first a secular priest—Joins the Franciscans in Rome—On the English mission—Seized and imprisoned—Tried and condemned to death for being a priest—His martyrdom.

UEEN MARY departed this life, trusting that her sister was as good as her word and that she would continue the work of restoration. On January 15, 1559, Princess Elizabeth submitted to the ancient Catholic coronation ceremonies, received Holy Communion and under solemn oath promised allegiance to the Pope and the Church of Rome. Deep down in her heart, however, the unscrupulous and treacherous queen was contemplating a final and decisive blow at Catholic doctrine and worship. No sooner was she firmly seated on the throne, to which she well knew Mary Stuart, Queen of Scotland, had a better right, than she threw off the mask and began undoing the work of her saintly predecessor.

During the reign of her father, Henry VIII, the English hierarchy proved all too pliant to the will of their monarch. Now, however, having learned by experience that schism and heresy were practically inseparable, the bishops firmly opposed every encroachment of the government on the rights of the Church and of the Holy See. Elizabeth, therefore, justly fearing a too rigorous pursuit of her project might enkindle a general uprising against her, counseled her ministers to proceed slowly and cautiously. After 1570, however, when Pope Pius V, after much pleading and long waiting, finally excommunicated Elizabeth and freed the people from allegiance to her, the storm of persecution against Catholics broke forth in full fury. It is not our purpose here to depict in detail how this terrible woman, supported by a few cringing courtiers, abused her Catholic subjects and at last succeeded in establishing Anglicanism as the State religion. Suffice it to say, during the forty-five years of her reign, "good Queen Bess" proved in her public as well as in her private life a worthy daughter of Henry VIII and Anne Boleyn.

With deep regret the English Franciscans witnessed this second storm of religious persecution gather over the country.[1] As to themselves, they knew quite well that Elizabeth hated them in particular for the boldness and determination with which in years gone by they had opposed her worthless mother, questioned her own legitimacy, championed the rights of the papacy, and, during the preceding reign, helped to reestablish Catholic doctrine and worship. Little then were they surprised when on June 12, 1559, one of her first measures was to seize their friary at Greenwich and to banish all the members of their Order from England. Many of the friars refused to leave the country, while others trusting in Divine Providence, once more wandered into exile and at last found a home among their brethren on the continent.

In the Province of Lower Germany, Davenport tells us, many of the English friars distinguished themselves as men of eminent virtue and learning. Since his banishment under Henry VIII, Fr. Henry Holstam had been twice appointed visitor of this province and, in 1549, he was elected its provincial minister. Other English friars taught theology in the Franciscan convent at Louvain so successfully that to them, as Fr. Pinchart later admitted, the members of the province were indebted for their

---

[1] Unless otherwise stated, our sources of information regarding the English Franciscans at home and abroad during the reign of Elizabeth are Fr. Angelus Mason, *Certamen Seraphicum;* Fr. Luke Wadding, *Annales Minorum;* Fr. Anthony Parkinson, *Antiquities of the English Franciscans,* whose authorities besides Mason are chiefly Fr. Francis Davenport, Fr. Francis Gonzaga, Anthony Wood and Jeremy Collier.

learning. Among those who ended their days in this province was Fr. John Elstow, who apparently returned to Lower Germany, when Elizabeth expelled the Order from England.

Fr. Thomas Bourchier was a descendant of the earls of Bath. He received his classical education at Magdalen College, Oxford, and joined the Franciscans at Greenwich toward the close of Queen Mary's reign. Later, together with Fr. Thomas Langton, also an English exile, he continued his studies at the Sorbonne in Paris and subsequently obtained the doctor's degree. Thereupon, he went to Rome and lived in the famous Franciscan friary of Ara Coeli. Here he died about the year 1586. Pits who knew the eminent friar in Rome tells us that he was a man of extraordinary piety and learning and deserved well of his Order and of the Church of Christ. He is the author of the much-quoted *Historia Ecclesiastica,* a brief account of the martyrdom of the Franciscans in England, Belgium, and Ireland between the years 1536 and 1582.

Fr. John Standish, who distinguished himself during Queen Mary's reign as a zealous and fearless defender of the Sacred Scriptures, was a nephew of Fr. Henry Standish, at one time provincial of the English Franciscans and later Bishop of Asaph. Fr. John was clothed with the habit of St. Francis shortly before the first outbreak of the persecution under Henry VIII. When the dissolution of religious houses began, he went to Paris and after the usual course of studies merited the doctor's degree in theology. He returned to his native land during the restoration and departed this life shortly before the outbreak of the second storm. Pits says that Fr. John was "a man celebrated for learning, piety, faith and zeal for the honor of God."

Fr. George Dennis was born of a prominent family in Devonshire. In 1545, when the English laid siege to Boulogne, he served his country as royal standard-bearer. In 1558, however, he renounced the world and joined the Franciscans at Greenwich. He was still a novice, when Elizabeth banished the friars. Filled with holy zeal, Fr. George refused to leave the Order and departed with his brethren for the continent. About the year 1585, the saintly friar died and was buried in the Franciscan convent of Liege, where he had spent the greater part of his holy life.

In the second year of Elizabeth's reign, Fr. Stephen Fox likewise left England and came to the convent of St. Francis in Antwerp. Some time later, when the city was plundered by the heretics, he was again forced to flee. With about twenty English Poor Clares, he at first went to Rouen and later proceeded to Lisbon in Portugal, where Philip II had a convent erected for the nuns. Fr. Stephen died in Lisbon, in 1588, and was laid to rest in the church of the Poor Clares.

Another English Franciscan priest, who probably belonged to the Greenwich community, was Fr. John Richel. He entered the Order during the reign of Henry VIII and lived to witness the utter ruin of the once glorious Franciscan province in England. Seventy-two years of his life he spent as a true and faithful son of St. Francis, highly esteemed for virtue and holiness. The venerable jubilarian passed to his eternal reward in the friary at Louvain about the year 1599, having attained the ripe old age of ninety-seven years.

When Elizabeth banished the Franciscans, a certain Fr. Richard (his surname is not known) for a time defied the queen and bravely continued to labor for the spiritual welfare of his persecuted countrymen. At last, however, he was arrested for being a priest and thrown into prison. After a long and severe confinement, he was for some reason or other set free and banished. He spent the remainder of his life in the Franciscan province of Andalusia in Spain and died at Herez de la Frontera, in 1619. So great was his reputation for sanctity that after his death the townsfolk cut bits of cloth from his habit, and treasured them as the relics of a saint.[2]

Of the English Franciscans who were living in exile, Fr. John

---

[2] Thomas Felton, martyred for the faith in 1588, and Henry More, a nephew of Bl. Thomas More, were not Franciscans, as is frequently stated, but Minims. This on the authority of Fr. Livarius Oliger in *The Catholic Encyclopedia*, Vol. X, p. 325.

Gray alone attained the martyr's crown. He was the son of a noble and wealthy English family,[3] and at the time of his martyrdom resided in the Franciscan convent at Brussels. During the absence of Don Juan of Austria, a horde of fanatical sectaries entered the city and set about molesting the Catholics and plundering the churches. As in England, so also here the Franciscans were especially odious to the heretics. On June 5, 1579, their friary was assailed. When the porter, Fr. James Leisman, an English lay Brother, saw the mob approaching, he barricaded the doors and warned his brethren of the impending danger. While the terror-stricken friars made good their escape, one of the community was both unable and unwilling to flee. It was Fr. John Gray, a man of seventy winters, who had spent the greater part of his religious life in exile. "Let us stay in God's house," he exhorted the fleeing friars; "where can we die so happily as in the presence of the Blessed Sacrament, on the holy spot where we hope to be buried." But his words fell on deaf ears; Fr. James alone remained with the aged and infirm priest.

By this time, the infuriated mob had forced their way into the friary. Meeting the porter, they beat him with cudgels until he lost consciousness. Leaving him for dead, they rushed madly to the church, where they found Fr. John kneeling before the Blessed Sacrament. Like ravenous wolves, they seized him and began to insult and maltreat him. Hardly knowing what he did, so great were his pain and terror, the venerable friar begged his enemies to spare him. "What," cried the ruffians, "shall we spare thee, thou wretch!" Thereupon one of the mob drew his sword and dealt the innocent priest a severe blow on the head. Mortally wounded the martyr fell to the floor and with a kindly, "I certainly forgive you," he passed to his eternal reward. Bourchier relates that Fr. John bore the stigmata of St.

---

[3] Bourchier, whose *Hist. Eccle. de Mart. FF. Ord. D. Francisci*, is our chief source of information regarding this friar, affirms with other chroniclers that he was of Scotch extraction.

Francis on his feet, adding that he himself had the privilege of seeing them. The martyred priest was known far and wide for his great sanctity. Hence, when the people heard that he had laid down his life for the faith, they hastened to the friary to do homage to his mortal remains. Bourchier further attests that a miracle was wrought through intercession of the martyr. A man who was near death, on learning what had happened in the Franciscan friary, asked that a cloth dipped in the martyr's blood be brought to him. On receiving it, the dying man kissed it reverently, whereupon he was immediately restored to health.

Not all the friars left their country and died in exile. A large percentage ignored Elizabeth's orders, remained secretly with their flock, and sought in every way to counteract the efforts of those illiterate and malevolent preachers to whom the government entrusted the dissemination of heresy. Needless to say, indescribable hardships and countless obstacles confronted the friars at every turn. Robbed of their cherished friaries, they wandered about from place to place, discharging their religious and priestly duties as best they might. To be ordained priest; to shelter, aid, or support a priest; to celebrate or assist at the Sacrifice of Mass; to administer or receive the sacraments—all these were crimes punishable with fines or imprisonment, and eventually with death on the scaffold. Towns and hamlets were infested with spies who, like Topcliffe, were ever on the alert for priests and religious and glorified in ferreting out their secret hiding-places. Hence we can readily conceive how constant fear and anxiety lest their labor of love be cut short and the people grow weak for want of spiritual sustenance, frequently drove the hunted friars into secluded caves and holes, where for weeks and months they eked out a miserable existence. Accustomed, as they were, to community life with its thousand charms and blessings, their condition was particularly distressing. They no longer had their friaries whither they might return after a day's arduous labor to find peace and rest. No longer could they seek the fatherly counsels of a prudent superior or share the sympathy and geniality of a loving fellow friar. All this was a thing of the past; they were now thrown on their own resources. They dared not appear publicly in their habit or with any distinctive mark of their sacred character, but had to go about in disguise and under assumed names, on which account, we may suppose, they were in many cases unable to identify themselves before the people on whose charity they depended for the necessaries of life.

Still, if the lot of the wandering friars was hard and distressing, their wonted zeal for the things of God was none the less fervent and self-sacrificing. We find, therefore, that all through the reign of Elizabeth there were always Franciscans in the mission-fields of England, ready to suffer everything, even death itself, for the salvation of immortal souls. Prudence, of course, demanded that they perform their duties in the greatest secrecy. Hence it is that to-day we find so little recorded regarding the activity of these men of God, and are restricted for a general estimate of their life and labors to a few isolated facts that chanced to come to the notice of the chroniclers.

A number of friars were at last captured by the royal emissaries and thrown into prison, where they ended their days in misery and oblivion. Thus it is known that, in 1583, a certain Fr. Thomas Ackrick lay confined as prisoner in Hull Castle.[4] Others, like Fr. Tonstall, vexed the government by the boldness with which they toiled in the vineyard of the Lord. Others, finally, defied and baffled the queen's priest-catchers. Thus, for instance, Fr. Gregory Basset was thought to be in hiding in Herefordshire; but, although his enemies were constantly on the look-out for him, they apparently never succeeded in getting him into their clutches. In fine, so great was the number of Franciscans in England at this time that, as Hope says, "even in the first year of Elizabeth's reign the government was greatly irritated against them, and attributed to their zeal the want of

---

[4] Thaddeus, *The Franciscans in England*, p. 19.

unity among Protestants."[5] Only regarding a few individuals have some interesting details been transmitted to posterity.

One of the first priests to suffer martyrdom during the reign of Elizabeth was Fr. John Storrens. Nothing is known regarding the early life of this friar except the fact that he was a native of England. At the time of Queen Mary, he was teaching at Oxford and held the offices of chancellor of the university and grand-inquisitor in the government's proceedings against heresy. It was very likely when Elizabeth ascended the throne and a second rupture with the Holy See threatened the Church in England, that he departed for Belgium and there joined the Franciscan Order. Meanwhile, Elizabeth had reopened hostilities against her Catholic subjects. This induced Fr. John to return to his native land. How long he succeeded in evading the queen's spies, is not known. At last, however, he was seized, cast into a prison, and, after undergoing the severest hardships, sentenced to death. At the place of execution, the heroic friar fearlessly exhorted the attending populace to remain true to their holy faith. Then at the command of the sheriff he ascended the scaffold. While the executioner was placing the rope about his neck, a loud murmur of disapproval arose among the bystanders. There was evident danger that a tumult would ensue; wherefore the executioners cut him down alive and without delay ripped him open, tore out his palpitating heart and entrails, and ruthlessly split open his head. The martyrdom took place in 1572, two years after Elizabeth had been excommunicated by the Pope.[6]

---

[5] Hope, *Franciscan Martyrs in England*, p. 86.

[6] Gaudentius, *Bedeutung und Verdiensts des Franziskanerordens gegen den Protestantismus*, pp. 170 seq., whose sources of information regarding this friar are Hueber's *Menologium*, the *Franciscan Martyrology*, Sannig's Tripl. Chronic., Gonzaga, and Barrezus. Strange to say, Fr. John Storrens is not mentioned in any of the English sources at our disposal; his name does not appear on the list of those who were beatified by Pope Leo XIII, on December 9, 1886; nor on the list of those whose cause of beatification was proposed to the Sacred Congregation, in the same year on December 4. See

In his famous *Certamen Seraphicum,* Mason brings at some length what a religious priest related about a certain Fr. John, commonly known as the "Old Beggar." When by order of Elizabeth, the Franciscans had to quit England this saintly friar found refuge in the house of Roger Lockwood in the parish of Leyland, county Lancaster. Here he resided till about the year 1590, when death summoned him to a better life. So popular was Fr. John for virtue and holiness, that the Earl of Derby prevailed upon the queen to allow the harmless friar to wear his religious habit in public, although the penal laws against Catholics were then in full force. Heaven favored Fr. John with the gift of working miracles. And when old age and bodily infirmities no longer permitted him to wander about in discharge of his priestly duties, the people flocked to him from all parts of northern England, in order to obtain help from him in their spiritual and temporal needs. That he was a Franciscan and not a Benedictine, as some claim, is quite certain from the testimony of the woman who served him in his illness. She was still living when Mason wrote his *Certamen Seraphicum* and testified that Fr. John never received or touched money, and that he himself had told her he was a mendicant and a beggar. Her testimony is strengthened by that of William Walton, one of the friar's penitents, who maintained that his father confessor went about barefoot and wore the grey habit and the cord of St. Francis.

About the same time that Fr. John closed his remarkable career, another English Franciscan, Fr. Laurence Collier, succumbed to the hardships of prison life. For a long time he succeeded in escaping the vigilance of the notorious priest-catchers. But at last, probably at Stafford, he was seized and committed to prison, where after two years of intense suffering he departed this life to share the glory and bliss of the next.

Another Franciscan whose name sheds luster on the history of the English province during these troublous times was Fr.

Acta Minorum, Vol. VI.

Nelson, a priest of singular holiness and undaunted zeal. He entered the Order during the period of restoration. Subsequently, during the entire reigns of Elizabeth and James I, Fr. Nelson toiled and suffered in the English missions. As usual, the details regarding his long and untiring activity were perhaps never recorded. All we know is that he spent the last thirty years of his life in the house of a Catholic gentleman, two miles distant from Hereford. Here, too, about the year 1628, the holy friar breathed his last and entered the realms of eternal joy to receive the reward for his long and faithful service in the Order of St. Francis.

Fr. William Stanney (Staney) was active in England at the end of the sixteenth and the beginning of the seventeenth centuries. He was a man of acknowledged virtue and learning, and, in 1598, received the official seal of the English province from Ven. Fr. Godfrey Buckley, shortly before the latter's martyrdom. That same year perhaps, the zealous missionary was taken prisoner and confined in Marshalsea. History does not tell us how he regained his liberty. But it is certain that in 1601 he was appointed commissary of the English Franciscans. Of this he himself informs us in the foreword to his *Treatise of the Third Order of St. Francis*, a sort of manual which he wrote for the use of secular Tertiaries, and which was published at Douai in 1617. It was probably in 1610 that he received Fr. John Gennings into the Franciscan Order, to whom also, a few years later, he entrusted the seal of the province.[7] We may say, therefore, that Fr. William forms the connecting link between the first and the second Franciscan Province of England. Whether he had any share in the founding of the Second Province, undertaken by Fr. Gennings a few years after his reception into the Order, does not appear from the records. All we know is that in 1620 he summoned to England one of the nuns of the Third Order Regular, who had established themselves at Brussels and were under the direction of Fr.

---

[7] Thaddeus, p. 27.

Gennings. "After this year," Thaddeus concludes, "no further mention occurs of Father Staney. It must only be added that in the annals of the Order he is praised for his integrity and holiness of life."[8]

Before the close of the century, at a time when the province was almost extinct, another English Franciscan sealed his missionary career with the glorious crown of martyrdom.[9] John Buckley, *alias* Jones, was born about the year 1530 of a prominent and wealthy family in Carnarvonshire. Like the majority of the people in Wales, his parents had remained staunch and fervent Catholics. Hence they did not object to their son's embracing the sacerdotal state. The place and time of his ordination, however, is a matter of mere conjecture. Since in later life he was commonly regarded an "old" priest, it seems probable that he received Holy Orders during the reign of Queen Mary. No doubt, he foresaw what hardships his sacred profession would involve, when, in 1559, Elizabeth ascended the throne. Perhaps to prepare himself for the coming conflict, he, in 1561, departed for Belgium in company of his friend William Allen, who subsequently became a priest and cardinal. That he returned with Allen a year later, seems quite probable. His name is not found on the records of the English College at Douai, from which we may conclude that he was active in England before 1568, the year in which Allen founded the famous missionary college.

Unfortunately, we are left in complete darkness regarding the future martyr's priestly career previous to 1582. We can

---

[8] Ibidem, p. 20.

[9] Hope, *Franciscan Martyrs in England,* pp. 89-98; and Stone, *Faithful Unto Death,* pp. 107-113. They base their narrative on a letter of Father Henry Garnet, S. J., to the Father General of the Society; on a manuscript in the library of the University of Louvain, in which the friar's trial and execution are described apparently by an eye-witness; on the *Life of F. John Gerard, S. J.,* by Morris; and on Challoner's *Memoirs of Missionary Priests.* See also Mason, *Certamen Seraphicum,* pp. 16 seq.; and Parkinson, *Antiquities of the English Franciscans,* pp. 258 seq.

imagine, however, what his lot must have been if we consider the perils and trials which at the time beset the life of the English missionaries. He wandered about in disguise and under the *aliases* John or Griffith Jones, Robert or Herbert Buckley. Neither is it known how long he succeeded in escaping the clutches of the priest-catchers. Certain is only that he lay confined in Marshalsea, a London prison, before June, 1582, and that he was again at large in October, 1586, under which date his name appears on the list of "priests that have been prisoners and were out upon bond." Fr. John, as we have heard, was of a prominent and wealthy family, and hence it is not unlikely that some friend of his at court had him released. A year later, however, we find him again a prisoner, this time in Wisbeach Castle, which fact, according to Hope, "proves that he possessed an independent fortune; for Elizabeth was economical in her cruel tyranny, and only those who could maintain themselves were sent to Wisbeach, while poorer prisoners were either banished or hanged."[10] It was probably here that Fr. John, leading with his fellow captives a sort of community life, conceived a liking for the religious state and resolved, on regaining his liberty, to join the Order of St. Francis, once so widespread, popular, and active in England.[11]

Whether the zealous priest was at last banished, or whether he succeeded in escaping from prison, has not been recorded. All we know is that, in 1590, he left Wisbeach Castle and forthwith proceeded to Pontoise in France, where he applied at the Conventual friary for admission into the Order. His request was granted, and henceforth he was known as Fr. Godfrey. Soon after he departed for Rome, where he joined the

---

[10] Hope, p. 91.

[11] Stone thinks (p. 108) that "possibly, at Wisbeach, he encountered some holy Franciscan, in prison for the same cause as himself, whose example inflamed him with a desire for the religious life."

Franciscans and spent three years in their friary of Ara Coeli.[12] "To one," says Hope, "who had already borne the cross and practiced the hardships of poverty, the further sacrifice of his worldly goods would have cost little. But it needed more than ordinary humility to enter religion at nearly sixty years of age, and by placing himself among the novices, to submit himself to religious superiors, who were probably his inferiors in years, suffering and spiritual experience." Many a time during these three years of retirement, Fr. Godfrey must have thought of and prayed for his persecuted countrymen, whose condition had by this time become well-nigh unbearable. He longed to live and labor once more in their midst, and perhaps even hoped to gain in the end, like so many of his brethren, the crown of martyrdom. After completing his religious training, he asked his superiors to send him to the English missions. Filled with holy joy on learning that his request had been granted, he visited Pope Clement VIII to beg his apostolic blessing. When informed of the friar's intention, the Holy Father embraced him tenderly, blessed him, and said, "Go, for I believe you are a true son of St. Francis. Pray to God for me and his Holy Church."

That same year, 1593, Fr. Godfrey arrived in London. Fr. Gerard informs us that the aged friar was the first to be received into the house which he had secured as a hiding-place for priests. He stayed in London a few months and then repaired to the country districts, where, it seems, he was henceforth known as Godfrey Maurice.[13] Hampered by the usual difficulties and hardships, he labored here "about three years," as Fr. Garnet writes, "in tilling the vineyard of Christ with no small profit." Then of a sudden his activity was cut short. He was captured and thrown into prison, where, we

---

[12] That he was at first a Conventual and shortly after joined the Franciscans, we learn from Parkinson, p. 259. See also Stone, p. 108.

[13] Garnet calls him Godofredus Mauricius. The missionaries at the time were compelled to go under assumed names. Hence it is often very difficult at the present day to determine their real name.

learn from Fr. Garnet's letter, he remained "about two years, during the latter part of which time he was treated with less rigor and had a certain amount of liberty. The quantity of good he did was incredible, through the great concourse of Catholics that came to him."[14] The zeal and sanctity of this worthy son of St. Francis had by this time attracted the attention of his brethren. They chose him minister provincial of the English Franciscans and entrusted to him the official seal of the province. Shortly before his martyrdom, Fr. Godfrey delivered this seal into the hands of Fr. William Stanney, thereby appointing him to succeed in the office.

The liberties which the imprisoned friar enjoyed and the zeal with which he discharged his priestly duties, at last roused the envy and indignation of Topcliffe. Determined to trump up some charge that would bring him to the scaffold, the notorious priest-catcher began to make inquiries regarding his previous history. His efforts were not in vain. In the spring of 1598, one of his spies reported that Fr. Godfrey before his arrest had been hiding for two days in the house of Mrs. Jane Wiseman, had said Mass there, and had received alms from her and from Mr. Robert Barnes.[15] The accusation was serious, and Topcliffe hastened to profit by it. Accordingly, Fr. Godfrey was indicted and summoned to appear, on July 13, before the King's Bench in Westminster. When challenged with going abroad to be ordained priest by authority of Rome and then returning to England in defiance of the laws, the man of God fearlessly confessed:

"If this be a crime I must own myself guilty; for I am a priest, and I came over to England to gain as many souls as I could to Christ. But I deny that I have ever intermeddled

---

[14] According to Mason, p. 17, he was apprehended soon after his landing in England and cast into prison, where he remained some years. See also *Annales Minorum*, Vol. XIX, p. 294; Parkinson, p. 260.

[15] Both, Mr. Barnes and Mrs. Wiseman, were tried and condemned to death. Their sentence was commuted to imprisonment.

directly or indirectly in any manner of treason."

"You are not charged with any matter of treason," the lord chief justice explained, "neither is there any matter of treason to be objected against you, except that you are a priest and have come into England; nor is there anything further needed. For by your own confession you are within the compass of the law."

Disgust and dissatisfaction with Elizabeth's bloody measures against Catholics had of late become noticeable among the lower classes. The judges were therefore evidently anxious to shake off the responsibility of another public execution; hence they urged the prisoner to demand a trial by jury.

"I will not have my blood required of men ignorant in the law," objected the disinterested and zealous priest; "I place myself and my cause before God and the Bench. You have made the laws, and therefore you must know best what is the meaning of them."

Upon this the judges were constrained to pass sentence and condemned Fr. Godfrey to be hanged, drawn, and quartered. But, to prevent all unnecessary commotion among the people, it was decided that the execution should take place at seven o'clock in the morning. When the sentence of death was read, the venerable priest knelt down and returned thanks to God for the singular privilege of dying in defence of his faith and sacred profession.

On the morning of July 22, 1598, the executioners took the gentle friar from his dungeon, fastened him to a hurdle, and dragged him through the streets of London. Arriving at St. Thomas' Waterings, where everything was in readiness for the grewsome tragedy, they released him from his painful position and led him to the gallows. After saying a short prayer, the man of God rose to his feet, and fearlessly facing his enemies, he solemnly called Heaven to witness that neither from Mr. Barnes nor from Mrs. Wiseman had he ever received one penny in silver.

"But gold they did give you," snapped Topcliffe.

"Nor yet gold," was the speedy but calm reply. Anxious, lest his friends be made to suffer unjustly on his account, he further declared that he had not said Mass in their presence.

"No," fell in Topcliffe sarcastically, "for they were public prayers, there being no superaltar."

"There are no such things, Master Topcliffe," boldly retorted the friar; "neither did I say any public prayers at all in their hearing."

At a loss for a suitable answer, the queen's servile creature accused his victim of having said private prayers. This was a charge that involved the martyr alone, and without reserve he gave vent to his feelings.

"I confess," he avowed earnestly, "with thanks to Almighty God for that grace, that I said such short and secret prayers as I have ever used since I was newly risen. And so I will do as long as I live, do you, Mr. Topcliffe, what you will."

Then he fell on his knees and prayed, while Topcliffe turning to the spectators, read a paper, the contents of which, he trusted, would establish the friar's disloyalty to the queen, and thus create public sentiment against him. We shall see how poorly he succeeded.

Having prayed about a quarter of an hour, Fr. Godfrey arose and with Topcliffe's assistance climbed into the cart that was standing under the gallows. Then first was it noticed that the hangman had forgotten to bring a rope and immediately a horseman was sent into the city to fetch one.

In the meantime, the martyr turning toward the people again proclaimed his allegiance to the queen and the realm. He further averred that, according to the declaration of the lord chief justice, he had come here to die not because he was a traitor, but because he was a priest and a Franciscan. This statement the under-marshal confirmed, whereupon one of the spectators protested that an innocent man was about to be executed.

"Patience awhile, sir," broke in Topcliffe quite alarmed at

the menacing attitude of the people; "you shall soon see what manner of innocent he is. Tell me," he cried, turning to the friar, "if the Pope excommunicated the queen, or tried to turn her out of her kingdom in order to encourage Papistry, what would you do, or what would you advise others to do?"

When Fr. Godfrey, ignoring this question, once more asserted that he prayed every day for the spiritual and temporal welfare of the queen, Topcliffe interposed saying that he as well as all other priests and Catholics were disloyal subjects of her majesty and would kill her if they could.

This base insinuation wounded the martyr's sense of truth and justice.

"I am certain," he challenged his lying accuser, "that I myself, and all other priests and Catholics, are ready to suffer much more for the good of the queen than you are, Master Topcliffe, though your cruelty alone has been sufficient to make her odious to all the priests in Christendom." An hour had now elapsed, when suddenly, "A reprieve! a reprieve!" resounded on every side. Soon the horseman drew up to the place of execution. "Ay, ay, here it is!" he exclaimed, showing a rope to the excited multitude.

Without delay, Topcliffe issued orders. The rope was fastened to the gallows, while one of the hangmen leaped into the cart and placed the noose about the friar's neck. Seizing the reins, he was about to whip off the horses, when of a sudden three stalwart fellows rushed forward, held back the terrified animals, and boldly demanded that the man of God be permitted to finish speaking. Topcliffe trembled with rage; but he dared not ignore the demand of the riotous multitude. Meanwhile, all eyes rested on the unoffending friar who was gazing heavenward and praying aloud, "Sweet Jesus, have mercy on my soul." With a sneer, the under-marshal remarked that he had forgotten the Blessed Virgin; whereupon, the servant of God added, "Blessed queen of heaven, be my advocate and pray for me now and ever."

After a moment of quiet prayer, the martyr again exclaimed,

"Sweet Jesus, have mercy on my soul." Then he gave a priest in the crowd the usual sign and received the last absolution,[16] whereupon he turned to the people and asked them to say one *Credo* and to pray for him. Impatient over the long delay, Topcliffe began to rebuke and ridicule the martyr, who in reply calmly begged not to be disturbed in his last prayers, since he had come to die for the faith. Once more he commended his soul to God, when with a sudden jolt the cart was drawn from under him and the form of the holy man was seen dangling from the gallows.

Alarmed at the disaffection that the sight of the martyr awakened in the multitude surrounding the gallows, Topcliffe allowed him to hang until life was extinct. Then the corpse was taken down and subjected to the usual barbarities. The head was exposed on a pole in Southwark; but the cheerful and smiling countenance it wore attracted such wide attention that after two days officials came and removed the head, having first disfigured the face most shamefully. The quarters were hung on four trees that skirted the roads leading to Newington and Lambeth. Two prominent young gentlemen, Challoner relates, were thrown into prison for attempting to remove them. According to the same historian, one of the martyr's arms was preserved for many years at Pontoise. "Such," writes Fr. Garnet, "was the most happy end of this saint. May God make us all partakers of his merits." In his *Franciscan Martyrology,* Fr. Arturus a Monasterio, on July 22, commemorates Fr. Godfrey as a martyr of the Order. The cause of his beatification was introduced on December 4, 1886, his name appearing on the list of English martyrs, drawn up under that date and presented to the Sacred Congregation.[17]

Venerable Godfrey Buckley closes the long line of

---

[16] Very likely, Father Garnet was present at the execution. Three days later, we know, he penned his valuable letter. See Hope, p. 93, footnote, on the authority of Challoner.

[17] See *Acta Minorum,* Vol. VI (1887), pp. 49 seq.

Franciscans who suffered and died for the faith in England, since the year 1534. The fact that he and Fr. John Storrens are the only Franciscans known to have undergone public martyrdom for the faith during the reign of Queen Elizabeth, shows clearly the deplorable state of the province at the end of the sixteenth century. With a heavy heart, no doubt, Fr. William Stanney took over the official seal, little thinking that at that very moment God was fashioning the heart and mind of a young convert in the English College at Douai, who was destined one day to breathe new life and vigor into the declining province.

PART SECOND
UNDER THE STUARTS
1603-1649

CHAPTER I
THE SECOND ENGLISH PROVINCE

Its founder: Fr. John Gennings—His remarkable conversion from Protestantism—Priest and missionary in England—He enters the Franciscan Order—First steps toward the restoration of the English Province—Action of the general chapter in its behalf—A friary at Douai in Flanders—The province canonically established—Fr. John Gennings, the first provincial—Franciscan missions in England—Extent of the province before 1649—Character of the friars—Their activity against Protestantism.

THE banishment of the Franciscans on June 12, 1559, and the subsequent seizure of their friaries was a blow from which the province never recovered. Although, as we have seen, a number of friars defied Queen Elizabeth and remained in England, the adverse conditions under which they labored, the long reign of Elizabeth, and the relentless severity of her measures against the Catholic Church and its institutions, necessarily effected the gradual extinction of the province. It is touching to read how for almost half a century these persecuted friars, surrounded by dangers and hardships of every description, sought to uphold at least the essentials of their holy Rule. The official seal of the province was handed on from one martyr or confessor to another, who thus maintained to some extent the regular succession of superiors and the obedience of the few scattered friars.[1] Not less indicative of their zeal is the fact that, even at this time when to be a friar and a priest meant exile or imprisonment, English youths applied for admission into the Order, and after completing their novitiate and studies joined the brethren in the missions.[2] Such recruits, however, were few

---

[1] Mason, *Certamen Seraphicum*, p. 19.

[2] Parkinson, *Antiquities of the English Franciscans*, p. 261.

and far-between, while the older friars who had survived the first storm of persecution passed one by one to a better life. Hence, as years wore on without any abatement in the Government's hostile attitude, the number of friars grew smaller and smaller. In his *Annales Minorum* under the year 1587, Wadding commemorates the English province as having perished "by the fury of the heretics."[3] Finally, in the statistics of the Order drawn up at the general chapter, in 1623, the name of the English Province is marked with a cross to indicate that canonically speaking it no longer existed.[4]

During the reign of Queen Elizabeth, there lived in Litchfield Staffordshire, a Protestant family by the name of Gennings.[5] They had two sons, Edmund and John. The elder of these, Edmund, at an early age, chanced to come under Catholic influence, which soon resulted in his return to the old faith. Not long after his conversion, he left England and came to Douai, where he studied for some years at the English College.[6] On March 18, 1590, at Soissons, he was ordained priest. Although physically unfit for the arduous life of a missionary, he was anxious to labor among his countrymen, and immediately after his ordination he received permission to set out for England.

At the time of Edmund's conversion, his brother John was a mere child. Reared and educated in Protestantism, nothing was farther from his mind than to follow in the footsteps of his brother. In fact, the news that Edmund had become a Catholic and, what was worse, a priest served only to steel the heart of John against everything that might influence his creed and mode of life. After the death of his parents, he proceeded to

---

[3] *Annales Minorum*, Vol. XXII, an. 1587, num. XC.

[4] Stone, *Faithful Unto Death*, p. 124.

[5] The subsequent narrative is based on *The Life and Death of Mr. Edmund Gennings, Priest*, written by the martyr's brother John and published at Saint-Omer in 1614. The Life was reprinted in the *Annals of Our Lady of the Angels*, Vol. XIII (1888), Nos. V-VII.

[6] See *Douai Diaries*, p. 14. 31.

London, where he soon fell a victim to the godless spirit of the times. Many a time, no doubt, the young man thought of his brother, never for a moment surmising what a great change he himself would shortly undergo. Much less did he suspect that the man whom one morning in the summer of 1590 he saw walking ahead of him by St. Paul's Church and anxiously looking round to see who followed, was none other than his own brother. A few days later, while walking along Ludgate Hill, he encountered the same person. This time, his curiosity was roused. From the anxious look and bearing of the man, John concluded that something must be weighing on his mind. He was, therefore, not surprised, when the former approached and courteously greeted him.

"What countryman are you?" queried the stranger.

"I am a Staffordshireman," replied John.

"And your name?" civilly demanded the other.

"My name is John Gennings," the youth answered, becoming interested.

At these words, the troubled look on the countenance of the stranger vanished. He raised his eyes to heaven in an attitude of prayer. Then, smiling affectionately on the young man before him, he said calmly:

"I am your kinsman; my name is Ironmonger and I am very glad to see you well. What has become of your brother Edmund?"

The mention of this name touched John to the quick. That man, he mused, knows more about Edmund than his question implies. But he shrewdly repressed his feelings.

"I heard," he answered with apparent coldness, "that my brother went to Rome to the Pope and became a notable Papist and a traitor to both God and his country. If he returns, he will infallibly be hanged."

"I have heard," sweetly retorted the other, "that your brother is a very honest man and loves both the queen and his country, but God above all. But tell me, good cousin John, do you not know him if you see him?"

At this, the young man became alarmed. What, he reflected, if this man were my brother.

"No," he rejoined with evident uneasiness, "I can not tell where he is. I greatly fear, however, that I have a brother a Papist priest, and that you are the man. If this is so, you will discredit me and all my friends. In this I can never follow you, although in other matters I can respect you."

When the good priest heard this spirited profession of heresy from the lips of his erring brother, he could restrain his feelings no longer.

"Indeed," he confessed, deeply touched, "I am your brother; for your love have I taken great pains to seek you. I beg of you to keep secret the knowledge of my arrival."

"Not for a world," John assured him, "will I disclose your return. But," he hastily added, "I desire you to come no more unto me, for I fear greatly the danger of the law and the penalty of the new-made statute in concealing you." The two brothers had by this time entered a tavern, where, of course, it was impossible for Edmund to discuss that which above all had induced him to search for his brother. But, to his deep regret, he soon learned that John was a staunch and thoroughgoing Protestant, whom for the present there was little chance of bringing back to the fold of Christ. He told him, therefore, of his intended departure out of town, at the same time assuring him that within a month he would return and confer with him at length on some very important affair. How earnestly would Edmund then and there have sought to win his brother for Christ, if on parting he had foreseen that he would never see him again in this life.

"And thus," wrote John in later years, "the two brothers parted, the one to his function of converting souls, the other to meditate how to corrupt his own; the one to spend his time in studying how to persuade, the other how to withstand; the one purposed to make haste back again, hoping to save a soul, brotherly love thereunto provoking; the other wishing his brother never to return, through fear of being converted, licentious liberty perverting in him brotherly love."

Eager for service in the vineyard of the Lord, Edmund left London and went to the country districts. Many a time during the ensuing year, his thoughts reverted to his unhappy brother, whom he knew to be treading dangerous paths. He had promised to see him again within a month; but for some reason or other he was prevented from going to London, much, we may readily suppose, to the satisfaction of John. Finally, in the fall of 1591, he could fulfill his promise. He came to London, trusting that this time he would find his brother better disposed. But God had decreed that something more than mere argument and persuasion was to bring about the conversion of John. On November 8, while Edmund was saying Mass in the house of Mr. Swithin Wells in Gray's Inn Fields, Topcliffe suddenly forced his way in and led the assembled Catholics off to Newgate prison. On December 4, they were brought to trial, pronounced guilty of high treason and condemned to death. Six days later, Edmund together with his host, Mr. Wells, was hanged, drawn, and quartered before the very house where he had celebrated his last Mass.

Hardened in heresy and sin, John Gennings was determined that Edmund's martyrdom for the faith, the news of which he received with cold indifference, should not in any way influence his own conduct. He was a Protestant and a Protestant he would remain. Wonderful, however, and irresistible are the eternal decrees of the Most High. How in the end the grace of God triumphed over the obstinacy of this young man, we shall let him relate in his own words.

"This much loved brother," he wrote, referring to himself in the third person, "this John Gennings, being in London at the very time of his (Edmund's) execution, hearing of the same, rather rejoiced than any way bewailed the untimely and bloody end of his nearest kinsman, hoping thereby to be rid of all persuasions which he suspected he should receive from him touching the Catholic Religion. But about ten days after his execution, toward night, having spent all that day in sport and jollity, being weary with play, he returned home, where to repose himself he went into a secret chamber. He was no sooner there set down, but forthwith his heart began to be heavy and his head melancholy, and he began to weigh how idly he had spent that day. Amidst these thoughts, there was presently represented to his mind a strange imagination and apprehension of the death of his brother; and amongst other things, how he had, not long before, forsaken all earthly pleasures, and, for his religion only, endured intolerable torments. Then within himself he made long discourses concerning his religion and his brother's, comparing the Catholic manner of living with his and finding the one to embrace pain and mortification, and the other to seek pleasure; the one to live strictly, and the other licentiously; the one to fear sin, and the other to run into all kinds of sin; he was struck with exceeding terror and remorse. He wept bitterly, desiring God, after his fashion, to illuminate his understanding, that he might see and perceive the truth.

"Oh, what great joy and consolation did he feel at that instant! What reverence on the sudden did he begin to bear to the Blessed Virgin, and to the Saints of God, which before he had never scarcely so much as heard of! What strange emotions, as it were inspirations, with exceeding readiness of will to change his religion, took possession of his soul! And what heavenly conception had he now of his brother's felicity! He imagined he saw him; he thought he heard him. In this ecstasy of mind, he made a vow upon the spot, as he lay prostrate on the ground, to forsake kindred and country, to find out the true knowledge of his brother's faith; which vow he soon after performed, and departed from England without giving notice to any of his friends, and went beyond the seas to execute his promise."

The conversion of John Gennings to the faith of his forefathers was as sincere as it was miraculous. The image of his sainted brother, whose cruel martyrdom had at first left him so strangely indifferent, was now constantly before his mind.

What only a few years since he had so greatly abhorred, Edmund's priestly profession, this same he now had a mind to embrace. He entered the English College at Douai, where he spent several years enriching his soul with that learning and virtue which so eminently qualified him for his later career. Finally, in 1607, he was ordained priest[7] and the next year was permitted to depart for the missions in England. It was apparently about two years after his arrival that he met Fr. William Stanney, Commissary of the English Franciscans. Very likely, he told the saintly friar the wonderful story of his conversion, and made known to him how ever since, he felt himself drawn to the religious life and to the Order of St. Francis. Fr. William soon detected the excellent qualities of the zealous priest and his sincere and deep devotion to the Order he wished to join. It was probably in 1610 that he vested him with the habit of St. Francis and sent him abroad to the friary at Ypres, there to be trained in the Franciscan mode of life and to study the Rule and the Statutes of the Order.[8]

Fr. John Gennings, as he was henceforth known, proved a true and worthy follower of St. Francis. The love he bore the Order to which he now belonged engendered in his heart a lively interest for everything that pertained to its glory and welfare. Hearing how the Franciscans, ever since the first outbreak of the religious persecution in his native land, had suffered and died for the faith, and how in consequence their province was well-nigh extinct, Fr. John conceived an ardent longing to restore the province to its one-time prestige and prosperity. A voice within seemed to tell him that Divine Providence had decreed its restoration and had chosen him as the instrument to accomplish it. This remarkable desire was not merely a transient notion that would fade and die with the first

---

[7] See *Douai Diaries,* p. 14, 34.

[8] "It does not appear quite certain," Thaddeus observes, "in what year Father Gennings joined the Franciscan Order. The dates given in his mortuary bill and his epitaph do not agree." *(The Franciscans in England,* p. 27, footnote.)

religious fervor. Evidently, it was the working of divine grace, growing stronger and more urgent as years went on. Such, at least, must have been the conviction of Fr. William. As commissary, he knew only too well into what a state of collapse the province had by this time fallen. Hence he was interested in his confrere's ceaseless reference to its possible restoration. Convinced of his ability as he was of his zeal and virtue, Fr. William delivered into his hands the ancient seal of the province,[9] thereby officially empowering him to work for its return to the place of distinction it once had enjoyed in the Order.

Not long after, Fr. Gennings learned that several priests and students of the English College at Douai wished to become Franciscans and join the province he intended to restore. Without delay he proposed the matter to Fr. Andrew a Soto, commissary general of the Belgian Provinces. The commissary favored the project and granted him all necessary faculties. Accordingly, in 1616, a residence was procured at Gravelines, and the first community assembled consisting of six Fathers and three novices. At the same time, probably for lack of sufficient accommodations, other novices destined for the English Province spent the year of probation in the friary at Ypres.

On June 8, 1618, the Franciscans held their general chapter at Salamanca, in Spain. It was here that the work of Fr. John Gennings, till then sanctioned only by the commissary general, received the approbation of the highest authorities of the Order. Among other things it was decreed that, as Fr. John Gennings had proposed, a friary should be erected at Douai. The king of Spain offered no opposition, but preferred to leave the final decision to her highness, the archduchess Isabella, who was then governing the Spanish Netherlands, and to the civil authorities of the university town. The archduchess, owing to the intervention of her confessor, Fr. Andrew a Soto, readily

---

[9] Mason, p. 19; Thaddeus, p. 27.

gave her consent, while the magistrates of the city even granted a site on which to erect the friary and college.[10]

On October 30, of the same year, the friars came to Douai and rented a private house, which for the present was to serve as convent. The next step of Fr. John Gennings was to solicit alms. Most generously did the nobility in England and the Benedictine abbots of St. Vedast and Marchienne respond to his appeal. The work on the buildings, therefore, progressed quite rapidly, and in 1621, the friars could enter their new home, which they dedicated to St. Bonaventure. To the first community belonged FF. John Gennings, Antony Clarke (Clercke), Francis Davenport, and Bonaventure Jackson, whom the commissary general appointed first superior. In 1624, the friary was made a guardianate with Fr. Bonaventure as first guardian.

At the general chapter, in 1618, the English friars living in Belgium, England, and Scotland were placed under obedience to the commissary general of the Belgian Provinces. Probably that same year, or shortly after, Fr. John Gennings became Vicar of England.[11] It was in this capacity that, in 1625, he sent Fr. Francis Davenport to Rome, that he might interest the general chapter in the cause of the English friars. The result of this mission was a letter from the minister general, Fr. Bernardine de Senis, to Fr. John Gennings, by virtue of which the English Franciscans were associated into a custody, and the zealous vicar was appointed the first custos enjoying the full power of a provincial.[12] Four years later, the minister general, moved by the entreaties not only of the Fathers but of leading Catholics, commissioned Fr. Joseph Bergagne, who had meanwhile become commissary general, to assemble the

---

[10] Mason, pp. 21 seq.; *Annales Minorum*, Vol. XXV, an. 1618, num. VIII.

[11] Fr. William Stanney, Commissary of England, was still living at this time. It is probably owing to this fact that Fr. John Gennings was appointed Vicar and not Commissary of England. See Thaddeus, p. 288.

[12] For a copy of this letter see Mason, p. 23; Thaddeus, p. 37.

English friars for the first provincial chapter. After some delay, on the first Sunday of Advent, November 14, 1630, the meeting was held in the convent of the Franciscan Sisters at Brussels. First the letters patent of the minister general were read,[13] giving the English Province a regular existence and, as is customary in such cases, instituting the first provincial superiors. Fr. John Gennings was declared Minister Provincial, and Fr. Francis Davenport Custos, while FF. Bonaventure Jackson, Nicholas Day, Francis Bel, and Jerome Pickford were appointed Definitors. Thereupon, the assembled Fathers proceeded with the minor appointments, of which a few are of interest. Fr. Francis Bel was elected guardian of St. Bonaventure's friary at Douai and professor of the Hebrew language. FF. Francis Davenport and William a S. Augustino were appointed professors of theology, Fr. Lawrence a S. Edmundo professor of philosophy and master of novices. Among the regulations was a decree providing "that for the better and easier direction of the brethren and despatch of business, the Provincial when residing in England, may appoint a commissary, invested with his authority, for our brethren in Belgium; and, when residing in Belgium, he may in like manner provide for England."[14]

During the fifteen years that witnessed the realization of Fr. Genning's project, the missions in England had not been neglected. It was providential that the restoration of the province coincided with the accession of Charles I (1625-1649). Like his predecessor, the king was well disposed toward his Catholic subjects; barring a few of the penal laws which the Puritan party compelled him to revive, the first years of his reign were generally speaking a period of religious peace and toleration. Naturally, Fr. John Gennings and his first companions availed themselves of these favorable conditions

---

[13] For a copy of these letters patent see Mason, p. 34; Thaddeus, p. 48.

[14] For a copy of the official regulations drawn up at this chapter see Thaddeus, pp. 49 seq.

and extended the field of their activity. From the report of Panzani, the papal envoy to England, we learn that, in 1634, there were twenty Franciscans on the English missions.[15] Already at the first chapter, in 1530, FF. Bonaventure Jackson and George Perrot could be assigned guardians of the London and Reading districts. By 1640, six new districts had been added; viz., Dorset (Dorchester) and York in 1632, Greenwich in 1634, Leicester in 1637, Oxford and Chichester in 1640. Seven years later, these vast mission territories were rearranged into eight guardianates; viz., London, York, Cambridge, Bristol, Oxford, Newcastle, Worcester, and Greenwich. Of these, the first seven comprised thirty-eight various shires or counties, while Greenwich, though situated in the London district, had a guardian of its own. These districts were governed by so-called titular guardians, who looked after the friars and the missions under their jurisdiction and also took part in the provincial chapters. The minister provincial or, in his absence, the commissary resided at London, where, too, after 1637, the provincial chapters were regularly held.[16]

Among the first Franciscans to be affiliated with the province were FF. Nicholas Day, Francis Bel, and John Baptist Bullaker; they were summoned from the Province of the Immaculate Conception in Spain, where they had entered the Order and made their profession. Other recruits, like FF. Jerome Pickford, George Perrot, and Paul Heath, came from the English College and from the neighborhood of Douai. Even on the missions in England, Fr. Gennings succeeded in gaining recruits for the ever increasing province. Thus we know that Fr. John Talbot, a secular priest, received the habit and spent his year of probation in England. Within a few years, the youthful province grew quite vigorous. This is evident from the fact, that in 1634, at the provincial chapter, the following were approved for preaching and hearing confessions: FF. William Anderton,

---

[15] The Catholic Encyclopedia, *Vol. V, p. 450.*

[16] Thaddeus, pp. 56 seq.

Peter Cape, Christopher Colman, Augustine East, Lewis of Nazareth, Vincent of St. Blase, Francis of St. Bonaventure, Bonaventure of St. Thomas, Lewis Wrest. In short, before the ill-fated year 1649, the province already numbered fifty-three members, not including the clerics who in that year were still pursuing their studies at Douai. By 1649, however, seventeen members of the province had passed to their eternal reward. Among these were the five who suffered and died for the faith during the Puritan Revolution.[17]

Like their brethren a century before, the members of the second province were faithful and zealous followers of St. Francis. At first they styled themselves *of the Regular Observance,* but later took the name *of Recollects.* "They were induced to make this change," says Thaddeus, "chiefly by two considerations. One was that probably all the Provinces over which the Commissary General presided were termed *of Recollects;* the other that there was already an establishment of Recollects at Douai. ... The people, seeing that the English friars were of the same Order, gave them also the same name. ... From the year 1676 the term Recollects is inserted in all their documents, and they also had the inscription of the old seal, *Regularis Observantiae,* changed on a new one then made into *Recollectorum.*"[18] As Parkinson rightly observes, "these Recollects were no separate body distinct from the rest of the Observants, but made up a part of it, giving themselves first to the contemplative life, as the most proper preparation for the better discharging the duties of the active; as also for the recovering their spirit when dissipated by preaching, teaching, ruling as superiors, or other similar exercises of obedience and charity."[19] How jealously they guarded the Franciscan vow of poverty, we see from the regulations drawn up at the provincial

---

[17] The above data have been compiled from Thaddeus's list of the members of the Second Province, pp. 190-320.

[18] Thaddeus, p. 59.

[19] Quoted by Parkinson, p. 215.

chapter in 1637. According to these, no friar was allowed to keep money about his person, nor to deposit it or to have it deposited without a written permission of the provincial. Furthermore, it was strictly forbidden to accept or to assign for oneself, for the province, or for the friary at Douai any rents given as alms either temporarily or for life. Neither could money be "received as alms for things curious, precious or superfluous, in food, clothing, and the rest which may be called extravagant considering the condition of the mission, according to the judgment of the provincial minister." "The faithful observance of these regulations," Thaddeus remarks, "was undoubtedly a great safeguard for the Franciscans on the English mission."[20] Like all true sons of St. Francis, they also fostered a deep and tender devotion to Mary the Mother of God. To her they recommended the conversion of England; and in 1632, it was decreed that daily on the missions the litany in her honor should be said after the principal Mass and the *Tota pulchra* after compline.[21]

No less remarkable than the growth of the youthful province, was the activity its early members unfolded. While a number of them labored in Belgium, especially at Douai,[22] instructing and training the clerics for their future missionary career and ministering to the spiritual and corporal needs of the people, others, after taking the prescribed oath,[23] set out for the English missions. The scenes of their activity in England were hallowed by the labors and sufferings of their brethren, who a hundred years before had resisted the fury of the first storm against the Church. It was, no doubt, the sacred memory of

---

[20] Thaddeus, p. 61.

[21] Ibidem, p. 79.

[22] The province had a residence also at Aire and at Bruges. Thaddeus, p. 58.

[23] By this oath, which the friars had to swear and sign before departing for the missions in England, they promised "that whenever they should be recalled, or sent back by their superiors, they would obey and conform to the command, circumstances notwithstanding." See Thaddeus, p. 58.

those Franciscan heroes that made their heirs forget the hardships and privations they encountered in the discharge of their duties. The Catholic faith could not be preached publicly; it was merely tolerated, and that only because the king secretly favored the Catholics and as yet was powerful enough to oppose his Puritan parliaments; while everyone knew that the queen professed and practiced the proscribed religion. Well regulated parishes and schools, of course, there were none. Accordingly, the friars' sphere of activity lay principally within the narrow confines of individual families. These they would visit from time to time and either minister to their spiritual needs or endeavor to bring them back to the faith of their forefathers. Already in 1638, regulations were made strictly obliging the friars frequently to catechize the children and others, either in their own homes or at the priest's residence.

Since these families were often widely scattered over the country, it was impossible for the friars to remain long in one place. Hence there was danger that the fruits of their visit would be lost before their next return. This naturally led to a phase of activity which speaks volumes for the zeal and learning of these early friars. To instruct and strengthen their scattered flock in the faith, they were wont to leave with the families their writings, in which they not only expounded Catholic doctrine but also defended it against the sectaries who were infesting the country. The literary productions of the friars previous to 1649 number no less than fifty books and pamphlets. These were printed in the friary at Douai where as early as 1638 a printing press was set up and placed in charge of Fr. Bonaventure a S. Thomas.[24] Unquestionably, the most prolific and versatile writer of this period was Fr. Paul Heath. His works, thirty in all, embrace Scotistic philosophy and theology, and many treatises on ascetical, historical, and controversial topics.[25] Fr. Bonaventure Jackson wrote the

---

[24] Thaddeus, pp. 78, 301.

[25] For a list of these works see Mason, p. vii; also Thaddeus, pp. 106 seq.

Manuduction to the Palace of Truth, a book of instruction for such as had wandered from the fold of Christ. Worthy of special mention is also the famous *Certamen Seraphicum (Seraphic Conflict)*, written by Fr. Angelus Mason and published at Douai in 1649. It is in the main a detailed account of the five Franciscans who were martyred for the faith during the last years of Charles I. The fact that its author was a contemporary and a fellow friar of the men whose life and martyrdom he recounts, makes this work especially valuable to the student of Franciscan history. The same may be said of two translations into English, St. Peter of Alcantara's *On Mental Prayer*, by Fr. Giles Willoughby, and St. Bonaventure's (?) *Stimulus amoris* (The Goad of Divine Love), by Fr. Augustine East. Among the writings of Fr. Christopher Colman we find a didactic poem entitled *Death's Duel*,[26] a book of verse on the religious controversies of the times, and the *Life of St. Angela*, a translation. That the friars were active in behalf of the Third Order of St. Francis is plain from the fact that Fr. Francis Bel wrote a treatise on its Rule, while Fr. Angelus Mason composed a manual in Latin and English for the use of Tertiaries.

Needless to say, the influence of these zealous and learned friars roused the hatred of the Puritans, which in the case of one friar at least broke out into open hostility. As early as 1633, Fr. Bonaventure Jackson, who three years before had been appointed guardian of the London district, was a prisoner in Newgate. This we learn from a letter, dated December 18, 1633, in which the writer, a secular priest laboring in the metropolis, states that Fr. Bonaventure was among the four prisoners "within this fortnight ... released upon bond." Furthermore, the *Certamen Seraphicum* says of him that "having been called to England by Father Gennings, (he) labored with great fruit of salvation, earning praise and gratitude, and having suffered persecution, affliction and imprisonment, died an eminent

---

[26] The poem is reprinted in *Franciscan Biographies*, published by the Catholic Truth Society.

confessor."[27]

Another Franciscan whose zeal for the true faith and influence over the ruling classes proved a constant menace to Protestantism was Fr. Francis Davenport. He was unquestionably one of the ablest theologians and controversialists of his time. Mason describes him as a most profound and versatile Scotist,[28] while Wood assures us that "he was excellently well versed in school divinity, in the fathers and councils, in philosophers, and in ecclesiastical and profane histories; ... all which accomplishments made his company acceptable to great and worthy persons."[29] As chaplain to Queen Maria Henrietta, the consort of Charles I, he was frequently at court, where on account of his erudition and pleasing manners, he commanded the respect not only of the queen and her Catholic household but also of the king and of Laud, archbishop of Canterbury. So great, indeed, was his influence that, in 1640, the House of Commons sent a complaint to the Lords, deploring the rapid increase of Popery in the realm and ascribing it to the writings and conferences of this formidable friar. The one desire of his heart was to effect a reunion of England with the Holy See. Accordingly, in his *Deus, Natura, Gratia*, a dogmatical treatise on divine grace, he brought by way of appendix an explanation of the Thirty-Nine Articles. In interpreting these, however, he was more zealous than judicious, making certain concessions to heresy and schism which the Church could not countenance. The book was, therefore, severely criticized by both the Catholic and the Protestant party, and the well-meaning friar had to undergo the humiliation of seeing it placed on the index by the Spanish Inquisition. It would probably have met a similar fate at Rome but for the intervention of Panzani, the papal envoy in London. "Thus," to quote Stone, "it was possible to go too far even in a good cause; Rome saw what we now see plainly, but what the

---

[27] Thaddeus, p. 75.

[28] Mason, p. 81.

moving characters in the drama could not see. The nation, instead of being ripe for conversion, was in reality drifting away from the Church, and a Puritan reaction was about to set in, almost as disastrous in its consequences as Henry the Eighth's schism, or Elizabeth's apostacy."[29]

---

[29] Quoted by Dodd, *Church History of England,* Vol. III, p. 105. Stone, p. 120.

CHAPTER II
VEN. WILLIAM WARD, FRANCISCAN TERTIARY

Troublous reign of Charles I—Puritan animosity against "Papists"—William Ward, a Protestant at Oxford—Returns to the old faith—Ordained priest—Seized on his return to England—Three years in prison—Thirty years of unceasing toil and hardship—A true follower of St. Francis—In Newgate for being a priest—Sentenced to death—Martyred at Tyburn.

AFTER three years of constant quarreling with the Commons, who demanded that the penal laws against Catholics be enforced, Charles I, in 1628, prorogued parliament and for the next twelve years ruled without it. During this period, as we have seen, Catholics enjoyed an interval of comparative peace and toleration. The Puritans, however, embittered by the consequent increase of "popery," left nothing undone to undermine the authority of Charles and to bring archbishop Laud of Canterbury to justice for treasonable leanings toward Rome. To create a spirit of fanaticism among the lower classes, unscrupulous pamphleteers deluged the country with their writings, in which they railed at the Pope and the Church and represented the king as a secret friend and protector of the detested Catholics. Had Charles been a strong and resolute character, his game of double-dealing would have neither emboldened the agitators of Puritanism nor undermined the throne on which he thought himself securely seated. He made principle subservient to policy, and this temporizing attitude proved his undoing.

Matters came to a head when, in 1640, the threatening attitude of the Scots compelled the king to reconvene parliament.

Now the Puritans, who controlled the House of Commons, had an opportunity to aim a deadly blow at the Church. At once they raised the cry of "no popery," and flatly refused to vote the necessary war subsidies unless the king rigorously enforced the penal laws against the Catholics, whom they falsely accused of favoring and aiding the Scots. Deserted by the terrified Lords, Charles reluctantly consented and "gave orders that all Catholics should quit the court, and be expelled from the army; that the houses of recusants should be searched for arms; and that the priests should be banished from the realm within thirty days."[1] But, by thus giving way to the fanatic Commons, the king signed his own death warrant. With unexampled insolence, they now publicly assailed their sovereign with keen invectives for having favored and protected Catholics, contrary to existing laws. From religious fanaticism the popular mind went over to political revolutionism; to the cry of "no popery" was added the clamor for "no royalty." What followed is well known. "A century of revolution," Stone aptly remarks, "begun with a king's act of defiance hurled at the highest spiritual authority on earth, was ending with a people's renunciation of all kingly authority."[2] The public execution of the unhappy monarch, in 1649, is one of the saddest and most shocking events in English history, and shows how the allegiance of a people to a temporal sovereign stands and falls with their allegiance to him whom Christ vested with supreme authority in matters spiritual.

Having seized the reigns of government, the Puritan "army of saints," under the cloak of zeal for "pure religion" and civil liberty, immediately began a bloody persecution of Catholics who deemed it their duty to support the king as the embodiment of lawful authority. During this religious and political upheaval, five Franciscans suffered death for the faith. Before detailing their life and martyrdom, however, we must acquaint the reader with one who, though not a member of the province, still, as a Tertiary of St. Francis, deserves more than

---

[1] Lingard, *History of England*, Vol. VII, p. 229.

[2] Stone, *Faithful Unto Death*, p. 211.

a passing notice in the story of the English Franciscans.[3] His saintly life and death will show how the spirit of St. Francis was breathing in England even at a time when the once glorious province had fallen to ruin.

F. William Ward[4] was born of Protestant parents about the year 1560, at Thornby in Westmoreland.[5] Of his early life nothing is known beyond the fact that his parents, who were of the wealthy class, had him educated at Oxford, where after completing his studies he was for seven years associated with Brasenose College. The renewed hostility of Queen Elizabeth against the Church of Rome and the subsequent sufferings of the Catholics must have made a deep and lasting impression on him. Examining the tenets of the proscribed religion and seeking the counsel of Catholic friends, he gradually perceived on which side truth and justice lay. It is probable that to avoid opposition on the part of his Protestant family, who would surely have resented his contemplated conversion to Catholicism, William accompanied Mr. Dutton, a Catholic gentleman, to Spain and there embraced the religion of his

---

[3] That Venerable William Ward belonged to the Third Order of St. Francis is sufficiently attested by Mason in his *Certamen Seraphicum*. On page 50, he makes mention "of the martyrdom of Mr. Ward, a priest of the venerable secular clergy, whom I shall justly call our confrere, as the cord of St. Francis, with which on the scaffold he was girded next to the skin, amply testifies."

[4] His real name, according to *The Catholic Encyclopedia*, was Webster. Under this name he is also registered in the Douai Diaries.

[5] Our sources of information regarding his life and martyrdom are the following: Dodd, *Church History of England,* Vol. III, p. 95; his chief sources were the *Athenae Oxonienses* of Anthony Wood and a manuscript account of the martyr's life written by a fellow priest of his acquaintance.—Hope, *Franciscan Martyrs in England,* pp. 117 seq.; the author seems to have drawn chiefly from De Marsys, who was an eye-witness of the martyrdoms he relates.—Stone, *Faithful Unto Death,* p. 128, who refers the reader to Challoner's *Memoirs of Missionary Priests.*—Spillmann, *Katholikenverfolgung in England,* Part IV, p. 23, who likewise drew from Challoner.—*The Catholic Encyclopedia,* Vol. XV, p. 552.

forefathers. He left England a skeptical Protestant, he returned a devout and practical Catholic. In time, Dodd informs us, he even succeeded in bringing his mother to the fold of Christ. Indeed, so openly did he practice his religion that he was repeatedly arrested and imprisoned. This, however, only confirmed him in the faith and filled his heart with a burning zeal to take the step he had long been contemplating.

In 1604, he left for the continent; and on September 16, the authorities of the English College at Douai admitted him as a candidate of the priesthood, despite the fact that he was already over forty years of age. On June 1, 1608, he was ordained priest; and a few months later, on October 14, he again set sail for England.[6] The ship, however, was driven to the coast of Scotland. English harbors at that time were infested with spies eager to detect a priest among the landing voyagers. F. William Ward did not escape their vigilance. He was seized and without much ado thrown into a dark and loathsome prison. Here he suffered for three years, until by some chance or other he was set free. Thereupon, he departed for his native land, where he soon engaged in ministering to the needs of the scattered Catholics.

The remaining thirty years of his life, from 1611 to 1641, were spent chiefly in and about London, the very hotbed of irreligion and persecution. They represent one long unbroken period of indefatigable zeal and devotion, beset with untold trials that would have discouraged a less fervent and self-denying spirit. Time and again, the heroic priest was arrested, imprisoned, and banished. His biographers tell us that the time he spent in the various prisons aggregated no less than twenty years. But nothing could quench the fire that glowed in his priestly soul. He always returned to his beloved flock with renewed zeal, anxiously hoping that the day would come when he would be permitted to seal his faith with his blood.

It was probably at the time when the English Franciscans

---

[6] See *Douai Diaries*, pp. 19, 24, 285.

undertook the restoration of their province, that F. William Ward became acquainted with the friars and joined the Third Order of St. Francis. His private no less than his public life was that of a true and wholesouled Tertiary. Personal sanctity lent special weight to his priestly exhortations, so that he was one of the most popular priests on the mission. Like a true follower of St. Francis, he loved and practiced holy poverty in a heroic degree and chose the poorest and meanest districts of London and its vicinity as the field of his activity. Although he possessed abundant riches, he was so niggardly with himself in food and clothing that his friends ascribed it to an avaricious spirit. How different would have been their verdict had they known that he was denying himself the comforts of life only to have more to bestow on his cherished poor. These he would seek out in their wretched hovels and with loving condescension minister to their spiritual and material needs.

Naturally of a somber, almost repulsive disposition, F. William Ward was known to be a very exacting confessor and spiritual director. Still, his impartial frankness and justice toward all who came to him won their confidence. Catholics, rich and poor, eagerly sought his advice and consolation in those dark days of political and religious dissensions. Even ladies of rank placed themselves under his direction, declaring that, despite the severity with which he censured sin and inculcated virtue, they preferred him to all other confessors.

Thus for thirty years, frequently interrupted by imprisonment and exile, this heroic Tertiary priest braved the hardships of the times in the discharge of his sacred office. Meanwhile, the endless agitation of the Puritans against the king and against the Catholics grew more and more aggressive, so that by 1640 it became evident that another bloody persecution would break out. F. William Ward viewed these conditions with mingled feelings of sorrow and joy. He grieved at the thought of the sufferings and hardships it would again create for the helpless Catholics; but his heart rejoiced over the prospect it gave him of yet winning the coveted martyr's crown. When, therefore, his nephew, who was likewise a priest on the mission, requested him to have regard for his old age, to quit London, and to flee to the country, where a safe refuge had been prepared for him, the intrepid priest of eighty years earnestly replied that he was not like the hireling who flies at the approach of the wolf and abandons his flock to its ravenous fury; only imprisonment and death could separate him from those whose shepherd he had been these many years. He was willing to brave death for the good of his people.

In March, 1641, parliament issued a warrant for the arrest of all priests who should be found in England after April 7. Among those who defied the government and remained with their scattered flock was F. William Ward. His frequent visits to the house of Mr. Wooton, one of his nephews, had long roused the suspicion of a certain Mr. Thomas Mayhew (Mayo), an apostate Catholic and a notorious priest catcher. About midnight, on July 15, 1641, this worthless creature without warning entered the house, forced his way into the apartments of the aged priest, and having literally dragged him out of bed, hurried him off to Newgate prison. Eight days later he was tried at the Old Bailey in London. Among the witnesses that deposed against him was Mayhew. He had known the prisoner for a long time, he declared, and had received the sacraments of Penance and Communion at his hands. After hearing two more witnesses, who likewise declared they knew him to be a priest, the judge asked the prisoner whether these accusations were true.

"No one," came the fearless reply, "is obliged to accuse himself. But if you wish to arrive at the truth and to convict me, produce witnesses without reproach, and not like this Mayhew, who may well lie before men since he has broken the faith which he vowed to God."

In a similar manner, he could have discomfited the other witnesses. But fear of again foregoing the martyr's crown sealed his lips. His heart leaped for joy, therefore, when the jury after a brief consultation returned a verdict of guilty and the judge condemned him to be hanged, drawn, and quartered on the following Monday.

On Sunday, the day before his martyrdom, he obtained leave to converse with a priest who was also a prisoner. What passed between them we can readily imagine. Early next morning, F. William Ward said holy Mass and administered Holy Communion to a number of imprisoned Catholics. His aged brow, otherwise grave and austere, was now radiant with joy, reflecting the peace and happiness that reigned in his soul. When offered a better coat than he was wont to wear, he said cheerfully:

"You are right to dress me better than usual, since I am going to a more splendid banquet and a more joyful wedding than any at which I have ever been present."

He gave a twenty-shilling piece to the jailer, who on leaving said blandly:

"Good bye, Mr. Ward. I hope we shall meet again, in heaven."

"By no means," replied the martyr, "unless you change your life and become a Catholic. This is the truth, in defense of which I am about to shed my blood."

About eight o'clock, the holy priest was led from his dungeon, fastened to a hurdle, and dragged to Tyburn. Many of the bystanders wept at sight of the feeble old man on his bed of pain.

"Why do you weep, my son?" he said to a young man whom he recognized as one of his penitents.

"For love of you, my father," came the touching reply.

"If you love me," returned the martyr calmly, "weep not for my death. I can yet live if I will, but it is my joy to die for this cause, and therefore you have no reason to weep."

Having arrived at the place of execution, he was taken from the hurdle and ordered to mount the cart that stood beneath the gibbet. Then turning to the presiding officer, he said in broken accents:

"Mr. Sheriff, I would have you all here assembled understand that I am condemned to death for being a Romish priest, although no proof of it was adduced in court. Hence they have dealt unjustly with me. Now, however, I proclaim of my own free will that for well-nigh forty years I have been a priest, for which I thank God. That on this account I have been condemned to death, fills me with joy and I deem it a great distinction, because I die for my Lord and Master, Jesus Christ."

When the sheriff offered him life and liberty if he would renounce his faith, the valiant champion beaming with joy exclaimed:

"If God had given me a thousand lives, I should deem myself happy to sacrifice them all for my priesthood and the Catholic Church."

Upon this the sheriff objected that he was to die not for being a Catholic, but for seducing the people.

"I have seduced no one," replied the martyr with indignation, "but I have led many in the way of salvation. Would to God that I had converted more—nay, even all England! Believe, I entreat you, that it is the love which I have for you that makes me speak thus; for if you wish to enter into Paradise you must embrace the Catholic religion, which was so long revered by your ancestors."

When asked whether he was related to Bishop Ward of Gloucester, he replied in the negative, adding that his real name was William Webster.

Seeing now that the executioners were making ready to carry out the sentence, the venerable priest knelt down and prayed. At last, the sheriff interrupted him asking whether there was anything he wished.

"Yes," he replied with a look to heaven, "from all my heart I shall pray God to bless the king, the queen, and the whole royal family as also the government, the people, and the entire kingdom. Then I should like to give a little alms to needy Catholics, but I see none here."

"Give it to the executioner," cried the people, "that he might deal mercifully with you."

"What mercy can he show me," retorted the martyr with a

smile, pointing to the gibbet and the fire. "Nor," he continued serenely, "do I even desire him to lessen the merit of my sufferings."

Thereupon, he handed the sheriff forty shillings to be distributed among needy Catholics. To the executioner he gave a half crown, while the driver of the hurdle received two shillings. Then throwing his ring, breviary, and handkerchief to the crowd, he permitted the rope to be placed about his neck. When the cart with a sudden jolt began to move from under his feet, he raised his eyes to heaven and exclaimed, "Jesus, Jesus, Jesus, receive my soul!" Immediately he was cut down and while still living subjected to the cruel and inhuman butchery. Seizing his heart the executioner held it up to the excited rabble and cried, "Behold the heart of a traitor!" But the valiant martyr was beyond the reach of human torture and insult. In the mansions of the King of kings, he was already in possession of that glorious crown for which he had labored and yearned so many years.[7]

---

[7] His name appears on the list of English martyrs whose cause of beatification was introduced on December 4, 1886. See *Acta Minorum*, an. VI (1887), p. 51.

CHAPTER III
FR. CHRISTOPHER COLMAN, O. F. M.

Of Catholic parentage—Student at the Jesuit College in Douai—Returns to England—The Catholic gentleman—Joins the Franciscans in Douai—Ordained priest—Summoned to England—Arrested and released—Missionary labors—The persecution revived—Fr. Christopher one of the first to he seized—In Newgate—Condemned to death—Execution delayed and prevented by the war—Sufferings and death in prison.

E have seen how, despite the unsettled times, the English Franciscans united once more into a province and eagerly cast in their lot with the Jesuits and the secular clergy on the missions. Neither the stress of present hardships nor the forebodings of another war on the Church could unman these champions of the Cross. Like their fellow friars a century before, they were ready to suffer all for the restoration of Christ's kingdom in unhappy England. Their zeal for the furtherance and preservation of the faith brought them in touch with all classes of society. Though their forces were scant, yet it was owing in no small measure to their ever widening activity and influence that the anti-Catholic hatred of the Puritans at last burst forth into an all-consuming flame. Hence, when the news of the martyrdom of the well-known and much-esteemed Tertiary priest Venerable William Ward reached the friars, they clearly saw what was in store for them and by redoubled prayers and penances prepared themselves for the inevitable conflict. Their provincial at the time was Fr. George Perrot, a man whom the death records of the province commemorate as "a lover of the brethren."[1] He, too, was aware of the calamity that would soon befall the youthful province; and we may imagine how, like another John Forest, he sounded

---

[1] Thaddeus, *The Franciscans in England,* p. 286.

the alarm among his devoted subjects, exhorting them to remain loyal and steadfast in the hour of trial.

History tells us with what courage the persecuted friars faced the enemy. Only after the executioner's knife had done its deadly work, did these fearless shepherds of souls cease to labor for the well-being of their beloved flock. Between October, 1642, and August, 1646, four members of the province mounted the scaffold and died for the faith, while one friar at last succumbed to the hardships of prison life.[2] Though small in itself, this number must appear considerable, if one remembers that at the time hardly more than thirty Franciscans were engaged on the missions in England, and that before the year 1649, in all only twenty-one Catholics underwent public martyrdom for the faith.[3]

Among the first victims of Puritan animosity and intolerance toward the Church of Rome was Fr. Christopher Colman.[4] He descended from an ancient and prominent Catholic family whose ancestral estate lay at Cannock in Staffordshire.[5] The parents of the future Franciscan friar, whose baptismal name was Walter, remained true to the faith of their forefathers and taught their son from early youth to value virtue higher than worldly wealth and distinction. Anxious to give him a thoroughly Catholic education, they defied the penal

---

[2] For the life and martyrdom of these five friars, that will engage our attention in the subsequent chapters, our chief source of information is the *Certamen Seraphicum,* written and published in 1649 by their confrere and contemporary, Fr. Angelus Mason.

[3] This number is based on Spillmann's *Katholikenverfolgung in England,* Part IV, pp. 235-320. Of these twenty-one martyrs, nine were secular priests, three Benedictines, four Jesuits, four Franciscans and one a layman.

[4] Thaddeus has embellished the *Franciscan Biographies* with an account of this friar, from which we have freely drawn for the present sketch.

[5] Thaddeus supposes his grandfather to have been the Walter Colman whom the records of the royal visitation, in 1583, represent as having forfeited the title of armiger and the right to armorial bearings, probably because he rejected the spiritual supremacy of Queen Elizabeth.

laws and sent him to the English College at Douai. Walter must have been about fifteen years of age when he accompanied F. William Eaton (Eiton), a priest, and two students to the continent. On June 20, 1585, he entered the college and registered, as was customary at the time, under the assumed name of Combe.[6] The ensuing year, however, on November 28, he was called home, perhaps, as Thaddeus suggests, on account of the illness or death of his mother. In 1593, his father entered upon a second marriage. Thereupon, Walter returned to the college at Douai.

After completing his studies, Walter went back to England, probably because his father being advanced in years wished him, as the eldest of his sons, to assume charge of the family estate. Wealth and social standing did not hinder him from closely following the dictates of his faith and conscience. Hence, he soon learned from experience what difficulties loyal Catholics had to contend with in the exercise of their religion. This knowledge in turn strengthened or, at least, engendered in his heart the desire to devote himself entirely to the service of the Church by renouncing worldly pleasures and promises for the nobler but wearier life of a missionary priest. Apparently, the only obstacle that as yet prevented him from taking this step was a loving and dutiful regard for his aged father.[7] About 1620, however, his father passed to a better life. Now Walter was free to answer what he believed to be a call from above.

It is very probable that during his sojourn in Flanders, Walter heard it told how Edmund Gennings had laid down his life for the faith and how John, the martyr's brother, had thereby been converted to Catholicism. Like him, these two brothers were natives of Staffordshire, a circumstance that

---

[6] Presumably an abbreviation of Comberford, the name of his mother. See the *Douai Diaries*, pp. 206, 213.

[7] It Is reported that a Walter Colman, presumably the martyr's father, was still living in 1617.

must have roused his interest all the more, especially when he learned that John Gennings had become a priest and Franciscan and had undertaken the restoration of his Order in England. It was, therefore, natural that he should decide to proceed to Douai and seek admission into the newly founded Franciscan friary. Accordingly, he settled his temporal affairs and about the year 1625[8] left England to execute his design. We can imagine the joy and gratification of Fr. John Gennings, when he was informed by Fr. Francis Davenport, then superior of the friary at Douai, that Walter Colman had arrived and desired to join the Franciscan Order. Needless to say, he readily granted the necessary faculties for his reception, and in due time the superior clothed the worthy postulant with the habit of St. Francis and bestowed on him the name of Christopher of St. Clare.

Despite the fact that he was already over fifty years of age and a man of learning, refinement, and experience, he vied with the youngest member of the community in ready submission to his superiors. For him the year of novitiate was in very deed a time of probation. Acts of penance and mortification were not wanting to prove his constancy and sincerity. But nothing could be too humiliating for him who had come to serve God and not himself. During his novitiate, an incident occurred that shows how he fostered the spirit of childlike obedience and heroic penance. Endowed by nature with a taste and talent for poetry, he had written for his own edification a number of verses on death. Hearing of this, the novice master told him one day to get the poem and to read it to the community during recreation. Gladly the novice obeyed. Hardly had he finished reading the poem, when he was told to throw it into the fire.

---

[8] In support of this date, Thaddeus argues that Mason in his *Certamen Seraphicum* "seems to use the term *Preses* purposely instead of *Guardian*. Father Bonaventure Jackson was Guardian at Douai in 1624; but, as he was wanted on the English Missions, Father Davenport was appointed to succeed him, apparently with the title of *Preses*, until the year 1626, when, at the meeting of the Officials of the Province, he was made Guardian."

That such a demand was mortifying for a man of his age and attainments goes without saying. But, to the edification of the assembled brethren, he obeyed without the least sign of reluctance or discontent. After his novitiate, he spent the next few years in prayer and study. At last, in 1633 (or 1634), he was raised to the priesthood, whereupon Fr. John Gennings summoned him to the missions in England. He had hardly set foot on English soil, when government spies suspecting his character placed him under arrest. Later, on searching him, they found that below the secular dress he wore a queer sort of shirt.

"What kind of man is this," they exclaimed, "who travels in such clothes?"

How differently the holy man would have fared, had his enemies known that the object of the uncivil remark was the tunic of a Franciscan friar. But his ready wit was equal to the emergency.

"Are you not ashamed," he fell in with seeming indignation, "thus to display the poverty and distress of a gentleman who has spent all his money in traveling, and now returns poor to his native land?"

This bold rejoinder, however, did not allay the suspicion of his enemies. They would, at least, satisfy themselves as to the religious convictions of the prisoner and demanded that he take the oath of allegiance.[9] Now, of course, there was no alternative. With equal intrepidity he declared that he was a Catholic and would never swear the tendered oath; whereupon he was led off to prison.

This time, it seems, the confinement of Fr. Christopher was of short duration. The intolerant Puritans were not as yet in full

---

[9] This oath, enacted with other penal laws in 1606 after the Gunpowder Plot, had to be taken by all who refused to swear that they were not Catholics. In 1625, the king was forced by the House of Commons to reenforce the oath. It had been condemned by a papal brief as partly derogatory to the rights of the Holy See. Hence, Catholics were bound in conscience to reject it.

control of affairs. The imprisoned friar found means to communicate with former friends, who readily used their wealth and influence in his behalf. On obtaining his liberty, he immediately proceeded on his journey to London, where he exercised the functions of his sacred ministry. As during the first years of his religious life, so now the earnest truths about death formed the constant topic of his meditations. After his novitiate, he rewrote with the consent of his superiors the poem he had been told to consign to the flames. On the mission, this child of his pensive muse must have still been very dear to him; for, despite the cares of his sacred calling, he completed the poem and published it. It is entitled *Death's Duel* and is dedicated to the Queen of England, Maria Henrietta. "In this poem," Mason remarks, "he teaches all men the way and manner of dying well; he invites all to meditate earnestly on death; graphically he describes the vanity of this deceitful world and with no little elegance of style vividly depicts how vice must be shunned and virtue practiced."[10]

After laboring a number of years in England, Fr. Christopher yearned for the more retired and regular life of the convent, and obtained leave to return for a time to Douai. Here, apart from the bustle of the world, he divided his time between prayer and study. When free from the religious exercises of the community, he worked at a poem on the controversies of the times and translated the life of St. Angela Merici into English. Apparently, he tarried at Douai only a year or so, and then refreshed in soul and body again departed for the missions. "His wit and brilliant talents," says Hope, "his placid and cheerful temper, and the polished manners which he had acquired in his social position in the world, made him generally popular, and helped on his missionary work."[11] For a long time, we are told, even professional priest catchers failed to detect the real character of the handsome and well-dressed gentleman

---

[10] Mason, p. 218.

[11] Hope, *Franciscan Martyrs in England*, p. 126.

Fr. Christopher Colman, O.F.M.

whom every now and then they chanced to meet on the streets of the metropolis.

For several years, Fr. Christopher braved the perils that beset his holy profession. The Puritan faction had gradually become more and more aggressive until, in the spring of 1641, the Commons compelled Charles to decree a rigorous enforcement of the penal laws against Catholics. Among the first priests apprehended and imprisoned was Fr. Christopher. After repeated hearings before various magistrates, the zealous friar together with five secular priests and two Benedictines was placed, on December 8 of the same year, at the bar of the Old Bailey. Here, a certain Wadsworth, an apostate Catholic, testified on oath that he knew Fr. Christopher to be a Franciscan and priest, having seen him clad with the habit of the Franciscans in their friary at Douai. On this evidence, the judge declared the accused guilty of treason and condemned him to be hanged, drawn, and quartered on the following Monday. Thereupon the aged friar and his six[12] companions were brought back to Newgate.

During the remainder of the week, while they lay in prison preparing themselves for the final conflict, the French ambassador made efforts for their release. Accordingly, the king reprieved the sentence of the court and asked the advice of both houses of parliament regarding a pardon for the condemned priests, suggesting that it might quiet the rising rebellion in Ireland. The Puritan Commons proved obstinate and demanded that at least four of the priests, among them Fr. Christopher, be dealt with according to the law. Then, after much debating, both houses voted the death of all six,[13] and in the end the king found it expedient to yield. "If you think the execution of these persons," his message read, "so very necessary to the great and pious work of reformation, we refer it wholly to you, declaring hereby, that upon such your

---

[12] One of their number had been acquitted, probably for lack of evidence.

[13] One of the condemned priests had already died.

resolution signified to the ministers of justice, our warrant for their reprieve is determined, and the law to have its course." In this way, the weak monarch shook the responsibility from his own shoulders and left the innocent victims of his temporizing policy to the mercy of the Puritans. As yet, however, these were not so well established in power as to proceed without royal sanction. Hence, it seems, the affair was dropped.[14] Soon, also, the Civil War broke out, during which the six priests were either forgotten or purposely left in their dismal dungeon to die a more terrible death by disease and starvation.

Well-nigh intolerable must have been the lot of Fr. Christopher, considering his age and character as well as the fearful conditions prevailing in Newgate in those days. Chained down in a gloomy, dank, and fetid dungeon, surrounded by filth and vermin, entirely shut off from the outer world, with nothing to break the grave-like silence but the gnawing of rats and the curses of vicious criminals, the venerable old man must have undergone a thousand martyrdoms. Money, it is true, might have procured him clean straw for bedding or more nutritious food to relieve his hunger and restore his declining strength; but as a poor Franciscan he had not wherewith to secure the good will of the jailer. Friends, too, might have come to his rescue, even though they would thereby imperil their own safety; but the Civil War with all its dangers and hardships for Catholics was now in full swing, while London was in the hands of the parliamentarians. Least of all could Fr. Francis Davenport, by whom he had been received into the Order, and his fellow friars relieve his misery. The welfare of their persecuted flock forbade them to expose themselves to the fury of the Puritans.

Hence, for three or four years, while four of his brethren mounted the scaffold and died a martyr's death for the faith, Fr. Christopher had patiently to wait till God should summon him

---

[14] Thaddeus, on the authority of Clarendon. See also Hope, p. 218; and Stone, *Faithful Unto Death*, p. 130.

to his eternal reward. "Not for him," Stone touchingly remarks, "was the glory of shedding his blood for the Faith, surrounded by a crowd of witnesses; for him were only the lingering torments of abandonment and the ignominy of the Cross."[15] At last, however, sickness and privation had done their work, and his tried soul exchanged the gloom of the prison for the glory of God's blissful mansions. In the *Franciscan Martyrology,* he is commemorated on November 1, in these terms: "In London, Blessed Christopher a Sancta Clara, Martyr, who, having been cast into a loathsome prison for the confession of the Catholic religion and sentenced to death, weakened by squalor and hunger, gave up his soul to God in prayer."[16]

Surely, the last moment had no terrors for one who in life had so diligently studied how to die. Many a time, no doubt, when lying cold and hungry on his bed of straw, he recalled to mind the poem he had written years before and paused to reflect on the words:

>Consider wisely what thou hast to do
>In this vain world with serious meditation,
>How short the time, what's likely to ensue,
>And frustrate not the end of thy creation.
>Since here is naught whereon thou canst rely
>But to be born, to labor, and to die.

---

[15] Stone, p. 132.

[16] His name does not appear, however, on the official list of December 4, 1886. See *Acta Minorum,* Vol. VI (1887), p. 49 seq. Accordingly, the title of Venerable is not prefixed to his name.

CHAPTER IV
VENERABLE JOHN BAPTIST BULLAKER, O.F.M.

Studies with the Jesuits at Saint-Omer and at Valladolid—Desires to become a Franciscan—Enters the Order—Novitiate and years of study—Joins the English Province—Departs for England—Arrested and imprisoned at Plymouth—In Exeter jail—Before the judges—Conveyed to London for trial—Liberated—Twelve years of missionary labors—Betrayed and captured while saying Mass—Court proceedings against him—Tried for being a priest—Condemned to death—Martyrdom at Tyburn.

T was in the year 1622 that Thomas Bullaker, the only son of a distinguished Catholic physician in Chichester, took leave of home and kindred and boarded a ship that was about to set sail for Flanders.[1] Had the civil authorities surmised that the comely youth of some eighteen summers was bound for the English College at Saint-Omer to study for the priesthood, they would undoubtedly have intercepted him and brought action against his parents for violating the penal laws then in force. To forestall this, Thomas had disclosed his intention to the Spanish ambassador in London, who alleging important business matters obtained for him the necessary passport.

Arriving in Flanders, Thomas at once proceeded to the English College at Saint-Omer. The Jesuit Fathers in charge of the institution soon detected the excellent qualities of the young Englishman, and perhaps also expressed to him their hope of one day numbering him among their own.

That Thomas shortly after his arrival bound himself in some way to their Order, seems at least probable. He had been with

---

[1] Mason bases his life sketch of Fr. Bullaker in the *Certamen Seraphicum* (pp. 35-70) on the writings of the martyr and on other trustworthy testimonies. These writings, he tells us (p. 33), were preserved at his time in the archives of the English Franciscans at Douai.

them only three weeks when they sent him for the higher studies to Valladolid in Spain. Here he registered as an *alumnus iuratus* of the English College under the assumed name of Thomas Tailer.[2]

But his mind was agitated with grave doubts regarding his vocation. More and more he felt himself drawn to the Franciscans. Alone in a strange country, without an acquaintance among the Franciscans, he was at a loss how to proceed. Fearing at the same time lest the college authorities might dissuade him from what he so earnestly desired, he kept the matter secret. With greater zeal than prudence, he spent long hours of the night in prayer and meditation, slept on the bare floor, and subjected his body to the pangs of the scourge and cilice. This he continued for some weeks when he began to realize that his health was declining. He at length took courage and revealed to Father Baker, S. J., his confessor, the secret of his heart. How happy he was when the zealous priest consoled him and assured him of his support. He then made a ten days' retreat, at the end of which he was determined to enter the Order of St. Francis.

Without delay, the Jesuit Fathers made the necessary arrangements with the provincial of the Spanish Franciscans. There was a friary about six miles from Valladolid, on a site called Abrojo, *i.e.,* Thistle, on account of the wildness of the surrounding landscape. Here on the feast of Corpus Christi, 1622, Thomas received the Franciscan habit and the name John Baptist. Here, too, he spent the year of novitiate, edifying all by his love of prayer and mortification. After his profession, he finished his course in philosophy and then studied theology at Valladolid, Avila, and Segovia. Finally, at the age of twenty-four, he was ordained priest. Having reached the goal of his youthful aspirations, his soul, long since inspired by the example of so many of his brethren, went out wholly to the foreign missions. But "at this first starting point," as Stone

---

[2] Stone, *Faithful Unto Death,* p. 133.

observes, "he was prevented by the virtue of religious obedience from making a second mistake as to his vocation."[3] Shortly after his ordination, a number of friars had again been selected for the flourishing missions which the province had in the West Indies. Fr. John Baptist asked leave to join them. But the provincial put him off, telling him to remember England, which was equally in need of missionaries, and which as his native country ought to have the first claim on his interest and zeal. The young priest willingly submitted and henceforth endeavored to fit himself in every way for a missionary career among his neglected countrymen.

Thus about a year elapsed when the provincial informed him that he might follow the summons of the Belgium commissary and join his brethren on the missions in England. Fr. John was overjoyed and devoted ten days to prayer and meditation. Then having changed his habit for a secular dress, which he obtained for charity, he set out for Bordeaux. Traveling alone and on foot though an unknown, desolate, and swampy country, the poor friar must have suffered greatly from anguish and fatigue. At last, after many hardships, he reached the French seaport and secured passage on a ship bound for England. From his modest bearing, the captain of the ship suspected his priestly character, and, on landing at Plymouth, reported his suspicion to the mayor of the city, who without further inquiry had the friar arrested and cast into prison. Here he languished for eight days. The weather was extremely cold, which added greatly to his sufferings. Lacking the means to secure sufficient and wholesome nourishment, he would have succumbed to hunger, had not some fellow prisoners shared their meager rations with him. His next place of confinement was the county jail of Exeter, where thrown among criminals of the lowest type he was to await the opening of the Lenten assizes.

At last, the circuit judges came to Exeter, and one of the first

---

[3] Ibidem, p. 135.

to be summoned for trial was Fr. John. After the usual questions as to age and profession, the judge asked him whether he was willing to take the oath of allegiance according to the meaning it had in England.

"As far as the allegiance that becomes a faithful subject is concerned," replied the friar, "I will obey the king in all that belongs to him. If necessary, I will confirm this by an oath and prove it by my conduct should an occasion present itself. In the proposed oath, however, there are certain clauses regarding the Supreme Pontiff, Christ's Vicar on earth, which I do not fully understand. Hence, with your leave, I absolutely refuse to take it."

The judge objected that there were priests who held the oath could be taken.

"From this you must not conclude, however, that it can," was the quick reply. "Whether your assertion is based on facts, I do not know. At all events, after due consideration, I feel convinced that the oath can not be taken."

Thereupon, he was asked whom he would obey, the king or the Pope, were they to issue contrary and conflicting orders.

"I imagine," the friar explained, "that we must obey the commands of him who proceeds along the lines of truth and justice."

Still bent on ensnaring him, the judge cunningly insisted that he should state who he thought should decide in that matter. But the wary friar detected the trap and refused to answer.

It seems that his quick-witted and straightforward rejoinders had won the favor of the judge, who finally gave him a gentle hint as to how he might escape the law.

"Perhaps you will change your mind in the near future," he said; "you may ask now for leisure to give the matter further consideration."

"What my opinion may be hereafter," put in the prisoner, "I can not at present discover. Nevertheless, I humbly request that judgment in my case be deferred."

Deeply resenting the attitude of the judge, the captain of the ship now stepped forward and produced a book, which he declared to be a missal and as such a positive proof that the prisoner on whose person it had been found was a priest. Though no one in court was able to read the book, all agreed that its content was dangerous to the commonwealth. Finally, someone who knew a little Spanish examined it and loudly contended that it was merely a volume of Spanish plays. Now, of course, peals of laughter rang through the court room, much to the discomfiture of the ever-zealous captain.

For the present, Fr. John Baptist was brought back to prison. A few days later the jailer received orders from the Privy Council to send the suspected priest to London, where he would be tried within the next twenty days. But this was only a ruse to effect his release. Hatred against priests was not so violent just then; and influential friends of the friars had succeeded in interesting the higher authorities in his behalf.

On gaining his freedom, he began at once to search for his brethren in the great metropolis. He had hardly taken up his abode with the friars, when the hardships he had of late been subjected to began to tell on him. He was stricken with a severe fever, from the effects of which he never fully recovered. Nevertheless, as priest and missionary, he sacrificed himself entirely for the welfare of his flock, gaining the esteem of all by his sterling piety and by his untiring zeal for souls. In 1638, he was formally incorporated into the English province.[4] In what esteem the brethren held him may be seen from the fact that he was made secretary of the provincial; and in 1640, he became titular guardian of the newly formed district of Chichester,[5] his native city.

---

[4] Thaddeus, *The Franciscans in England*, p. 206.

[5] Mason, p. 49. Thaddeus says (p. 206) that he was appointed guardian of Oxford. The two districts, Oxford and Chichester, were established in the same year, 1640. Perhaps Fr. John Baptist was at first appointed for both places or was soon transferred to Oxford, since Chichester was his native place and he could escape detection more easily at Oxford.

Twelve years had elapsed since his arrival on the English mission. All this while, he had hoped and prayed for the privilege of dying a martyr's death. But it was a time when priests were comparatively safe, so that he gradually despaired of the martyr's crown and longed for the life of seclusion and prayer he had enjoyed during the first years of his religious profession. Accordingly, he asked and obtained permission to return to the continent. He was on the point of leaving England, when the smoldering embers of Puritan hatred against Catholics were again fanned into a devastating flame by the rebellious Commons. Now, of course, he decided to remain; especially when he learned how the Tertiary martyr, Venerable William Ward, had been captured, tried, and executed for being a priest. Hoping to share his happy lot, he hastened to London, the hotbed of Puritan intolerance.[6] Friends, however, compelled him to seek a place of safety. A few weeks later, he heard how a number of priests had been seized and thrown into prison.[7] Again he ventured into the thick of the fray, but again he was forced to retire. At last, regardless of friendly entreaties, he went a third time to London and sought out the provincial, Fr. George Perrot, who gave him permission to remain in the city.

With undaunted zeal, the heroic friar undertook the hazardous task of ministering to the persecuted Catholics. He visited the loathsome prisons and the gloomy homes of the aged, poor, and sick, administering the sacraments as best he might, distributing whatever alms he could gather, and confirming all in the faith by his noble example of self-denial and by the words of cheer that gushed from his God-loving soul. He was lodging in one of the most dangerous parts of the city, when one day the priest catchers suddenly entered the very house where he was staying.

"Am I the priest whom you are seeking?" he asked, fearlessly stepping up to them.

---

[6] Spillman, *Katholikenverfolgung in England*, Part IV, p. 261.

[7] Mason thinks that among them was Fr. Christopher Colman (p. 51).

Baffled by his boldness, they replied in the negative.

"But, besides me there is no other here," he hastily subjoined, fearing they might depart without making further investigation. On the following day, they returned and again searched the house. Fr. John Baptist was sitting at dinner and had his breviary lying beside him on the table. The door to his room stood ajar. On passing, the spies looked in, but, strange to say, they took no notice of him. At this second defeat of his most ardent desire, the man of God was much disturbed. On the one hand, he longed for the martyr's crown; on the other hand, he dreaded to cross the designs of Providence. Now he redoubled his prayers and penances, beseeching "the Father of mercies and the God of all consolation to deign at last to hear him and to number him in the ranks of the martyrs."

In a letter to a fellow priest, Fr. John Baptist recounts the particulars of his arrest and trial.[8] "In 1642, on September 11, which fell on a Sunday," he writes, "it pleased the Most High and Almighty to soothe my anguish and to console me, his unworthiest servant, with the prospect of obtaining what I had so long yearned and prayed for." At the time of his seizure he was staying in the house of Lady Powel, a very pious and charitable gentlewoman. One of her maids, however, was secretly in league with the anti-Catholic party, and it was through her greed and treachery that Fr. John fell into the hands of the priest catchers.[9] Having finished his breviary and morning meditation on the above-mentioned day, the saintly friar vested for holy Mass. Little did he think that at that very moment the pursuivants were standing in the street below, ready to enter the house at a given signal and surprise him at the sacred functions. Just as he was intoning the *Gloria,*

---

[8] For a copy of this letter see Mason, pp. 53-63.

[9] This we learn from De Marsys, who at the time of the Puritan Revolution was in the service of Comte d'Harcourt, the French ambassador at the English court. He was present at the trial and execution of Venerable Bullaker. See Hope, *Franciscan Martyrs in England,* pp. 140 seq.

Wadsworth[10] rushed in and dragged him from the altar.

"Oh, why didst thou not wait till after the consecration?" exclaimed the friar. "The precious body of my Saviour would have strengthened me against thy violence, under which my weakness may now succumb."

Blinded with hatred and rage, the heartless zealot insisted that his victim accompany him through the streets of London, clad in the priestly vestments. Only after being warned of the possible danger to himself, did the base informer relent. Thereupon, he confiscated all the vestments, books, rosaries, pictures and oilstocks, and ordered the friar to follow him to headquarters.[11]

A half-hour after their arrival, the sheriff entered and asked Fr. John whether he was a priest. Glad that his hour had come, the man of God assured him that he was.

"What! Durst thou violate the laws of the kingdom, which strictly forbid any person of that profession to set foot on English soil?"

"Those laws are wicked and opposed to Christian justice; therefore, I cared not a straw for them. If you pursue the course you have begun," he added fearlessly, "I dare say, before the lapse of many years, you will pass a law making it treason to believe in Jesus Christ."

Then, to bear out his assertion, he referred with glowing indignation to the recent outrage which the intolerant Puritans had committed against Christ by defacing and pulling down the crucifix in Cheapside. This reproach, of course, infuriated the sheriff and his attendants.

"Where in Holy Writ does Christ command that a picture or a statue of himself be made?"

---

[10] The same who captured Ven. William Ward.

[11] Lady Powel and her twelve-year-old son, who was serving the martyr's Mass on the morning of his seizure, were likewise arrested and brought before the sheriff. According to De Marsys, the three prisoners were subsequently thrown into different prisons. See Hope, p. 143.

"Albeit, in the sacred pages, he does not command it expressly," the friar explained, "still, the custom is sanctioned by the natural law with which the divine by no means conflicts. Sound reason and experience, however, tell us that the insult offered an image touches him whom the image represents."

Then asking whether they would prosecute for treason the man who would outrage the king's image, he argued that more traitorous by far is one who abuses Christ's image, as they had done.

"What has brought thee to England?" demanded the sheriff, eager to change the subject.

"To lead back my countrymen to the fold of Christ, whence they have strayed; this was the purpose of my sending and of my coming."

"By whom hast thou been sent? By the Pope?"

"By those whom the Sovereign Pontiff has vested with due authority and power."

Satisfied that the prisoner was a priest, the sheriff gave the pursuivants the necessary instructions and departed. What followed we will let Fr. John relate.

"What now troubled them above all," he writes, "was how to lead me off without danger of death through the dense throng that had gathered at the door and was waiting for me. For this reason, the pursuivants decided to ask for an escort, so that I might safely accompany them to prison. Accordingly, to avoid the fury of the mob, I was taken through a rear door that led into another street. On the way to the prison known as Newgate, we passed by the house of the constable, who together with my captors gave me company. Now this house happened to be a tavern, and thither they brought me, that I might get something to drink. While we were here, Wadsworth, the head of the pursuivants, asked me all kinds of questions regarding my name and birthplace. On all these points, I openly confessed the truth, because I had made up my mind to conceal nothing. He further asked me with which gentlemen of the county of Sussex I was acquainted. I told him that years ago I had known two, who at one time were schoolmates of mine, but now belonged to the parliamentarians; that one of them was Mr. William Morley, and the other Mr. William Cauley, both of whom had been decorated with the order of knighthood. Then he asked me where I had studied. For some time, I answered, with the Fathers of the Society of Jesus at Valladolid in Spain; then, through the kindness of the said Fathers, I went to the friary at Abrojo, where I received the habit of the Seraphic Father Saint Francis, passed my novitiate, and made my profession. These things I told him quite freely, all of which he faithfully reported to parliament."

The next day, Fr. John Baptist was informed that parliamentary proceedings against him would begin on Tuesday, and that his two former schoolmates would preside as commissioners of parliament. Accordingly, on the following morning at seven o'clock, he was led from Newgate to Westminster. On a table in the courtroom, Wadsworth had spread out the sacred vestments and other articles he had seized in the house of Lady Powel. After examining them, one of the bystanders remarked that they were of rather ordinary grade.

"By my troth, much too precious for those who now possess them," returned the friar; "I'd have you know, however," he continued good-humoredly, "that I could have procured more costly things, had I not apprehended what has already come to pass."

"Despite the inferior quality of those vestments," sneered the presiding judge, "idolatry can be practiced as well in them as in more precious ones."

"Prithee, what sort of idolatry art thou referring to?"

"Is it not, indeed, criminal idolatry to worship bread as God?"

"We do not worship bread and wine in the august sacrifice of Mass. Under the appearances of bread and wine, we rightly adore and pay homage to Christ our Lord. Such, from the days of the Apostles down to the time of Martin Luther, has ever been the unanimous teaching and practice of the entire Church."

Just then, while rummaging the articles on the table, someone accidentally discovered the altar stone. After closely examining the inscribed crosses, he shouted triumphantly that he had found the number of the beast.[12] All eyes were turned on the speaker, while the friar could hardly refrain from laughing at the man's stupidity.

"Since there is such intimacy between thee and the beast," he quizzed, "have the goodness to tell me openly and plainly the beast's name."

The judge was evidently vexed at the prisoner's playful and fearless manner.

"On what grounds," he demanded sternly, "hast thou ventured to violate the laws of the country?"

"No other answer suggests itself to me just now than the one St. Peter, the Prince of the Apostles, and St. John the Evangelist offered on a similar occasion. When they were called upon to account for having preached the name of Jesus contrary to the command of the Jews, they replied: 'Decide for yourselves, whether it is right in the sight of God to hear you rather than God.' "

"Mr. Bullaker," Cauley interposed, "knowest thou not that it is written: 'Fear God and honor the king'?"

"In faith, I do know it; but I know, too," the martyr added, "that the same parliament which declared the priesthood treason, also established by law the episcopate, liturgy, and ecclesiastical offices and ceremonies, all of which you in the present parliament are undoing."

"What was wrongly ordered we are warranted to adjust."

"I certainly see you have tried and schemed to do so. But take my word for it, the very next parliament after this will reject and remodel the religion you are now striving to frame

---

[12] He refers to Apoc. 13:18, where the Evangelist portrays the antichrist.

and establish."

"That day thou wilt never live to see."

"Fully do I realize that the time of my dissolution is at hand; yet, what I have just foretold will come to pass."[13]

"A traitor! a traitor! Who are to be blamed for the present disturbances in England but thou and others like thee?"

"Would to God there were in this kingdom no other sort of traitors who will put it in more real and serious dangers. Of a truth, it matters little how many treasonable practices base calumny has laid to the charge of Catholics; I defy you to point out to me one case that has been proved against them."

Not daring to accept the challenge, they quickly retreated to safer ground.

"How old art thou," asked the judge, "and when didst thou receive holy orders?"

"There are a number of orders," the friar observed, "of which four are termed minor; then follow sub-deaconship, deaconship, and priesthood."

"We are speaking and inquiring about the last."

"That gentleman there, Mr. Cauley, knows my age better perhaps than I do."

"Thou are thirty-seven or thirty-eight years old."

"Deduct twenty-four, and the remainder will tell you how many years I've been a priest."

"How long hast thou been in England?"

"About twelve years."

"How many Franciscans are there in England."

"Think you I'm going to turn traitor to my brethren? Take it for granted, herein you shall never succeed. If I answer freely, to what concerns my own life, it is because I would have you know that I do not esteem my life more than myself. But in all that might injure others or imperil my brethren, I shall try to be extremely cautious."

---

[13] What he foretold came to pass in 1660, when the Puritan reign of terror ceased, and Charles II mounted the throne.

"My lords," broke in Wadsworth, "this man is so obstinate and so resolute in what pertains to his duty and office, that if you were to send him into exile by one port, he would not hesitate to come back by another."

"You are quite correct in your conjecture," replied the martyr with a smile.

After putting a few more questions, the court officials sent a written account of the proceedings to the chief justice and remanded the martyr to Newgate, to await his final trial and sentence.

When the general sessions opened, Fr. John Baptist was summoned before the judges. On entering the court, he blessed himself with the sign of the cross, saying in a loud voice: *By the sign of the cross deliver us from our enemies, O God!* Then the clerk ordered him to raise his hand, and having read the indictment, he asked:

"Guilty or not guilty?"

"If by *guilty* you mean a person that is harmful or criminal, I positively deny that I am guilty. I do not deny, however, that I am a priest."

"Sayest thou then thou are not guilty?"

"If the force and meaning of the term *not guilty* designates one wholly innocent of a crime, then I swear that I am not guilty. But, never shall I plead *not guilty* if you take it as a denial of my having been ordained priest; for I admit without reserve that I am a priest."

"Thou art a traitor! a traitor!"

"If besides such as I am, the kingdom harbored no other traitors, traitors who in very deed are enemies and subverted of their country, it would be now in a far better and happier condition than it is."

This bold rebuke struck home. For a moment there was deathlike silence, until someone broke the spell by calling him a seducer. At this, the martyr's countenance beamed with joy.

"Thou makest me exceedingly happy by bestowing upon me the same title that the Jews bestowed upon Christ. In sooth, thus was our Saviour once reproached by the Jews. There have always been priests in England. Saint Austin, the Apostle of England, was a priest; hither he was sent by the Sovereign Pontiff, Saint Gregory the Great. I too, am a priest, just as Saint Austin was."

"Thou hast come to this place not to preach, nor to insult and disgrace our laws, but to answer whether thou art guilty or not."

"I have never made myself guilty of a crime against my country or of a capital offence, and I shall never admit it. I do not deny, however, that I am a priest and that I was arrested while saying Mass. If you are trying to make me plead *not guilty* and thus gainsay my priesthood, you will never succeed; because I will never comply, even should I suffer a thousand deaths. At no time, will my conscience permit me to stoop so low as to admit that the priesthood is a crime. Of a truth, far from being a crime, it ought, I think, be held by all in high reverence and esteem."

"What, thou, miserable wretch, hast never sinned?"

"By your leave, this honorable assembly strains and misapplies the meaning of my words. Readily do I own that I am the greatest sinner on earth. What I maintained was that my being a priest or saying Mass does not make me guilty of a sin or crime. This is the sense in which my words were to be taken."

"Mr. Bullaker," ventured the registrar, "hast thou not time and again declared and confessed that thou art a priest? Now tell us, art thou guilty or not?"

"I consider myself innocent of a capital crime; that I am a priest, I readily grant."

"Art thou not aware that thou hast infringed the law and that according to the tenor of the law, thou art accused of treason?"

"The law that opposes and conflicts with the law of God, should be made light of, I imagine, seeing that I am annointed a priest of Christ, according to what the Royal Prophet, inspired by the Holy Spirit, foretold regarding priests, to wit: *Thou art a priest forever according to the order of Melchisedech.* But, forsooth, as you have set down the priesthood of Christ as treason, so logically you are apt to make the same provision regarding the faith in Christ Jesus himself."

"But such happens to be the law; and to violate the law is a sin against God, the author of all law."

"A very sound argument, indeed: it is the law, and to violate the law is a sin. Consequently, the Turks did right in passing a law that prohibits under pain of death the preaching of Christ or the promulgation of Christianity among them. Now, may I not from the form of your argument infer thus: therefore, whoever preaches the name of Christ among them is a traitor, inasmuch as he acts contrary to the law."

"If such were contrary to the law, it were indeed wrong to attempt it."

"Thou art a good partisan of Mohammed, my lord mayor, and a staunch defender of the Qur'an.[14] But, if such be the case, then we must conclude that the Apostles by preaching Christ contrary to the laws and edicts of the princes and emperors not only acted illegally, but actually committed sin, an assumption that offends pious ears."

"Thy reasoning is unsound; a distinction must be made between the Christian religion and the Catholic or papistical, between promulgating the former and promulgating the latter."

"As Saint Austin, the Apostle of our nation, came hither to convert the people, with the same intention and for the same purpose have I come hither, to convert the country to the true faith and to unite it to the Catholic Church."

"Ah, then perhaps thou art Saint Austin?"

"I am a priest of the same priestly order as Saint Austin, and for the conversion of the country have I been sent hither by the

---

[14] For obvious reasons, the martyr does not recount this apt and witty retort in his letter. Hope (p. 149) seems to have found it in the manuscript of De Marsys, who witnessed the trial.

same Apostolic See which supported and empowered him."

Not knowing what to reply, they laughed and again asked him whether he was guilty or not. The undaunted friar distinguished as before between the guilt of treason and the guilt of being a priest, denying the first but admitting the latter, if guilt it could be called. Then stepping forward with an air of bold defiance, he exclaimed:

"Whether the priesthood is a capital crime, Mr. registrar and thou, my lord mayor, I place before the tribunal of God, whose countenance beholds justice, and who will one day be our judge."

"We hope to do nothing that we can not render an account of," was the rejoinder.

"Never will I admit the priesthood to be a crime," repeated the martyr. "If it were such, then to be a priest were the same as being a traitor, and consequently every priest, inasmuch as he is a priest, is guilty of treason and must be put down as an enemy and betrayer of his country."

"And such, forsooth, he is; for to be a priest is contrary to the law."

"The parliament," he contended, "that enacted such a law against priests is far from being infallible, since it denies this prerogative to the universal Church of Christ, the pillar and ground of truth."[15]

Finally, realizing that they would never succeed in making their victim admit himself guilty of treason, they removed him from the bar and had him taken back to prison.

In the afternoon of the same day, Fr. John was again

---

[15] Here the martyr's account breaks off.—Lady Powel, we learn from De Marsys, freely admitted that she was a Catholic, and that she had harbored priests in her house. Eager to gain the crown of martyrdom, she steadfastly refused to renounce her faith. Hence, she was imprisoned and finally condemned to death. But, on the day set for her execution, when she was about to lie down on the hurdle, a messenger arrived from parliament with orders that she be taken back to prison and kept there till further notice. Shortly after, she was pardoned. See Stone, pp. 150 seq.; Hope, p. 150.

summoned to court. When told by the judge to acknowledge himself guilty of treason, he replied:

"This morning I proved my innocence; it is for thee now to acknowledge thyself guilty on account of the iniquitous sentence thou art about to pass. One day thou wilt have to give an account before the Judge of judges. Then every drop of blood thou art about to shed will rise up against thee, and death, far from being for thee, as it will be for thy victim, a passage to glory, will be an entrance to darkness and punishment that will last for all eternity."

"The punishment," laughed the impious judge, "matches its duration. But that's a long way off. Meanwhile I will pass upon thee a sentence which will send thee to pave the place with which thou dost threaten me."

"I hope in the mercy of God," declared the friar, "and I pray Him to grant a better lot even to my persecutors."[16]

Now the judge turned to the twelve jurymen and said:

"The prisoner is convicted of treason by his own confession. More evidence you need not. As to the rest, remember well your oath and duty to return a just verdict, having God in your mind."

After a brief deliberation, the jury unanimously declared that they were for referring the case to parliament, since the prisoner had sufficiently established his innocence. This angered the judge. Urging the friar's admission that he was a priest, he ignored the jury's verdict and sentenced the prisoner to death.

"According to the law," he said, "thou shalt return whence thou camest; thereupon, thou shalt be drawn on a hurdle to the place of execution, namely, to Tyburn, and put to death: thou shalt be hanged, cut down alive, disembowelled, and quartered."

At this, the friar fell on his knees, raised his eyes to heaven and intoned the *Te Deum*. Then rising, he thanked the assembly

---

[16] See Hope, p. 150.

and accompanied the guards back to Newgate.

Although the day for his execution had not been fixed, Fr. John realized that the long desired martyr's crown would soon be his. We can imagine how zealously he used his last days in prison to prepare himself for the final struggle. The time not spent in prayer and meditation he devoted to works of charity. The Capuchin friars, who had a convent near the royal palace, came to ask his prayers; they were living in great fear and anxiety, for the hatred of the Puritans had of late become more insolent and aggressive. Catholics from all parts of the city risked their own safety and visited him to ask his counsel and to obtain his priestly blessing. It was apparently during one of these visits that he was informed of the day appointed for his martyrdom.

"I thank thee heartily, my friend," he rejoined, smiling gently, "for these long desired and most happy tidings. Believe me, were it not for my utter lack of money, I should not let thee depart unrewarded; but thou shalt not be without compensation."

Great was the joy of his heart, when on Wednesday morning, October 16, the officers came and led him from prison. On passing out, he met Fr. Francis Bel, one of his confreres.[17]

"Brother," said the latter playfully, "I made profession before thee. Why takest thou precedence of me?"

"Such is the will of God," the martyr replied sweetly; "but thou wilt follow soon after me."

Since the day of his condemnation, it was observed, the sun had not shone over London. That morning, however, as if rejoicing over the friar's triumph, it burst forth in full splendor. With brutal violence, the officers thrust him upon the hurdle and tied him to it, with his face upward. The trip to Tyburn over the rough stony streets was attended by the usual sufferings and indignities. At last they came to the place of

---

[17] Mason, p. 178.

execution. Fr. John was unbound from the hurdle and brought to the scaffold. Far from trembling with fear at sight of the dreadful instruments of torture lying by, the martyr turned his eyes to heaven, knelt down, and prayed aloud. But he was soon interrupted by the sheriff, who asked him whether he had anything to say.

"Only this," came the calm reply, "I am greatly indebted to you and to my country for the very singular and unexpected favor I have received."

"What favor is it that so affects thee?"

"A favor of which I deem myself most unworthy, a favor for which I always yearned, but never dared to hope: to wit, to die in defence of the Catholic, Apostolic, and Roman faith. Yet, despite my unworthiness, the goodness of God has privileged me to prove my loyalty by the shedding of my blood."

Then, having mounted the ladder in compliance with the sheriff's orders, he turned to the assembled multitude and discoursed to them on the words of the Psalmist: *Thou art a priest forever according to the order of Melchisedech.* Fearing that he might mention the Real Presence in the Blessed Sacrament, one of the Protestant ministers interrupted him saying he was doing wrong in seducing the people with his false and pernicious doctrine. To this the martyr replied with sweet composure:

"Sir, patiently grant me leave to speak for the space of one brief hour. Thou art, indeed, a minister of the king of the English *(Anglorum),* but I am, though most unworthily, a minister of the King of Angels *(Angelorum).* Never had I a more sacred and exalted pulpit than the one I now occupy. Thou leavest no stone unturned to undo and pervert a simple and untutored people, blinded in dark ignorance. Let me then, I pray, owe thee this little favor, that at least from the scaffold I may extend a helping hand to them, and that my tongue may be unto them a plank by means of which they can escape shipwreck and destruction."

He had not yet finished his discourse, when the sheriff, who was listening with impatience and disgust, suddenly gave orders that the sentence of the court be carried out. While the executioners were making the final preparations, Fr. John raised his hands, as a sign to one of his brethren[18] in the throng, that he was prepared to receive absolution. Then, commending himself to the mercy of God, he was rudely thrust from the ladder, cut down while still alive, and subjected to the usual barbarities. Seizing his heart, the brutal executioner held it up to the frenzied multitude. "Behold the heart of a traitor!" he exclaimed and threw it into the fire. Having beheaded and quartered the body, they exposed the parts to public view, the head on London Bridge and the quarters on four gates of the city.[19] "But," concludes Mason, "the fetters, as it were, being broken, his most holy soul, freed from its narrow prison and escorted by a host of angels, winged its flight to heaven, where decorated with the victor's palm in token of his triumph, it exults in enduring peace, in undisturbed rest, and in the splendor of never-ending glory."[20]

---

[18] Very likely, it was Ven. Francis Bel.

[19] We are told that the afore-mentioned Franciscan rescued the martyr's heart from the flames. Other relics were either snatched from the fire or bought from the executioner by the servants of Count Egmont, who was present and later drew up a formal statement establishing the authenticity of the relics. The Franciscan nuns of the Convent of Our Lady of Dolors at Taunton have a forearm of the martyr, a corporal which was dipped in his blood, and another which he used at Mass on the morning of his arrest. See Hope, pp. 154 seq.

[20] His name appears on the list of December 4, 1887. He is likewise reckoned among the companions of Venerable Francis (Arthur) Bel, whose cause of beatification was again taken up in 1900. See Ortolani, *De Causis Beatorum et Servorum Dei Ordinis Minorum*, p. 14.

CHAPTER V
VENERABLE PAUL HEATH, O.F.M.

Of Protestant parentage—Student at Cambridge—Religious doubts—Conversion—Enters the Franciscan Order at Douai—Novitiate and years of study—Esteemed by the brethren—The scholar—The priest—The religious—Eager to join the English missionaries—Permission finally granted—Arrives in London—In Compter prison—Before the mayor and the commissioners of parliament—In Newgate—Before the judges—Sentenced to death—Martyred at Tyburn.

BOUT six weeks had elapsed since the martyrdom of Venerable John Baptist Bullaker, when a fellow friar of his, no less distinguished for sanctity than for learning, set out for the English missions, in the hope of gaining the martyr's crown. The story of his conversion from Protestantism, of his career in the Franciscan Order, and of his martyrdom for the faith, forms perhaps the fairest episode in the history of the Second English Province.

Venerable Paul Heath, the son of a Protestant family in Peterborough, Northamptonshire, received at his christening, on December 16, 1599, the name Henry. He was an unusually gifted child, and from early boyhood manifested an insatiable fondness for books. To give him the advantages of a liberal education, his parents sent him at the age of eighteen to the university of Cambridge. He matriculated at Corpus Christi College, where on account of his engaging manners and extraordinary diligence he soon won the esteem of his professors and associates. From one of his fellow students, who later became a Catholic and a Jesuit, we learn how earnestly Henry Heath devoted himself to his studies, how eagerly he sought the company of such as cared more for books than for pleasure, and how, even as a Protestant, he showed a decided aptitude and inclination for the life he was one day to embrace.

Serious doubts regarding the faith in which he had been reared began to trouble his mind; and the farther he advanced in his studies, the graver became his religious misgivings. Not less prudent than sincere, however, he kept the matter a close secret from all except a few intimate friends, who presently joined him in his search for the truth. Thus four years elapsed, when the authorities conferred on him the degree of bachelor of arts and placed him in charge of the college library. This appointment gave him an opportunity to delve into the rich mine of Catholic literature, largely the spoils of the confiscated monasteries.

At this time, no religious controversialist was more extolled in the Protestant circles at Cambridge than William Whitaker, a former master of the university. With absorbing interest, young Heath read and studied the canon's attack on Cardinal Bellarmine, who had openly questioned the literary honesty of the Protestant divine. Consulting the original sources to which the disputants referred, Henry noticed how accurately the learned Cardinal quoted his authorities, and how his less scrupulous adversary misquoted and misconstrued passages in order to buttress his theses. This roused the young man's suspicion and indignation. Night and day, he busied himself with the teaching of the Catholic Church and soon perceived how utterly untenable Protestantism was on logical and historical grounds. Meanwhile, the grace of God enlightened and strengthened him, so that after the lapse of about a year Henry was determined to embrace the old faith. It was probably through the imprudence or malice of a fellow student that the affair at last came to the notice of the university heads. Knowing what an influence he exerted over his associates, the authorities threatened him with imprisonment and expulsion. This only served to confirm the young man in his convictions.

He secretly left Cambridge and proceeded to London.[1]

Here, in the hotbed of Puritanism, Henry's constancy was put to a severe test.[2] He sought to interest the Spanish ambassador in his behalf; but in vain. Still more disheartening was his experience with Mr. George Jerningham, a well-known Catholic nobleman, who took him for a spy and sent him packing with bitter reproach.[3] Altogether at a loss how to prove his sincerity, Henry began to seek the aid of the Blessed Virgin, promising eventually to dedicate himself entirely to her service. The next time he met Mr. Jerningham, the nobleman's attitude was wholly changed. Through him he became acquainted with Rev. George Muscot, who after due preparation received him into the Church. Thereupon, provided with a letter of recommendation from the Spanish ambassador, he departed for the English College at Douai.

Henry Heath had been at the college but a short time, when two Franciscans from the neighboring friary came there. Their

---

[1] Mason, *Certamen Seraphicum*, pp. 73-146. The author drew the above facts regarding the university career of Fr. Heath from a letter which F. John Spencer, S. J., wrote on May 23, 1643, about a month after the martyr's death, declaring that he was an eye-witness of what he recounts. See Mason, p. 74.—Four of the martyr's friends likewise converted to the Catholic faith and embraced the religious state, one, apparently the above-mentioned F. Spencer, joining the Jesuit Order, and three becoming Franciscans. The names of the latter are not known. See Hope, *Franciscan Martyrs in England*, p. 157; Gaudentius, *Bedeutung und Verdienste des Franziskanerordens im Kampfe gegen den Protestantismus*, p. 176; Stone, *Faithful Unto Death*, p. 156.

[2] The subsequent facts concerning Fr. Paul's conversion and later career are vouched for by Mason, who for at least ten years shared the same roof with the martyr and hence had ample opportunity to observe his private and public life.

[3] In extenuation of the ambassador's and the nobleman's behavior, we must bear in mind that at the time government spies infested the country. With devilish cunning they frequently ingratiated themselves into Catholic households, in order to ferret out the names and hiding places of priests and of such as harbored them. An instance of this kind is related by Stone (p. 157), where a certain Beard repaid the hospitality of unwary Catholics by denouncing them to the authorities.

modest and mortified demeanor caught the fancy of the young convert, and he conceived an ardent desire to join their ranks. But his father confessor, whose advice he had sought, dissuaded him on the grounds that such a life would prove too difficult for him who had only recently embraced the true faith. But Henry had no peace. Again he began to pray to the Blessed Virgin, and again he experienced her aid. It was probably in May, 1624, that the superior of St. Bonaventure's, Fr. Jerome Pickford,[4] invested him with the habit of St. Francis and gave him the name Paul of St. Magdalene.

"I am scarcely able to relate," writes Mason, "what a saintly and angelic life he led in the seraphic lyceum. Indeed, the virtues that others acquire only in part and by degree, were united in him and sprang up all at once; both in the beginning of his conversion and in the novitiate, no one was more austere than he in self-abnegation and self-discipline, no one more conspicuous for contempt of the world, no one more assiduous in prayer, more perfect in renouncing his own will, more fervent in the love of God and of heavenly things." Having completed the year of probation, Fr. Paul was admitted to profession by Fr. George Perrot who was governing the friary in the absence of the superior.[5] The next three years, he studied theology under the direction of Fr. Francis Davenport, whereupon, in 1628, he was ordained priest.

The important offices which were subsequently entrusted to him show how highly the superiors esteemed the young priest's virtue and learning. The first chapter of the English province, held in 1630, appointed him vicar of Douai, professor of moral theology, and spiritual director of the student clerics.

---

[4] Fr. Bonaventure Jackson had, indeed, been appointed guardian of Douai in 1624; but we know, too, that he was called the same year to the mission in England.

[5] He was "governing the friary," says Mason (p. 80), "in the absence of the preses" (namely, Fr. Francis Davenport), who had been sent to Rome to plead the cause of the newly-founded English custody at the general chapter held on Pentecost, 1625.

Two years later, he succeeded Fr. Francis Bel[6] as guardian of the friary. In the same year, after the death of Fr. William of St. Augustine, he was appointed head professor of dogmatic theology. The provincial chapter of 1637 again elected him guardian, at the same time entrusting him with the responsible offices of custos and provincial commissary. All these offices, we are told, Fr. Paul discharged with great fidelity, although he deemed himself unfit and unworthy to be placed over others. The Flemish Franciscan, Fr. Peter Marchant, who presided at the chapter of 1637 and who was intimately acquainted with the members of the English province, informs us that Fr. Paul was "a mirror of meekness, integrity, and sincerity, a beacon light of holiness, a model of religious observance among the brethren, and in the science of theology a shining and glowing star among the luminaries of the Douai University."

Even before his ordination, Fr. Paul evinced a remarkable aptitude for the sacred sciences. With a penetrating intellect, retentive memory, and acute judgment he combined untiring zeal and energy. One day, Dr. Poletius, then *regius professor* at the local university, attended a public disputation which the clerics had prepared at the friary. The manner in which Fr. Paul defended his thesis won unstinted applause from the learned divine. "I will say candidly," he remarked later, "that never in my life did I hear a theologian defend his thesis in a more learned and skillful manner."

No wonder that after his ordination Fr. Paul was permitted to devote himself principally to teaching and writing. In order to deepen his knowledge of theology and better to qualify himself for the sacred duties imposed upon him, he carefully studied the writings of Holy Scripture and of the Holy Fathers, the decisions of the Councils, and the history of the Church written by Baronius. In speculative theology, he was an ardent and efficient expounder of Bl. John Duns Scotus, the founder of

---

[6] Fr. Bel had been commissioned by the general chapter to restore the Franciscan province in Scotland.

the Franciscan school. His lucid exposition and sound vindication of the Scotistic doctrine was the frequent topic of comment not only among his brethren but also among the professors and students of the neighboring university. His writings, of which Mason adduces thirty titles, embrace every branch of higher learning, philosophy, dogmatic and moral theology, canon law, ascetics, and history. A number of them are of a controversial character, directed against the English Protestants of his day. How valuable his services were to the province, we may judge from the fact that his superiors found it expedient to refuse him permission to leave for the English missions, because, as they averred, the welfare of the province demanded his services as teacher of the clerics.

Despite the manifold cares as superior and professor, Fr. Paul found ample time to discharge the various functions of his religious and priestly calling. In 1635, when the Franciscan Sisters settled at Nieuport, he became their extraordinary confessor. At the same time, he heard confessions at the convent of the Poor Clares at Aire. Like a true son of St. Francis, he cherished a singular love for the sick and needy. When he heard of families in distress, he would visit them and even beg alms with which to relieve their wants. In him the lowly and unlettered found a trusty friend, ever ready to instruct and advise them in the way of salvation. Sinners and heretics seemed to be the special objects of his priestly zeal. No way was too far, no weather too inclement, no other concern too pressing, no sacrifice too great, where the salvation of an erring soul was at stake. For their conversion he offered up his prayers and fasts and in the end won them over to Christ not so much by learned discussion as by the engaging humility and modesty of his demeanor. His success in this respect must have been extraordinary. Mason remarks that he could recount many instances of conversions wrought through the labors and prayers of Fr. Paul, but that he refrained from doing so, because the persons concerned were still among the living.

A fair glimpse into the inner life of this holy man is afforded us by his *Soliloquies or Documents of Christian Perfection*,[7] an ascetical treatise similar to the *Imitation of Christ* of Thomas à Kempis. His so-called "Daily Exercise,"[8] a sort of rule of life to which he obliged himself, shows how earnestly the saintly friar endeavored to guard against worldly principles and allurements and to make constant progress in holiness. Among these exercises or resolutions, a number are significant: daily to make a hundred aspirations of love to Jesus; constantly to mortify the eyes, the tongue, the passions, and the affections; to bear patiently with the shortcomings of others; to be fully resigned in time of discomfort and want; to seek only God and his service; to disregard the love and esteem of men; to refrain from all needless and protracted conversation with others; to perform all things in the spirit of obedience; in particular, to observe the following rules: (1) to renounce all right and authority over everything whatsoever, even over my good name and personal convenience, and willingly to suffer myself to be despoiled of all things for God's sake; (2) to offer myself as a servant to every creature and to do all possible good, expecting in return only crosses and afflictions; (3) to live as entirely dead to the defects of others, in order that I may continually lament my own defects.

Prayer and mortification constitute the fountain whence the saints of God draw light and strength for their exterior activity. Like the Seraph of Assisi, Fr. Paul was a great lover of prayer. Though the provincial constitutions exempted him from choir duty, he deemed it a privilege and an obligation to chant the divine office in common with the brethren. Many a time, after the others had finished the midnight chant and meditation and had retired to their rooms for a brief rest, he would pass the

---

[7] A third edition of these *Soliloquies,* together with a brief life sketch of Fr. Heath, was published in 1892 by the Franciscans of St. Bonaventure's College, Quaracchi, Italy.

[8] Contained in the *Vita Auctoris* prefacing the third edition of the Soliloquies.

remainder of the night in prayer and contemplation before the Blessed Sacrament. Especially dear to him was the Franciscan custom of praying with arms extended in the form of a cross. To encourage his brethren in the practice of this form of prayer, he used to tell them what singular favors he had obtained through it from God. Mason says that he often heard the saintly friar relate the following incident. A contagious disease had broken out in the community. Several friars had already died of it, and a number were dangerously ill. When Fr. Paul, who apparently was guardian at the time, felt the sickness coming on him, he went to the church and with his arms extended spent half an hour in prayer. Finally, overcome by fatigue, he dropped his arms and rose to his feet, only to find that the symptoms of the disease had entirely left him.

No less remarkable was his devotion to the Mother of God. To her intercession he ascribed his conversion to the true faith. He carefully carried out the promise he had made of entirely dedicating himself to her service. As a constant reminder of this pledge, he wore a little chain on his arm, which he never removed. Like Bl. John Duns Scotus, he was an ardent champion of her Immaculate Conception, defending and extolling this prerogative of Mary whenever an opportunity offered itself. In all difficulties, trials and temptations, he had recourse to Mary, his Mother, and constantly exhorted others to do likewise. It was to her that he took refuge when everybody and everything seemed to stand in the way of his joining the missionary friars in England. Shortly before his departure for England, he wrote a beautiful letter, or rather prayer, to his heavenly Queen.[9] In this letter, he again pledges her undying love and fidelity and thanks her for all the benefits he has till then received through her, recounting above all how she has helped him find the true faith and how she has obtained the same grace for his father, who at the time was a man of eighty years and was living as lay brother in the

---

[9] For a copy of this letter see Mason, pp. 103-109.

community at Douai.

On the subject of Fr. Paul's spirit of mortification, his biographer becomes quite eloquent. "Why," he asks, "should I mention those bodily penances, abstinences, and fasts which the Rule and the Statutes of the Order prescribed and which Fr. Paul observed so scrupulously that he looked on the least remissness in this regard as a serious matter?" To these austerities he was wont to add many more of his own choice. His bed was not the customary strawsack, but the floor, where without removing his habit he took a few hours of sleep. For years he was accustomed to fast on bread and thin broth, two or three days of every week. Next to the skin he constantly wore a hairshirt and an iron chain about the waist, and often disciplined himself even to blood. So great was his love of poverty and self-denial that he always reserved the shabbiest habit and the dingiest room for himself. Despite his learning and sanctity, he thought so little of himself that Mason can not help remarking how condescending and considerate he was in his dealings with the brethren over whom he was placed. Thus, in the solitude of the friary at Douai, did the man of God prepare himself for the supreme sacrifice of his life.

In 1641, it was learned at Douai that the persecutions had again broken out in England, and that seven priests were in prison awaiting execution. No one in the Franciscan convent was more affected by these sad tidings than Fr. Paul, especially since among the condemned priests was his former fellow novice and friend Fr. Christopher Colman. This is evident from the letter which he wrote to Fr. Colman on hearing of his imprisonment and impending martyrdom.

> To his eminently honored and ever beloved friends, the illustrious Colman and companions, Greetings.
>
> O most estimable men, most noble friends, most excellent champions of Jesus Christ! Your bodies are temples of the Holy Ghost, your souls are a celestial paradise, your blood is more precious than all the morning and evening sacrifices of Aaron

and all his sons. Alas! how great is my misfortune not to be permitted to come to you, in order to share your bondage and offer myself as a sacrifice with that burning love for Christ which has made you so steadfast in your trials, so triumphant over human threats, so resplendent with all gems of virtue that Solomon in all his pomp was not so glorious as you are. O loving Jesus, what crime have I committed that I am not allowed to share your fate? Since there is nothing I desire more in this life, nothing in very deed can satisfy me so long as I am separated from you. Humbly, therefore, I beseech you to pray for me, that I may come to you and never be severed from you.

Your unworthy servant,
P. Magdalene.[10]

As the days wore on, he was so carried away by the desire for martyrdom that he finally addressed a letter to the provincial, Fr. George Perrot, asking leave to come to England. He wrote in part:

Neither new nor singular is this my petition, but only what stones and plants and other insensible creatures strive after, inasmuch as all things by a spontaneous and innate force incline toward the center and end for which they have been created. You will not, I think, deem that soldier brave and magnanimous who, learning that the army of his general is drawn up on the field of battle, and that his fellow soldiers with drums and trumpets and other instruments of warfare are clamoring for a charge with the enemy, yet indulges himself in base sluggishness at home. It is true, I am unfit (I do not deny it) and altogether unworthy to discharge the office of an apostle and to contemplate encountering injury and reproach for the name of Jesus, but power is made perfect in infirmity, since God has chosen the foolish to confound the wise. Of this, too, I am convinced, that the obligation to serve Jesus Christ is as well incumbent on me as on

---

[10] Mason had an autograph copy of this letter. Referring to the salutation and subscription, he reminds the reader that their unusual and inappropriate form was owing to the religious troubles in England, where letters addressed to priests were often intercepted and confiscated by the heretics (p. 113).

others, and that I am certainly not less bound to suffer for him. May the most loving Lord inspire you with a speedy consent.

The provincial was deeply moved by this solemn appeal. But there was just then a dearth of superiors and teachers for the Douai friary. Of this he reminded Fr. Paul, promising, however, to summon him to the missions in good time. Impatiently the man of God waited for the call; but when it was not forthcoming, he finally approached the commissary provincial, Fr. Angelus Mason, fell on his knees before him, and amid a flood of tears disclosed the anxiety and grief that tortured his soul. The commissary, however, though hardly able to refrain from weeping, was loath to anticipate the decision of the provincial. Now the saintly friar had recourse to Mary, the Queen of Martyrs. In his childlike simplicity, he composed a beautiful letter to his heavenly Mother, asking her to intercede in his behalf as she had so often done before. With due permission, he undertook a pilgrimage to the shrine of Our Lady of Montague in Brabant. Passing through Ghent, he visited the commissary general, Fr. Peter Marchant, and opened his heart to him. But his pleading was again in vain, and confident that Mary would not forsake him, he continued his journey to Montague. On his way home, he once more sought out the commissary general, who at last felt himself constrained to grant the friar's request. "I opposed him," the commissary wrote later, "I tested his spirit, but his zeal ran too high, and I finally supplied him with an obedience under the condition that his immediate superior would subjoin his approval." Armed with this, the man of God hastened back to Douai and reported his success to Fr. Angelus Mason, who thereupon also granted the necessary permission, "calling God to witness," as we read in his *Certamen Seraphicum*, "that he was impelled by some hidden force to give his consent."

From that moment, Fr. Paul was a changed man. Naturally of a severe and somber aspect, his every look, word, and act henceforth reflected the joy and peace that reigned in his heart.

He seemed already in possession of heavenly bliss when he spoke of the glory of martyrdom, or when at the altar he offered up the august Sacrifice. Without delay, he made arrangements for his departure. Holy zeal for the strict observance of the Franciscan Rule prompted him to refuse the secular dress and the traveling money which the guardian offered him. It was a cold day in December, 1642, when he bade farewell to his brethren and set out for Dunkirk. Here again he refused to take money, but asked the guardian to have a sailor's suit made of his habit. Thus strangely attired, he boarded a ship for Dover. During the voyage he made friends with a German nobleman, who perceiving his destitute condition, paid his expenses, and on landing at Dover offered him money for his journey and subsequent stay in London. But refusing to accept any further assistance, the friar thanked the nobleman for his kindness, and despite the inclemency of the weather, set out to travel the forty miles on foot.

Night was setting in, when he reached the metropolis.[11] Not knowing whither to turn for food and lodging, he finally about eight o'clock ventured into a tavern near the bridge. But the innkeeper finding him without money turned him out into the cheerless night. Overcome with hunger and fatigue he sat down on a doorstep and reflected how to get information regarding Fr. Colman and others for whom he had letters. Here the master of the house found him, and startled by his strange appearance, sent for the constable. When the latter arrived with

---

[11] The following details regarding Fr. Paul's arrest and trials are founded on his own narrative in English, which was preserved in the friary at Douai and translated into Latin by Mason (pp. 119-123).—London was at the time in the hands of the parliamentarians. Their ultimate ascendancy in power and the late encounters between their army and that of the king proved but new incentives for them to take bloody reprisals on the Catholics, who were known as having espoused the King's cause. Several priests had recently been executed, among whom were Venerable William Ward and Venerable John Baptist Bullaker. On the very day of Fr. Paul's arrival in London, the Capuchins had been dragged from their convent near the royal palace and thrown into prison. See Hope, p. 176.

his assistants, he subjected the holy man to a strict examination. On searching him they discovered certain writings which he had sewed into his hat before leaving Dunkirk. These roused their suspicion; they arrested him and confined him for the night in the Compter prison.

The next morning, he was brought before the mayor. Not knowing that he was a priest, they told him that under pain of life imprisonment he would be required to take the oaths of supremacy and of allegiance. On hearing this, Fr. Paul resolved to disclose his priestly character when the time should come, and silently prayed to God for constancy. All looked askance at him when he entered the courtroom.

"Whose papers are those that were found on thy person?" inquired the mayor, eyeing him closely.[12]

"They are mine," replied the friar.

"What is their import?"

"I wrote them for thy government and parliament, in order that through them I might render an account of my faith, should I perchance be arrested in these perilous times."

"Why camest thou to England?"

"I came to save souls, just as Christ Himself for the salvation of souls came down from heaven and sent out His Apostles, with the command, *Going therefore, teach ye all nations; baptizing—*"

"Thou art a traitor!" interrupted the mayor.

"Then also Christ and His Apostles were traitors, because they, too, preached contrary to the laws of the infidels and heretics; wherefore, we must not abandon God for the sake of men, but obey God rather than men."

"Art thou a priest?" inquired the mayor, growing suspicious.

"The priesthood instituted by Christ is something honorable," the friar returned; "for Christ Himself, a priest, according to the order of Melchisedech, ordained His Apostles priests at the last supper and commanded them to consecrate

---

[12] The dialogue form is ours, based on the martyr's narrative.

His sacred body; elsewhere saying, *Receive ye the Holy Ghost. Whose sins you shall forgive, they are forgiven them; and whose sins you shall retain, they are retained.* Though unworthy of so great an honor, yet say I in reply to your question, I am a priest."

"Thou are not a priest according to the order of Melchisedech," objected a Protestant minister, "because thou art of the Order of St. Francis."[13]

"Indeed, sir," rejoined the friar, "by those words thou displayest thy ignorance. For the order of St. Francis is an order of religion, professing to follow the example of Jesus Christ; whilst the order of priesthood is an order of consecration for the purpose of consecrating the body and blood of Christ in the Blessed Sacrament. They, therefore, that receive the order of consecration are priests according to the order of Melchisedech, whether they be Franciscans or members of any other Institute."

"Why goest thou about in so poor and mean a dress?" at length broke in the mayor.

"Indeed, to be poor for Christ is to be rich; even Christ made Himself poor for our sake, and the Apostles of Christ following in His footsteps, forsook all."

This brought the hearing to an end. On leaving the courtroom, Fr. Paul said in a tone of sweet composure, "I find consolation in the example of the Apostles, *who went from the presence of the council, rejoicing that they were accounted worthy to suffer reproach for the name of Jesus.*" Since he had confessed himself a priest, he was conducted to Newgate and placed with criminals already condemned to death.

Some time later, he was summoned to appear before the commissioners of parliament. Here again he openly proclaimed and fearlessly defended his priestly character. When asked why he had come to England, he answered:

---

[13] They had learned that he was a Franciscan from the writings found in his hat.

"I came to free souls from the slavery of the devil and to convert them from heresy."

"From which heresy?" his enemies insisted.

"From the Protestant, Puritan, Brownist, Anabaptist, and many others; for as many as profess these are justly termed heretics."

According to De Marsys who was present at the trial, he steadfastly refused to reveal the names of those who had given him pecuniary assistance, and answered their various objections with such a display of learning and alertness as to elicit the admiration of the bystanders.[14]

During his confinement in Newgate, he penned the following letter to a priest:

> Very Reverend Father: Your consolations have filled my soul with joy. The judges have not yet passed sentence. I beseech the divine mercy, that it may turn out as I desire, to suffer death for my Lord Jesus Christ. Alas! Father, what else can I wish than to suffer with Christ, to be rejected with Christ, to be crucified with Christ, to encounter a thousand deaths in order to live forever with Christ? For, if it is a soldier's boast to be like unto his lord, far be it from me to glory in aught save in the cross of the Crucified. Let them come, therefore, let the executioners come, let them tear my body into bits, let them gnaw away my flesh with their teeth, let them pierce my sides and grind me to dust. For I am fully aware and I know for certain, how much it profiteth me to die for Christ. This momentary suffering secures the eternal measure of celestial glory. Reverend Father, pray for me, a miserable sinner, who in the wounds of the Crucified will ever be, until death is swallowed up by victory,
>
> Your Reverence's most devoted
> Fr. Paul of Saint Magdalene.

At the opening of the assizes, on April 11, the valiant champion was summoned for the final hearing. After the

---

[14] Hope, p. 180.

prescribed court formalities were gone through, he began to deliver an apology[15] which he had prepared for the occasion.

"Most noble lords," he said, "I deem myself fortunate in being permitted to propose and defend the justice of my cause before so venerable an assembly. At one time, to be candid, up to my twenty-fourth year, I was a Protestant, professing the same heresy that you now profess, but to quote Job, *let the day perish wherein I was born, and the night in which it was said: a man-child is conceived.* In like manner can I denounce and execrate the day on which I began to imbibe the Protestant superstition."

"Stop him instantly," exclaimed the judge, "or a padlock shall be put on his mouth. Evidently his sole purpose is to cast slurs and abuses on our religion; therefore, let him eschew all digression and reply directly to the accusation."

At this, the saintly friar again openly declared his priesthood, maintaining that the laws condemning priests were tyrannical and unchristian.

"Art thou guilty or not guilty?" they insisted.

"If the term *guilty* implies a crime, then I am not guilty; but if it involves what I have already confessed, then I am guilty."

"Art thou not a dead man?" suggested one of the bystanders.

"To die for Christ is the greatest glory," came the quick reply.

Without further ado, the judge condemned him to death. At this, the friar's face beamed with joy.

"I thank the most august assembly," he said, making a low bow, "for the singular honor bestowed upon me."[16]

In Newgate, Fr. Paul devoted much of his time to the spiritual comfort of his fellow prisoners and of the Catholics

---

[15] For a Latin version of this apology see Mason, pp. 126-138. The author observes (p. 126) that the martyr delivered the entire oration either in the court room after sentence of death had been pronounced or on the scaffold shortly before his execution.

[16] Here the martyr's narrative ends.

who flocked to him from all parts of the city. Many came to have him bless the cord with which they girded themselves in honor of St. Francis; others brought holy pictures and asked him to put his signature to them. More than five hundred persons, we are told, received the sacrament of Confession at his hands. Forty Protestant ministers, Mason relates, disputed with the prisoner on matters of faith. So completely did he expose the fallacy of Protestantism that afterwards, in the presence of the Spanish ambassador, many acknowledged their defeat and openly bewailed the sad lot of so learned and accomplished a man. The valiant friar, however, gloried in the assurance of soon winning that crown for which he had yearned so many years. When asked how he could be so happy with death staring him in the face, he replied, "I never doubted that my most merciful God would grant a special sweetness to those who lay down their life for justice and in defense of the faith, but never could I have conceived it to be so excessive as that which I now experience, and which so overwhelms and melts my soul that I can hardly bear it."[17]

How he must have rejoiced when at last it was told him that on the following Monday, April 27, he would be executed at Tyburn.[18] The little time he could spare from his charitable ministrations was spent in prayer and meditation. On the morning of the appointed day, he placed his signature to the following protestation:

> I, the undersigned, prepared through the grace and favor of my sweetest Jesus to offer my life today in defense of His holy law and of the Roman Catholic Church, and to render unto Him the most excellent homage I can conceive, next to the winning of

---

[17] Stone, p. 173. See also Gaudentius, who quotes Challoner, p. 179.

[18] Most authors and also the *Franciscan Martyrology* of Fr. Arturus assign April 17 as the day on which Fr. Paul suffered martyrdom. In this, they follow the Old Style of reckoning. From the martyr himself, who adopts the New Style, we learn that it was April 27. In either case, however, April 27 (N. S.) and April 17 (O. S.) was a Monday in 1643.

souls, do hereby with my whole heart declare unto all, but especially unto Catholics whom it more concerns, that the so-called oath of allegiance can not and ought not, with any restrictions or interpretations, be taken by them in its proposed form, without incurring grevious sin and the certain ruin of their souls, unless they repent. In defense of this I would lay down my life[19] just as readily as I would for any other article of, or for our entire, holy faith. I am fully convinced that I should not die righteously, were I to hold any other doctrine or opinion regarding that oath. In testimony whereof, now about to give my life for the cause of God, I subscribe with my own hand and name, in Newgate, Monday, April 27, 1643.

Thus I hold, Fr. Paul of St. Magdalene, now destined for the scaffold.[20]

This solemn declaration of faith the man of God read aloud on his way through prison. When the guards led him to the hurdle, he asked to be tied to the horses' tails and in this way dragged to the place of execution. But they ignored his request and having bound him to his bed of pain dashed off over the rough roads to Tyburn.

On reaching the place of execution, Fr. Paul was released

---

[19] It must be borne in mind that Venerable Heath suffered death not so much for refusing to take the prescribed oath, but primarily for being a priest and having come to England in defiance of the existing laws.

[20] Following is the attestation which shortly after, on May 8 (N. S.), three Jesuits drew up and together with the protestation presented to the Franciscans at Douai:

We, the undersigned, do testify that the reverend father and already glorious martyr, Father Paul of St. Magdalene, of the Order of St. Francis, called in the world Henry Heath, read the above protestation or resolution carefully, and that he wished to add the subscribed words to what he had read, in order to express himself more definitely regarding the injustice of that oath, and that he then said: With all my heart I affix my hand to this paper and am ready to sign it a thousand times with my blood. In testimony whereof, we, the undersigned, have placed our signature. On this, the 28th day of April, old style, 1643.

Thomas Harvey,
Simon de Mazaron,
William Jordan.

from the hurdle and commanded to mount the cart that was standing below the gallows. He obeyed, praying with a loud voice: *Into Thy hands, O Lord, I commend my spirit.* Then the rope was placed about his neck, and he was given leave to address the assembled multitude. He told the people that he had come to England in the hope of dying for the defense and propagation of the Roman Catholic Faith, and for this faith as well as for his priestly character was he now on the point of shedding his blood. Here, however, the Protestant ministers interrupted him, saying that he had been sentenced to death not on account of his faith, but because he was a seducer of the people.

"With no more right can I be called a seducer," returned the fearless martyr, "than my Lord Jesus Christ was called a seducer by the Jews."

Nettled by this bold retort, they ordered him to be silent. Thereupon, he asked leave of the sheriff to die like his divine Savior, stripped of his outer garments, assuring him that he had made such preparations of clothing as decency would demand. Instead of an answer, the sheriff told him to prepare for death. Raising his eyes to heaven, he remained motionless in prayer for about half an hour. Suddenly remembering that it was the feast of the Martyr-Pope, St. Anicetus, he intoned the hymn,

> Martyr of God, who following
> The instance of God's only Son,
> Hast triumphed o'er thy enemies,
> And triumphing hast heaven won.

Having recited the hymn to the end, he raised his hands, thereby signifying to a priest in the crowd that he was prepared to receive the last absolution. This same grace, the martyr himself imparted to one of the criminals who also was about to die, and who touched with contrition at sight of the saintly priest had asked to be reconciled with God.

At last, the executioners advanced to carry out the sentence.

While they were making the final preparations, Fr. Paul repeatedly invoked the names of Jesus and Mary, concluding, "O Jesus, forgive me my sins! Jesus, convert England! Jesus, have mercy on this country! O England, be converted to the Lord thy God!" Then, with a sudden jolt the cart was drawn from under his feet and the holy man hung suspended beneath the gallows. A brief struggle, and his soul passed to the mansions of eternal bliss. By a singular exception, he was not cut down until death had set in, whereupon the executioners proceeded to perform their bloody task. The head was placed on London Bridge, while the quarters were exposed on four gates of the city.[21] At the moment of Fr. Paul's death, tradition says, his aged father, who was still living as lay brother at Douai, saw a brilliant light ascending into heaven and turning to some of the brethren told them that his son had just then died for the faith. They believed in the truth of this vision when a few days later the news of his martyrdom arrived.[22]

In the *Franciscan Martyrology* of Fr. Arturus of Muenster, Venerable Paul Heath is commemorated on April 14, in these terms: "At London in England, B. Paul of St. Magdalene, Martyr, who shed his blood in defense of the Catholic faith."[23]

---

[21] Count Egmont was present at the execution and had his servants gather a number of the martyr's relics. The Franciscan nuns at Taunton treasure a piece of the rope with which Venerable Heath was hung, a bone about three inches long, and a corporal dipped in his blood. See Stone, p. 176.

[22] Thaddeus, p. 250. See also Hope, p. 186, and Gaudentius, p. 180, on the authority of Challoner. Mason does not mention this apparition, probably because the martyr's father was still living in 1649, the year when the *Certamen Seraphicum* was published. The venerable old lay brother died on December 29, 1652, at Douai.

[23] His name is on the list of the English martyrs, contained in the *Acta Minorum* (Vol. VI, p. 49 seq.). He is also among the companions of Venerable Francis Bel, whose cause of beatification received a new impulse in 1900. See Ortolani, *De Causis Beatorum et Servorum Dei Ordinis Minorum*, p. 14.

CHAPTER VI
VENERABLE FRANCIS BEL, O.F.M.

Of wealthy Catholic parents—Student at Saint-Omer and at Valladolid—Ordained priest—Seeks admission into the Franciscan Order—Novitiate and profession—Summoned to the English Province—Priestly zeal in Flanders—Provincial of Scotland—Missionary in England—His character—Arrested as royal spy—Suspected of being a priest—Conveyed to London for trial—Before the commissioners of parliament—In Newgate—His trial—Guilty of treason—Condemned to death—Last days in Newgate—Drawn to Tyburn—Martyrdom.

BOUT six miles from Worcester, in the parish of Hanbury, stood a beautiful residence, styled the Manor House of Temple-Broughton.[1] Here was born, on January 13, 1590, Venerable Francis Bel.[2] Though belonging to the wealthy class, his parents were widely known as staunch and practical Catholics. His mother, of an ancient family by the name of Daniel, is praised by Mason as a virtuous and accomplished woman. From her it was especially that Arthur, as the future martyr had been named in Baptism, acquired those habits of piety and refinement that characterized his later career.

After the death of his father, in 1598, Arthur remained till his thirteenth year with his mother, who meanwhile entrusted to private tutors his elementary education. Thereupon, she sent him to Acton Place in Suffolk, to join his two cousins in their

---

[1] Unless otherwise stated, our narrative is based on Mason, *Certamen Seraphicum*, pp. 147-181. The author's sources of information were the martyr's own account of his arrest and trial, and a life of the martyr written by Du Bosque, who was an eye-witness of what he relates (Mason, p. 180).

[2] We adopt this spelling of the friar's name in conformity with his own signature to a letter still preserved by the Franciscan Sisters at Taunton. Stone, *Faithful Unto Death*, p. 182, brings a photographic reprint of it.

studies and amusements. Here he remained till his twenty-fourth year.

Already as a boy, Arthur gave unmistakable signs of a higher calling. Hence his relatives were not surprised when he told them of his intention to embrace the priestly and religious state. His saintly mother was overjoyed when she heard of it and gladly gave her consent. Accordingly, in 1614, he bade farewell to his kindred and departed for the Jesuit College of Saint-Omer in Flanders. A year later, having learned that he wished to join their Order, the Fathers sent him to Valladolid in Spain. Here he devoted three years to the study of philosophy and theology; whereupon, in consideration of his unusual progress in virtue and learning, his superiors had him ordained priest.

Two years before this event, in 1616, the restoration of the English Franciscan Province, begun by Fr. John Gennings, had received the official approbation of the Belgian commissary. Since then, the province had made rapid progress. A number of English Franciscans had joined it, among whom was Fr. Nicholas Day, sometime professor of theology in the friary of Segovia, Spain. Father Bel probably heard of this, and knowing what the sons of St. Francis had suffered in England during the first period of the religious upheaval, he asked his superiors for permission to join the ranks of Fr. Gennings. Gladly they granted his request when they realized that it was more than a passing fancy. The rector of the college made the necessary arrangements with the provincial of the Spanish Franciscans, and on August 9, 1618, Fr. Sebastian de Salazar, guardian at Segovia, vested the pious Jesuit with the garb of St. Francis.

Although a priest, Fr. Francis deemed himself the least among his fellow novices. In humility, mortification, and prayer, he earnestly strove to become a worthy follower of the Saint whose name he was privileged henceforth to bear. The year of probation sped quickly by, and, on September 8, 1619, he made his profession in the hands of Fr. Joseph of St. Clare. With redoubled zeal, he now resumed his theological studies.

Before the end of the year, however, he received the following letter[3] from the commissary general:

> Whereas, our Most Reverend Father General, Benignus of Genua, has committed to me the care of sending to England and Scotland such fathers as seem suitable to labor in the Lord's vineyard, for the comfort of Catholics, who groan under the heavy yoke of persecution, and for the restoration and preservation of our Order in those parts; and as he has given me power to call English and Scotch Religious from any province whatever: I enjoin you, in whose zeal and piety I trust, in virtue of holy obedience, to come to these parts at your earliest convenience, in order to be sent into the Lord's harvest there, or to prepare yourself for the mission here among your countrymen, until you shall be judged fit to go. I herewith recommend you to our prelates as well as to the faithful of the places where you happen to stop on the way.
> Given at Brussels, on the last day of December, 1619.
>   Father Andrew a Soto,
>   Commissary General.

Fr. Francis immediately presented the letter to the Spanish provincial and with his consent and blessing set out for Flanders. Great was the joy at Douai when he arrived. The next two years he attended the Benedictine College of St. Vedast, in order to complete his theological course. At last, having passed the necessary examination, he received faculties to exercise his priestly office. During the year 1622, he served as confessor to the Poor Clares at Gravelines; whereupon he was appointed in the same capacity for the newly founded community of Franciscan Sisters of the Third Order at Brussels. Here the saintly and learned friar was active for seven successive years, directing the nuns on the road of perfection and counseling them in the management of their temporal affairs. To this day, the community, now residing at Taunton in Somerset, revere

---

[3] See Thaddeus, *The Franciscans in England,* p. 201.

the venerable martyr as their founder and chief benefactor.[4]

In the meantime, the number of English friars and their mission activity in England had increased to such an extent that, in 1629, the minister general thought it feasible to organize an independent province. The next year, as we have seen, the first provincial chapter was held in the convent of the Franciscan Sisters at Brussels. At this chapter Fr. Francis was declared provincial definitor and was appointed guardian and professor of Hebrew at Douai. His stay at St. Bonaventure's, however, was of short duration.

The Belgian commissary general, in 1632, sent him as provincial to Scotland with orders to reorganize the Franciscans in that country into a province. Accordingly, to the great sorrow of the brethren, Fr. Francis left for Toledo, Spain, to attend the general chapter, and from there he set out for Scotland. "It was certainly not Father Bel's fault," Thaddeus observes, "that his efforts were not crowned with success. But the time was not opportune for the restoration of the Order in Scotland."[5] After two years, therefore, Fr. Francis was permitted to take up mission work in England, as he had long desired. Here he spent the last nine years of his life, becoming titular guardian of London, in 1637, and provincial definitor for a second term, three years later.

Both in Belgium and on the English missions, Fr. Francis was beloved and esteemed by all who came in touch with him. Though severe with himself and zealous for the observance of the Rule, he was affable and obliging towards others, and governed by example rather than by precept. Naturally of a sunny disposition, his very look and word bespoke the inner joy that none but the humble and mortified know. In him the brethren found a charitable and sociable confrere, a prudent and solicitous superior. Fr. Angelus Mason, who was a novice

---

[4] They were compelled to quit France at the time of the French Revolution. See Thaddeus, p. 46.

[5] Thaddeus, p. 39.

at Douai in 1631, sums up his character in *Certamen Seraphicum,* by saying, "Father Francis Bel was a true son of the seraphic Father St. Francis."[6] He further tells us that the brethren wept when their beloved guardian departed for his mission in Scotland. Like Venerable Paul Heath, Fr. Francis was a man of prayer and recollection. He, too, fostered a tender devotion to Mary the Mother of God. In keeping with a vow he had made, he recited the Little Office of the Blessed Virgin every day; and to ensure proper attention, he was wont to say it in the seven languages with which he was conversant, Latin, Hebrew, Greek, Spanish, French, Flemish, and English.

Equally fervent was his love of prayer and mortification while on the missions in England. In fact, the nine last years of his life may be aptly styled one long preparation for martyrdom. "Francis du Mont," writes De Marsys, "had thus ample scope for observing the martyr, without being seen, and he has told me that he often saw Father Bel, with extended arms, absorbed in prayer, and that he would remain thus, for two or three hours together, several times a day. He also remarked that Father Bel was abstemious to the verge of singularity. ... I must add," he continues, "that Monsieur Langlois, Preacher to the Count d'Harcourt, who had the honor to converse with the martyr two days before his death, and to whom it had been given to sound the secret depths of his soul, declares that he recognized in him all the marks of perfect sanctity, of a mind long detached from all material things. I pray God that his example and his prayers may sow in us some seeds of holiness."[7] Such is the verdict of men who were intimately acquainted with the martyr.

Early in 1643, Fr. Joseph Bergaigne, then archbishop of Cambray, was directed by Pope Urban VIII to gather evidence regarding the martyrdoms that had recently taken place in England. On the committee appointed for this purpose by the

---

[6] Mason, p. 157.

[7] Quoted by Stone, pp. 206 seq.

Archbishop was Fr. Francis.[8] "It is probable," says Stone, "that the attention of parliament was directed to Father Bel, from the fact of his name appearing on the list of commissioners, for on the day that the report was published he was himself called upon to take his place among the martyrs."[9] Only a few months before, on October 16, he had met Venerable John Baptist Bullaker at Newgate and, we may suppose, had accompanied him to Tyburn, so that now he was in a position to give evidence in his case. Ever since, too, the thought of martyrdom, of which Fr. John Baptist had assured him, was uppermost in his mind. For the past twenty years he had been praying for this inestimable grace by daily reciting the thirty-fifth psalm. Little, however, did he think while investigating the recent martyrdoms, that his own was so close at hand.

It was on Monday, November 6, that the saintly missionary hired a horse at Brigstock in Northamptonshire and set out for London, where he had his headquarters. His appearance the next day at Stevenage, a little town in Hertfordshire, roused the suspicions of the garrison stationed there. Taking him for a royal spy, they searched him and found three papers written in Latin and Spanish. Two of these were of a devotional character; while the third, an indifferent note addressed to the Spanish ambassador, revealed the fact that he was a Franciscan.[10] Unable to decipher the writings, the soldiers summoned the local schoolmaster, who, to shield his ignorance, pompously declared that the papers contained very serious and dangerous matters. On this verdict the friar was arrested.

The next morning he was taken to Hertford and placed in

---

[8] Hope, *Franciscan Martyrs in England*, pp. 192 seq.—Fr. William Anderton also was on the commission. Thaddeus, p. 191.

[9] Stone, p. 183.

[10] The note read: "Most excellent sir, Father Francis Bel, of the Order of St. Francis, professed at Segovia, declares that he most gratefully accepts your offer to remain in your house; but he humbly requests not to be bound by the condition so destructive to his calling, that he should not leave the house on behalf of his neighbor's welfare, for such a condition he can not agree to.

the custody of Marshal Thomas Jones. During the day army officials and prominent citizens visited the suspected priest. In the course of the conversation a drummer stepped forward and asked him of what religion he was.

"I am a Catholic," replied the friar.

"A Roman Catholic?" insisted the other.

"Why, I told you I was an Englishman. How then can I be a Roman? As to the Catholic Church, however, there can be only one Catholic Church, of which I am a member. This, with the help of God, I will profess till my dying hour."

"Dost thou believe," another bystander broke in, "that the Pope is the supreme head of the Catholic Church?"

"I do," came the fearless reply; "neither did I ever doubt it."

This provoked a hot disputation between the friar and his enemies. To prove their heretical tenets, the latter brought several bibles. Finding the text very corrupt, the man of God severely rebuked his hearers for doing such violence to the word of God. The disputation continued for some time, when finally the Puritans, seeing themselves worsted, declared that in religious matters no certainty could be had. At this blindness and obstinacy, the friar grew warm with indignation.

"To call every religion doubtful," he contended, "is not the way to attract others to yours, but rather to confirm them in that Church's doctrine to which Christ has promised infallibility. All your efforts are directed to this: while declaring all religions to be in error, you attempt to draw me from that which can not err to that which needs must err, and thus you deprive me of what I possess and leave me nothing. In fine, you deal with my soul as you have dealt with my body, which you have robbed of all its clothes and instead have fitted out in rags. Rest assured, outside the Catholic Church there is no salvation; and I wish you all were like me, excepting my bonds."

Completely baffled by this boldness and sincerity, the crowd gradually dispersed; whereupon the friar was conducted before the civil authorities. On delivering his writings to the parliamentary commissioner, the marshal warned him to have the prisoner carefully guarded, because one of the papers contained an incantation by means of which he could escape through any prison bars.

"Art thou come from abroad?" asked the presiding officer, turning to the friar.

"I am," he answered.

"Hast thou received holy orders?"

"That is considered a crime; wherefore no one will answer such a question."

"The prisoner is mine, by right of my office," fell in the marshal, filled with rage. "I reserve him for further investigation."

With this, he advanced and once more subjected his victim to a most degrading examination. Finding a key on his person, the wretch demanded under threat of severe torture that the prisoner reveal the whereabouts of the lock to which the key belonged. Perceiving that it would not be to the detriment of his Catholic friends and benefactors, Fr. Francis replied that the porter of the Spanish ambassador had it.

During the following night, which the friar spent in close study, his keeper robbed him of all his clothes so that the next morning he was forced to don a tattered uniform given him by one of the soldiers. Thus scantily clad and with his hands bound behind him, he was placed on a horse and hastened off to London. In the various towns through which their journey led them, the servant of God became the laughing-stock of the people who gathered on the street corners to hail with insults and abuses this latest victim of Puritan intolerance.[11]

When they arrived in London, Marshal Jones confined his prisoner in a hotel and ordered him to send for his trunk. Fr. Francis complied, fearing a refusal might inconvenience his friends and benefactors. When the trunk arrived, the marshal

---

[11] "Helpless and half naked," the friar wrote in his account, "I rode on a hired horse, all too great a parade, however, for one who professes to carry the cross and to follow Christ."—Mason, p. 163.

took possession of all its contents.

Two guards now conducted the friar before the commissioners of parliament. While they were waiting at the door of the courtroom, the man of God was rebuked and insulted by the passers-by. At last, the commissioners were ready to receive them. After the preliminary questions regarding name, birthplace and religion had been answered, Mr. Corbet, one of the commissioners, began to ask the prisoner about certain persons mentioned in the papers that had been taken from him.

"Prithee, question me not about any third person," the friar rejoined, "because my conscience forbids me to injure others."[12]

"Such considerations are out of season," threw in Mr. Whitaker, "when the public weal is the issue."

"Is this thy writing?" they then demanded, producing the friar's note to the Spanish ambassador.

"It is," came the ready reply; "but it is only an imperfect sketch of what I had in mind to write."

"Art thou, as the writing shows, a member of the Order of St. Francis?"

Here the friar hesitated.[13]

"Several others," urged his enemies, "have been brought before us, who wisely admitted it."

"I am a poor penitent of the Order of St. Francis; but it is becoming for everyone to do penance."

"Art thou a priest?"

"That question should not be put; for, if I say yes, I own myself guilty of a crime; if I say no, my denial will implicate others."

"Is this thy breviary?"

"It is; and it contains many pious prayers dictated by the Holy Spirit."

---

[12] The dialogue form is ours, based on Mason's narrative.

[13] He feared for the convenience of his friends in the city, whom he endeavored to shield from harm throughout his trial.

"Aye, but interspersed with idolatrous ones that poison all the rest," broke in Whitaker.

"Forsooth, it is no breviary at all, but a missal," clamored some of the bystanders, examining the book from all sides.

Here Fr. Francis explained to them the difference between a Roman breviary and a Roman missal. In the meantime, the judges agreed on the sentence to be passed. The prisoner had admitted being a Franciscan; moreover, suspicions were strong that he was also a priest. For the present, therefore, he must be confined in Newgate.

The next day, Fr. Francis received a letter from the provincial urging him to come to Douai and take the place of Ven. Paul Heath. In reply, the man of God penned the following note:

Reverend Father—I received your behest with all due humility and readiness to follow it. Some twenty-four hours before it came to my notice, I had already begun to take the place of Fr. Heath in Newgate. As for the rest, I ask your prayers that I may persevere unto the end. With St. Andrew, I likewise entreat all Christians not to thwart my martyrdom.

Your poor brother,
Francis Bel.

To the letter from the commissary provincial, which arrived a few days later and also summoned him to Douai, he answered that he would obey as soon as the present impediment, for which he had no excuse, would be removed; then he playfully explained the nature of this impediment: how he had been arrested, tried, and thrown into Newgate. Expressing his desire to die for Christ, he at the same time declared his willingness to forgo this privilege if such were the will of God. After asking his superior to pray for him, he concluded with the assurance that, were he to escape the death sentence, he would use every lawful means to recover his liberty so as to be able to obey.

On December 7, the servant of God was summoned to the mayor's bench. His indictment having been read aloud, the judge asked him what he had to offer in his defence.

"Where are my accusers?" demanded the friar.

"Thou shalt face them to-morrow. For the present, declare whether thou art guilty or not."

"To cross the sea, receive holy orders, and return hither, I deem no crime. Therefore, I plead not guilty."

"Reply to the question!" snapped the judge. "What is thy answer?"

"The same that I already gave to the high commissioners; I have no other to give."

"That one we have; in addition, however, we now demand an answer in legal form; namely, art thou guilty or not guilty?"

"Very well, if such be the manner of your procedure, then I maintain that I am not guilty."

"By whom wouldst thou be judged?"

This question, it seems, perplexed the friar; he was at a loss what to say.

"By God and thy country!" suggested one of the bystanders.

"By God and my country," repeated the friar.

With this, the guards approached and led him back to Newgate.

The next morning, the feast of the Immaculate Conception, Fr. Francis was again placed at the bar. After swearing in the twelve jurymen, the judge ordered the witnesses to advance their accusations against the prisoner. Immediately, James Wadsworth and three other notorious apostates stepped forth and testified that they knew the prisoner to be a priest. One of them, Thomas Gage, made such a botch of it that he was sharply reproached by the bench and told to retire. Another, not having been sufficiently instructed what to say, had little evidence to offer. At last, when the witnesses had finished their wretched testimony, the judge turned to the prisoner.

"What hast thou to say in reply to these depositions?" he asked.

"The witnesses," boldly retorted the friar, "are men of ill repute, and therefore they should find no credence."

"Well, what objections hast thou to present against them?"

"All are apostates from the Catholic faith. Now, in all justice, men who have broken their troth with God can not and should not enjoy the confidence of their fellow men."

"Thy objection is without weight," they shouted. "Hast thou anything to propose to the jury in thy defence?"

"I have not; but I trust they are Christians. I am not a priest of the order of Levi," he subjoined, "according to the priesthood of Aaron; nor, indeed, would it be wise for one called by God to the priesthood to pass by the fountain itself and drink of the muddy water."

"Thou speakest mysteriously. Hast thou anything else to say?"

"Nothing; I refer you to the answers I gave at my trial before the high commissioners."

Thereupon a copy of the proceedings was presented to him. Having read it through, he handed it back without a word of comment. In the meantime, the jurymen went out for consultation. After a short time, they returned and declared the friar guilty of the charges brought against him. On hearing this, Fr. Francis thanked the jury, declaring that he was ready to die for his faith and profession. But sentence of death was not immediately passed. The judges, overawed by the noble and fearless bearing of the martyr, still hoped that in the end he would relent. Hence they gave orders that he be led back to prison, where he would have time to reflect on what was in store for him.

"Mr. Bel," said one of the judges, "you will be cut open while you are still alive, and with your own eyes you will see your entrails burnt before your face; wherefore we beseech you to abjure the Roman Church, or at least the priesthood, so as to avoid this disgraceful and cruel punishment."

"You can condemn me," retorted the man of God, "to a light and temporal punishment; but the Protector and Avenger of the innocent can condemn you to a punishment which shall last eternally."[14]

That same afternoon he was again cited to court to hear his sentence. Although he realized that he would be condemned to death, his heart was filled with inexpressible joy.

"My accusers," he said, "have borne witness against me; the twelve jurymen have pronounced me guilty. Most heartily I thank them; for with greatest readiness and joy I will die with Christ and his Apostles and Martyrs, inasmuch as their cause is my own. But since the matter on which I intend to speak is of equal and even greater importance than that of the prophets of old, I will invoke, as they did, heaven and earth. Be astonished, ye heavens, and be confounded, O earth! to behold a Christian State, professing Christ and his Gospel and yet condemning for treason the priesthood which was founded by Christ and which rests on the Gospel; the priesthood, I say, which upholds the Gospel and which in turn is upheld by the Gospel. For this reason I asked this morning, whether the jurymen were Christians; meaning that Christians would perhaps condemn priests of the order of Aaron but not of the order of Christ, and that Jews might condemn priests of Christ but not priests of Levi. What you then called mystical I shall now explain. If anyone has from God a vocation to the priesthood, let him seek it there where the succession is indisputably certain and where it has never been interrupted since the time of Christ, namely in Rome; not there, however, where it is doubtful and unquestionably defective, as is the case with the Protestants; for certain it is that in the Protestant Church there is no true priesthood."

Here the clerk interposed:

"We are to comply with the laws under which we were born and under which, you confessed, you, too, have been born."

"Quite correct, I admit," replied the friar; "forsooth, had I been born among pagans and infidels, I should submit to their laws in so far as they were not opposed to the law of God.

---

[14] This incident is taken from Hope, p. 206.

Know ye, therefore, that they who first enacted these laws, have long ago and irrevocably obtained what they deserved. Wherefore, let those be prudently and betimes on their guard and look to their consciences who are now charged or will yet be charged with the office of executing these laws."

"Is there anything else you would like to say?" queried the judge with cynic indifference.

"I have no more to say," returned the martyr. "I resign myself into your hands."

At a sign from the judge, the guards approached and shackled the friar's hands, a ceremony that was generally dispensed with in the case of priests. Then the judge arose and solemnly pronounced sentence of death. Fr. Francis was overjoyed when he heard it and with a loud voice intoned the *Te Deum.* Before leaving the courtroom, he turned to the judges and thanked them. They in turn reminded him of the terrible torments and death his obstinacy was preparing for him.

"I beseech God," said the friar with trembling voice, "to grant through his infinite mercy that not greater torments befall you in the next world than those that await me in this."

As usual, Catholics as well as Protestants flocked to Newgate to see the condemned priest during the two days preceding his execution. For all the saintly friar had a word of comfort or warning, as the case demanded. Many were moved to tears that one so gentle and refined in his manners should be condemned to a death so painful and revolting. But the valiant hero only rejoiced in the anticipation of the eternal reward that was to follow.

"I am astonished," he said repeatedly to his visitors, "that God should have been pleased to honor me with the crown of martyrdom, and that he should have chosen me, a miserable being, rather than the many holy men now in England, who are aspiring to this happiness."[15]

On Sunday morning, he celebrated Mass and administered

---

[15] Hope, p. 209.

Holy Communion to a number of Catholics. During the day, four Protestant ministers came at the behest of parliament to dispute with the martyr on doctrinal matters. But they were outwitted at every turn and in the end were compelled to beat an inglorious retreat, much to the satisfaction of the bystanders. Ever since sentence of death had been pronounced, the Spanish and the French ambassadors were taking steps for his acquittal. When Fr. Francis heard of it, however, he became sad and even reproached the prior of St. Magdalen, when the latter told him that they were trying to obtain grace for him.

"Alas! dost thou deem it a grace," he said, "to be robbed of the crown I have desired so long? Till now, I considered thee my friend; but, let me tell thee, if thou persist in thy design, I shall no longer regard thee as my friend, but as my greatest enemy. I beseech thee, do not prevent my martyrdom. I conjure thee, do not oppose my death which is my greatest happiness; whatever steps thou takest, I shall invoke the most holy Mother of God and St. Andrew that no one in the end may deprive me of the cross which I see before me."

When, at last, night set in, the man of God dismissed his visitors, saying it was his wish to be left alone the remaining few hours of his life, so as to prepare himself for the sacrifice he was to offer on the morrow. The entire night he spent in prayer and meditation. Early next morning he rose to say Mass for the last time and to give Holy Communion to several Catholics. He was still rapt in prayer, when the guards entered his cell and told him that his hour had come. Recommending himself to the Most High, he arose and followed them to the street. Without delay, they fastened him to the hurdle and then whipping up the four horses dashed off to Tyburn followed by a concourse of people.

Arriving at the place of execution, the holy man was transported with joy.

"Now I find myself in the place," he exclaimed, "which blessed Thomas Bullaker predicted to me!"

At the command of the sheriff, he ascended the cart and, as

was customary, addressed the people who had assembled in great numbers to witness the bloody spectacle.

"Listen, my dearest countrymen! If you wish to be freed of your miseries, it is necessary that you first put an end to your sins. For, without doubt, your great sins are the cause of your present calamities and misfortunes. Above all, however, arise from heresy in which you are engrossed these many years. For through heresy, I grieve to say, you are separated like decayed members from the body of Christ, or are cut like dead branches from the tree of the Church. If you continue to love the darkness more than the light, daily hardships will be your share. Certain it is, many tribulations and calamities will come upon this city of London and upon the entire kingdom of England, if they do not betimes leave off persecuting and harassing the priests and the Catholic people. Consider, I beseech you, and see the afflictions with which God even now visibly begins to punish you, and know for certain that all these punishments are signs of his love and the most evident assurance that he will not destroy you unless forced to do so. All these chastisements, wars, and misfortunes he inflicts upon you, so as in time to gather in the shipwrecked into the harbor of the Catholic Church. Do not, therefore, shamefully abuse his goodness and mercy; do not with violence, as it were, extort your perdition by provoking divine justice.[16] I am brought here to suffer death, but I wish before I suffer to tell you the cause. I am not even accused of any crime, but am condemned solely for being a priest of the Catholic Church. Were I a pagan priest, I should not wonder at being put to death in a Christian country; but that a Catholic priest should be put to death by those who profess to be Christians and to follow Jesus Christ and his Gospel, ought to surprise every reasonable person. It is said that the laws demand it. But these laws were iniquitously made and now they are being iniquitously executed. I declare

---

[16] So far Mason; the rest of the address and attending incidents are taken from Hope, pp. 212 seq.

before you all in the sight of God and of his Son Jesus Christ who will judge us, and I sign my declaration with my blood, that I die a true member of the Catholic Church."

"You mean to say the Roman Church," interrupted a Protestant.

"If you wish me thus to distinguish it," replied the martyr, "with all my heart I distinguish it from every Protestant Church and every sort of heresy, and call it the Roman Church. My parents lived and died in this religion. They brought me up in this faith, and if I had a longer life to spend I would profess it to my last moment, even though I had to suffer a thousand deaths and the greatest imaginable torments."

"Mr. Bel," broke in the sheriff, "we can not let you declaim any longer against our laws and give a wrong impression to the people. You know that you are going to die for having seduced the king's subjects."

"I see," answered the martyr, "a great multitude before me. This is why I wish to do them a good office and draw them back to the right way. They possess a part of the Catholic faith. They believe the incarnation of our Lord, his passion, and his resurrection. But this is not enough, and therefore I wish to declare to them the whole truth for the good of their souls."

"Help yourself! help yourself!" shouted some in the crowd.

"Those that are the victims of a false religion," the man of God quietly continued, "will not listen to the truth. But I protest to you that the Protestant religion is not of divine faith."

Here the sheriff interposed, forbidding the martyr to say any more against the Protestant religion. Whereupon, the latter with a look of sorrow and pity exclaimed:

"I forgive with my whole heart all who have contributed to my death, and I die joyfully for so glorious a cause."

A thief who also was to be executed felt such compunction at these words that he solemnly abjured the Anglican heresy and was absolved by the martyr. Finally, orders were given to carry out the sentence. While the cart was drawn from under him, the martyr raised his hands and received the last absolution from the prior of St. Magdalen. He had hung only a few seconds when the executioner cut him down. On removing his secular dress, they found that beneath it he wore the Franciscan habit and cord. At this sight the crowd was filled with admiration.

"What sort of men are these," they murmured, "who thus despise earthly comforts?"

Having finished their bloody work on the sacred corpse, the executioners exposed the quarters on the four gates of the city. Mason concludes his life sketch of Ven. Francis Bel by remarking that several miracles were thought to have been wrought through his intercession. Like his fellow friars who died for their faith and profession at this time, he, too, is now on the official list for eventual beatification.[17]

---

[17] See *Acta Minorum*, Vol. VI (1887), p. 49 seq., and also Ortolani, *De Causis Beatorum et Servorum Dei Ordinis Minorum*, p. 14.

CHAPTER VII
VENERABLE MARTIN WOODCOCK, O.F.M.

His Protestant father and Catholic mother—He embraces the old faith—Student at Saint-Omer and at Rome—Joins the Capuchins in Paris—Dismissed from the Order—Serious doubts regarding his vocation—Received into the Franciscan Order at Douai—Ordained priest—Longs to join the missionaries in England—Permission at last granted—Arrested on arriving in England—Sufferings in prison—Before the judges—Sentenced to death for being a priest—Martyrdom.

HE last Franciscan to die for the faith during the Puritan Revolution was Venerable Martin Woodcock.[1] Before, as well as after, his entrance into the Franciscan Order, his life was one long series of mental and bodily affliction, which he bore with heroic resignation to the will of Him whose judgments are incomprehensible and whose ways are unsearchable. "In the eyes of the world," Hope thoughtfully observes, "his life was a failure, for disappointment seemed ever to attend all his efforts in God's service. But in God's eyes his constant humiliations were the fitting preparation for the glorious crown which was predestined to him rather than to those of his brethren who might be deemed to have more worthily deserved it."[2]

Fr. Woodcock was a native of Lancashire. He saw the light of day in 1603 at Leyland, and in baptism received the name John. His father, Thomas Woodcock, was a Protestant, while his mother Dorothy, born of a good Catholic family named Anderton, was known for her piety and staunch adherence to the old faith. Unfortunately, all we know regarding John's

---

[1] For the present sketch, unless otherwise stated, we have drawn chiefly from Mason, *Certamen Seraphicum,* pp. 183-208.

[2] Hope, *Franciscan Martyrs in England,* p. 216.

boyhood and youth is the fact that, possibly to wrest her son from the influence of Protestant environment at home, his mother entrusted him at an early age to the care of his grandfather. With him he stayed till his twentieth year, when he abjured Protestantism and embraced the Catholic faith. In consequence, as he had foreseen, his Protestant father treated him very cruelly. But he esteemed the treasure of his faith higher than earthly comforts. Patiently he bore his father's taunts for almost two years. Then having come of age, he made shift to follow what he sincerely believed to be a summons from above to the holy priesthood. With a number of young men he accompanied F. Edward Squire, S. J., to the continent and soon found himself within the halls of the Jesuit College at Saint-Omer. After a year of study, during which he completed his classical training, he departed for the English College in Rome, where he intended to take up philosophy and theology.[3]

All this time, the young convert felt in his heart an earnest desire to enter some religious Order. Finally, after six months of prayer and deliberation, he decided to join the Capuchins. The procurator general of the Order, to whom he had gone for advice, mistook the Capuchins at Faubourg St. Jacques in Paris for an English community. Accordingly, he told John to enter the Order there. The young man immediately set out for the French metropolis, and on May 16, 1630, received the Capuchin habit. Soon, however, a storm of bitter trials was to dispel the joy and peace of his heart. He had been with the Capuchins only three months, when the superiors found it necessary to dismiss him from the Order. The novice was inconsolable when he heard of it. So ardent was his devotion to the life he had embraced that only by sheer force, as Mason tells us, could he be deprived of the lowly garb of St. Francis.

In a letter to a friend, the unhappy young man explained the

---

[3] Stone, *Faithful Unto Death*, p. 212.

reasons why the friars had sent him away.[4] His friends in England, and even his Catholic mother, had neglected to answer the letters which had been directed to them for information regarding his antecedents. Furthermore, his superiors could not discover what had prevailed on him to join their Order in Paris rather than in Rome; it seemed incredible to them that the procurator general should have mistaken their friary for a community of English Capuchins. Moreover, from letters received through the Jesuits in Rome, they learned that the novice's mother, elder brother, and other relatives strongly discountenanced his entering a religious Order, which fact the superiors anticipated would in the end create difficulties for him as well as for the Order. Again, not only was the young man of Protestant extraction, but he had also been reared among Protestants. Then, his precarious health evidently militated against vowing a life of seclusion and penance. Finally, there was little hope of his ever becoming conversant with the French tongue, while the decided predilection he manifested for the English Jesuits who had lately visited him caused considerable comment. Therefore, "without any fault of his own," as Mason concludes, John Woodcock was compelled to leave the Order. "God made use of the injustice of men," Stone remarks, "to work out his own design, for if Father Woodcock had remained with the Capuchins, he could never have attained the martyr's crown, they having at that time no mission in England, so that what was to him a source of grief and suffering at first, was ultimately the very means by which he was to ensure his happiness and reward."[5]

With a heavy heart, the young man left the quiet precincts of the convent where he had only begun to taste of the peace and consolation for which his spirit longed. Trusting in God for strength and guidance, he proceeded at once to Douai and

---

[4] Mason brings a Latin version of this letter, which at his time was preserved in the provincial archives at Douai.

[5] Stone, p. 214.

applied for admission among the English Franciscans. At the same time, however, serious doubts regarding his true vocation began to harrow his soul. Would not his father's being a Protestant debar him also from becoming a Franciscan? Had he not better complete his studies, receive ordination, and secure a living? What if the Franciscans at St. Bonaventure's also turned him off? How, in that event, could he earn a livelihood, deprived as he was of his inheritance? While pondering what course to pursue, it suddenly occurred to him how, when he left Rome for Paris, Fr. Luke Wadding,[6] the guardian of St. Isidore's, had drawn his attention to all these predicaments and had promised to receive him into the Irish College of Franciscans. It was at this juncture that the troubled student made the mistake of his life, as he himself later confessed. With more zeal than forethought, he withdrew his application to the friars at Douai and returned to Rome. But the end of his trials had not yet come. For some reason or other, he was not admitted among the Irish Franciscans, and again his heart became a prey to doubts and fears. To join the Order of St. Francis was his one and only desire. With deep regret he thought of the friars at Douai. Had he only joined them instead of applying to their Irish brethren in Rome. To be received into their midst now was more than he could reasonably hope or ask for. "Thus," as Mason says, "he was tossed about on all sides and found rest nowhere, until, after escaping from many dangers, and overcoming many difficulties, he fell back upon his original design, and returned to the place which in the first instance had been designated for him by God."[7]

A natural sense of shame forbade him to appear personally at the convent of St. Bonaventure, and he solicited by letter[8] the

---

[6] The famous historian of the Franciscan Order.

[7] Mason, p. 197.

[8] For a Latin version of this letter see Mason, p. 197.

aid of his friend Fr. William Anderton,[9] who was then a member of the community. This letter breathes a spirit of rare humility, winning sincerity, deep faith, and religious fervor. In it he begs his friend to plead his cause with the superiors of the province, to declare in his stead that "through some weakness of body and soul, and through a fear not altogether reprehensible," he had justly incurred their distrust and displeasure; that now, however, having regained his mental and bodily strength, he was better disposed and earnestly desired "to heed his first call rather than to expose himself any longer to the surging billows of this world and to the furious onslaughts of implacable enemies; wherefore, my dear Father William," he pleaded, "by our old friendship which in this misfortune above all intercedes for me with you; yes, by the tender love of our Lord Jesus Christ, I pray that pity on my miserable condition may move you successfully to endeavor to obtain favor and pardon for me. This is my desire, this I ask, this I wait for, for this I sigh and yearn, and I shall await its accomplishment solely out of pure love of God and of his glory. Farewell. That which formerly you saw me long for lightly, you will strive now, for love of Christ, to secure for me more efficaciously. This will be my happiness; nothing else will ever cause me greater joy. Farewell."

The superiors at St. Bonaventure's were deeply touched when they read this humble and sincere appeal. Evidently, it was the outburst of a soul that the All-Wise was leading heavenward through the perilous gloom of sorrow and affliction; and in their little community, perhaps, that tried soul was predestined at last to find spiritual peace and consolation. Thus the friars reasoned, and eager to further the designs of Providence, they informed the young man that he might come and join their ranks. Without delay, John Woodcock repaired to St. Bonaventure's, where Venerable Paul Heath, who at the

---

[9] Perhaps Fr. Martin was related to him; his mother's name, we know, was Anderton.

time was vicar of the friary, vested him with the Franciscan habit and gave him the name Fr. Martin of St. Felix.

Humility had opened for him the portals of the friary; and it was this same virtue that chiefly characterized his later career. Fr. Martin soon won the esteem and confidence of his superiors by his love of prayer and recollection and by the spirit of ready submission which he manifested on all occasions. Though of a weak constitution, he ate very sparingly and shortened his hours of sleep to satisfy his thirst for prayer. In the discharge of choir duty, he edified all by his promptness and devotion. Mason, who had occasion to observe him during the novitiate, assures us that Fr. Martin outstripped all his fellow novices in strict observance of the Rule and of other, even the slightest, disciplinary regulations. In short, so fully did he vindicate the hopes of his superiors and confreres, that after the year of probation he was admitted by unanimous consent to holy profession. He pronounced the vows in the hands of the guardian Venerable Francis Bel. Thus, by a singular coincidence Fr. Martin of St. Felix was vested and professed by two Franciscans who, like himself, were destined one day to shed their blood in defence of their holy faith and profession.

About two years after his profession, Fr. Martin was ordained priest, although he had not yet finished the usual course of studies. His health was very much impaired, and it was probably this circumstance together with his age,—he was now past thirty—that induced the provincial to have him receive ordination. Apparently, for the next three years, till 1637, he continued to study theology. Whereupon he was empowered to hear confessions and to preach and was approved for the mission in England. His first appointment was to Nieuport as confessor and spiritual adviser of the Franciscan Sisters residing in that place.[10] In 1640, the provincial chapter, which was held in London on April 19, appointed him chaplain and confessor to a certain Mr. Sheldon at Arras. But he lived

---

[10] Hope, p. 218.

with this gentleman only a short time, when his health broke down completely, owing to the austere life he had been leading and to the disinterested zeal with which he had discharged his priestly duties. The physicians declared his ailment very serious; wherefore, the superiors recalled him to Douai. Resigning himself entirely to the will of God, the saintly priest returned to St. Bonaventure's and, despite his physical debility, again took part in all the penitential exercises of the community.

Since his elevation to the priesthood, and especially since the renewal of anti-Catholic hostility in England, Fr. Martin had hoped and prayed for the day when he should be allowed to join his brethren on the missions. But his health had grown from bad to worse, so that he finally despaired of ever obtaining the necessary permission. Mingled feelings of joy and sorrow prevailed in the community at Douai when in the spring of 1643 the friars were informed that Venerable Paul Heath had won the martyr's crown. On Trinity Sunday they held a solemn service of thanksgiving. No one was more impressed by the sermon which a Capuchin preached on the occasion than Fr. Martin. To lay down his life for Christ again became the ever recurring burden of his thoughts and prayers. Several times he wrote to the provincial in England, Fr. George Perrot, asking leave to come to the missions. But for some reason or other his letters remained unanswered.

Meanwhile, the state of his health had become so alarming that the superiors ordered him to take the waters at Spa. It was here that he met Fr. Peter Marchant, the Belgian commissary general. With childlike confidence he told him how, ever since the glorious death of Fr. Heath, he had been yearning to join the missions. The commissary in turn bade him apply to his immediate superior, promising at the same time to use his influence in securing the necessary permission. Accordingly, the servant of God addressed the following letter[11] to Fr.

---

[11] For a copy of this letter see Mason, p. 201.

Angelus Mason, the provincial commissary:

> Reverend Father:
>
> Since Trinity Sunday, which I doubt not your Reverence remembers, and previously, I have written three consecutive letters to our Reverend Father Provincial in England, asking for permission to return thither, etc. Recently, I also wrote to the commissary general. But now after speaking to him personally, I have obtained in writing his free consent to my desire, provided it meets your approval, as he pointed out to me. He affixed his seal to it and returned it to me open, that I might read and sign it when I saw fit. This I did on my arrival here yesterday evening. After due consideration, however, I refrain from sending it to you, for fear it may be lost on the way, which would necessitate my beginning the whole matter anew. Trusting you will take me at my word, especially in an affair of this kind, in which I could not lie, I judged it better to inform you of it by these simple lines and to request your consent with return mail. By the tender love of the most sweet Jesus, I entreat you not to delay sending it. Indeed, I might propose to your Reverence the same urgent reasons which I have twice already laid before the above-mentioned superiors, though perhaps in a style little adequate to the subject. But I hope that this will not be necessary. Your Reverence knows me better than they do; nor have I less confidence in you than in them. Still, rather than fail in my cherished purpose, I assure you that, if it be your wish to try me, I am willing to rehearse the same reasons to your Reverence which I unfolded to them, though I by no means entreated them with importunity, but with modesty and with unpersuasive reasoning. Reverend Father, the season admits of no delay; winter is at the door and my health in consequence of this and other greater anxieties is not as robust as your Reverence and I myself might expect. Therefore, for the love of God, kneeling now in my room, I pray you to say Amen, and to send me your approval as soon as possible. What I have for its security I will send to you whenever and wherever you desire. Meanwhile, offering you my humble, submissive, and unfeigned love and service, I remain with confidence in you, ever yours, Friar Martin of St. Felix.

Great was the joy of the holy man when some time later the commissary general notified him that Fr. Angelus Mason had given his consent. The happy news seemed to restore the health of his body as it soothed the anguish of his soul. Without delay, he returned to St. Bonaventure's. On arriving there he learned that a short time before another of his confreres, Venerable Francis Bel, had suffered martyrdom for the faith. Now nothing could longer detain him. He hastened his preparation and before the end of the year departed for England, fortified with the blessing of the guardian. After a perilous voyage, he landed at Newcastle-on-Tyne, and immediately set out for Lancashire, hoping to find his relatives and to convert them to the true faith. But God had decreed otherwise. On the very night of his arrival, he was arrested on the suspicion of being a priest and brought before the magistrate, who without much ado had him thrown into the city jail.

Owing to the Civil War, which was then at its height, the circuit judges were prevented from holding regular sessions. Hence, for more than two years, Fr. Martin was left to languish in prison. During this time, he endured untold hardships. The prison was rank with filth and disease. The rations that the jailer or some Catholic friend brought to him, were coarse and hardly sufficient to sustain him. Many of his fellow prisoners were criminals of the lowest type; and the shameless and wicked conversation they carried on only added to the misery and distress of the saintly friar. But he bore all with heroic patience and divided his time between prayer and works of charity. From time to time, Catholics would venture into the prison to be instructed by him or to receive the sacraments at his hands. They were greatly edified and encouraged by the self-forgetting zeal with which he ministered to their spiritual needs. Even the Protestants were at a loss to explain how a man of his physical debility could survive and even be happy amid such privations. What sustained the servant of God, however, was the assurance that his cause was righteous, and that in the end God would reward him with the crown of martyrdom. How earnestly he yearned for this singular grace we learn from a letter of Fr. William Anderton, the same through whose intervention he had been admitted into the Franciscan Order. Fr. William was then engaged on the missions and succeeded in visiting his imprisoned confrere. "During the entire period of his confinement," he wrote, "he manifested a great desire for martyrdom, and always declared that, drawn especially by this hope, he had crossed over to England."

At length the long looked-for moment arrived. The crushing defeat which Cromwell's Ironsides inflicted on the king's forces at Naseby had decided the war in favor of the parliamentarians. Hence, the Puritans had free scope to satisfy their vengeance on the Catholics. The judges soon after resumed their regular circuits and early in August, 1646, came to Lancaster. Among the first to be summoned before them was Fr. Martin. On being asked whether he was a priest, the friar fearlessly replied in the affirmative and also admitted that he was a Franciscan. More was not needed, and without further questioning the judges condemned him to suffer the death of a traitor. On hearing his sentence, Fr. Martin raised his eyes to heaven and with a loud voice exclaimed, "Praise be to God! Thanks be to God!" Meanwhile, the guards approached and conducted him back to prison.

Owing probably to the fact that the prisons were overcrowded, the execution of Fr. Martin and of the two secular priests who had been condemned with him, was fixed for the following morning. At daybreak, therefore, on August 7, the three priests were taken from their dungeon and led out into the streets. Here they were fastened to hurdles and amid the taunts and jeers of a blood-thirsty rabble hurried off to the place of execution. The humility and patience with which the friar bore these insults elicited the secret sympathy of many, so that even Protestants were heard to remark, "If ever there was a true martyr in the Roman Church, this is one."

The first to mount the ladder that rested against the scaffold was Fr. Martin. When the executioner had placed the rope about his neck, the martyr addressed the people. Having told them that he was about to suffer death solely for being a Roman Catholic priest, he began to discourse on the only true and saving faith. Suddenly, however, at a signal from the sheriff, the executioner overturned the ladder. It is related that the rope broke and that the martyr fell unconscious to the ground. But he soon came to and rose to his feet. At the command of the sheriff he reascended the ladder, and patiently suffered the executioner to readjust the rope. Then with a sudden jerk the ladder was again thrust aside, and the friar hung suspended between heaven and earth. Immediately he was cut down and the bloody work began.[12] When the executioner seized his heart, the martyr was heard to invoke the name of Jesus. "He praised God in life," Mason concludes, "he called upon God in death, and after death he enjoys God in everlasting happiness."[13]

---

[12] The head of the martyr, we learn from Hope (p. 228), was preserved in the Franciscan friary at Douai till the French Revolution, when the friars were compelled to seek refuge in England. The Franciscan Sisters at Taunton possess one of his arm-bones.

[13] Mason, p. 208. Fr. Mason is the last of this period whose cause of beatification was introduced on December 4, 1886, and was advanced a step farther in 1900. See *Acta Minorum,* Vol. VI, pp. 49 seq., and Ortolani, *De Causis Beatorum et Servorum Dei Ordinis Minorum,* p. 14.

CHAPTER VIII
CONCLUSION

Franciscans in prison during the Commonwealth—Early reign of Charles II—Peace and prosperity—Death of Fr. John Gennings—Activity and influence of the friars—The Maryland Mission—Franciscans and the Titus Oates Plot—Two martyrs: Ven. John Wall and Ven. Charles Mahoney—Four die in prison—Ominous signs—Fall of King James II—Franciscans forced to flee from the continent—Many of their number seized and imprisoned—Peace restored—The province at the height of prosperity—Two Franciscans die in prison: FF. Paul Atkinson and Germanus Holmes—Decline of the province—Subversive State laws—The French Revolution—Franciscans flee to England—Their number gradually decreases—The province canonically dissolved.

HE reader may wish to know how the English Franciscans fared after the execution of Charles I and the ultimate triumph of Puritanism. We will conclude our narrative, therefore, with a brief account of the Second Province during the remaining two centuries of its existence.[1] Naturally, the eleven years that Oliver Cromwell and the Puritans were in power proved another period of sufferings for Catholics. Among the many priests who languished in the prisons at this time we find a number of Franciscans. Under the year 1653, the chapter register has the following entry: "Three fathers have suffered imprisonment, and have with danger of their lives undergone their trial, showing great constancy." Another entry was made three years later, reading: "Since the last chapter three fathers have suffered imprisonment." One of these, it seems, was Fr. Lewis Wrest. After a long confinement in Lancaster Castle, he at last obtained his freedom and returned to Douai, where he died in

---

[1] The following facts and figures are compiled chiefly from Thaddeus, *The Franciscans in England*.

1669, aged 73 years. Whether the other friars were also set at liberty or were left to die a lingering death in prison, is not known.

The Catholics looked forward to brighter days when the royalist party at last gained the upper hand and, in 1660, placed Charles II on his rightful throne. The popularity which the Franciscans enjoyed at this time and later, is best seen from the many bequests made to them, and from the fact that so many young men applied for admission into their ranks. Since 1649, not less than 175 new members were added to the province, so that by the end of the century the total number of friars (living and deceased) amounted to 228, of whom 89 were still living in 1700. Their zeal for the strict observance of the Franciscan vow of poverty was truly remarkable. In 1676, the superiors of the province drew up a solemn declaration, in which, among other things, they protested: "We repudiate all property in common as well as in private, admitting only the use of what is necessary, given us either as a free gift or alms or as retribution for our labors: not as if we had a strict right to those things, but being content with their simple use." The instructions with which the provincial in 1704 sent Fr. John Capistran Eyston to England, show what spirit guided the friars on the mission. "Be courteous, civil, and obliging to all," he tells the young priest, "familiar with few, and with none of the other sex. Compassionate the poor, helping them when you can. Be tender and careful of the sick. ... Omit not daily mental prayer, nor an annual recollection. ... Let not your manners contradict your doctrine, nor life and actions belie your words. Be zealous for the conversion of souls, but temper zeal with prudence and discretion. Meddle as little as may be with the temporal concerns of your flock, or economy of families; and be not forward in recommending servants or making matches. Remember, perfect expropriation is our great treasure, which we must endeavor to preserve by renouncing all dominion: in the case of money we ought to be very moderate; and in all matters of moment have recourse, if possible, to the Superiors."

About six months after the accession of Charles II, the friars on the mission received the sad news that the founder of their province, Fr. John Gennings, had passed away. After the first provincial chapter in 1630, he at once returned to England and continued to labor there as missionary till 1659. In that year, he attended as commissary provincial the chapter held in London. Being now over ninety years of age, and wishing to prepare for his last hour, he asked and obtained leave to return to the friary at Douai. Here, on November 12, 1660, he passed quietly to a better life. He had served three terms as provincial and had repeatedly held the offices of custos and definitor. In 1651, he published his *Institutio Missionariorum,* in which he bequeathed to his brethren the fruits of his long experience as missionary in England. The records describe him as "a man of exemplary and blameless life, steadfast in his purpose, and beloved by all."

Of the Franciscans conspicuous for their activity and influence we mention only a few. Fr. Francis Davenport, whom, before the outbreak of the Civil War, parliament had designated as greatly responsible for the increase of popery, was still exerting a wide influence, especially at court. In 1670, he effected the conversion of Anne, the Duchess of York; and it was, without doubt, largely owing to him, as one of Queen Catherine's chaplains, that Charles II was at heart so favorably disposed toward Catholics. Fr. Francis died in 1680; he had spent fifty-seven years on the missions and had held the highest offices in the province. Another learned and influential Franciscan at this time was Fr. John Baptist Canes. Among his writings we note especially *Fiat lux,* a controversial work on the religious troubles then agitating England. Selected by the Catholic party to defend the faith against Dr. Stillingfleet, the learned friar wrote and published his *Diaphanta* or *Exposure of Dr. Stillingfleet's Arguments against the Catholic Religion.* Other distinguished writers on historical, ascetical, and dogmatical subjects, were Fr. Angelus Mason, who is known especially for his valuable *Certamen Seraphicum,* the work which formed our chief source of information regarding the five Franciscans who suffered during the Civil War; Fr. John Cross, who wrote on ascetics and Scotistic philosophy; and Fr. Antony Le Grand, who is recognized as "the first philosopher of the age that reduced the Cartesian system to the method of the schools."

But the second province did not restrict its activity to England. In 1672, the chapter answered the appeal of the Jesuits, who were then serving the English Catholics in the Maryland colony, by sending FF. Polycarp Wicksted and Basil Hobart to their assistance. Three more friars joined the American mission in 1675. They labored here with the sons of St. Ignatius in "fraternal charity and offices of mutual friendship," as the Jesuit Records put it, until the year 1689, when the English crown passed over to the Prince of Orange, and the prosperity of the Maryland mission came to an end. Lord Baltimore was deposed as governor of the colony, and in 1692 Protestantism was established there by law. But the Catholic missionaries did not forsake their flock. In fact, as late as 1699, two Franciscans again set out for the English colony. One of these, Fr. James Haddock, was active there till his death which occurred in 1720.

During the religious persecution that broke out in 1678, in consequence of the Titus Oates Plot, two Franciscans died on the scaffold for their faith and sacred profession, while four underwent the hardships of prison life. Venerable John Wall, known in religion as Joachim of St. Anne, was laboring successfully in Worcestershire when, in December, 1678, he was arrested at Rushock Court. On his refusal to take the oaths of allegiance and supremacy, he was cast into the jail at Worcester. Here he languished till the following April, when he was brought to trial and condemned to death. Four months elapsed, however, before orders were given for his execution. The people of Worcester were opposed to it, maintaining that till then no one had been executed in their city solely for being a priest. Like so many others, Fr. John was, therefore, taken to London, in order that the more serious charge of complicity in the supposed plot against the king's life might be proved

Conclusion

against him. How little his enemies succeeded in their base design, we learn from a letter which the friar wrote to a friend of his, on July 18, shortly after his return from London.[2]

> Sir:—With my service I return you thanks for the twenty shillings. I am safe returned from London, whither I was sent to be examined by Mr. Oates and Bedloe, Dugdale and Prance, to see if any of them had anything against me, as guilty of concerning these great disturbances of the times. I was very strictly examined by all four, several times over, in that month I stayed in London; and thanks be to God I was after the last examination, publicly declared innocent and free of all plots whatever by Mr. Bedloe, who examined me last; and he was so kind to me, that he told me publicly that if I would but comply in matter of religion, that he would pawn his life for me that for all I was condemned yet I should not die. I was also offered the same after my first examination, though I should have been never so guilty if I would have done what was against my conscience. But I told them I would not buy my life at so dear a rate as to wrong my conscience. How God will dispose of all of us that are condemned none know. Some think it is concluded we all must die; and yet, because it will not appear grateful in the eyes of rational and moral men to see us die merely for conscience' sake, I have been several times informed from London, since I came down, that if possible some will do their best to bring some of us, some way or other, into a plot, though we have all at London been declared innocent after strict examination. God's will be done! The greater the injury and injustice done against us by men to take away our lives, the greater our glory in eternal life before God. This is the last persecution that will be in England; therefore I hope God will give all His holy grace to make the best use of it. All these things have been sufficiently prophesied long since; and I do no way question the truth, though it is like some will suffer first, of whom I have a strong imagination I shall be one. God's will be done in earth as it is in heaven, and in mercy bring me happy thither!

---

[2] This letter and other details regarding Venerable John Wall are taken from Hope, *Franciscan Martyrs in England,* pp. 236 seq.

I subscribe, sir, your faithful servant,
Francis Webb.³

The holy man's presentiment that he would be among the first of the condemned priests to die for the faith proved correct. Feelings of joy and gratitude thrilled his noble soul when he learned that his execution would take place on August 22. Prayer and acts of penance filled out the remaining days of his life. Shortly before his martyrdom he received the sacraments at the hands of a priest who obtained permission to visit him in prison. On the appointed morning, he was drawn on a hurdle to Red Hill, near Worcester, and martyred in the usual bloody manner. His mangled remains were laid to rest in the Catholic churchyard of St. Oswald, while his head was given to Fr. Leo Randolph, who had it conveyed to the brethren at Douai.

Ten days before, another Franciscan suffered death for the same cause in another part of England. It was Venerable Charles Mahony, a member of the Irish Province. Apparently, he had been ordained priest only a short time before, and was on his way to Ireland, when the ship on which he sailed stranded on the coast of Wales. While he was traveling through this region, government spies detected his priestly character and arrested him. At his trial, which took place at Denbigh, Fr. Charles openly confessed that he was a priest. Accordingly, he was condemned to death and sent to Ruthin, where on August 12, 1679, he obtained the crown of martyrdom.

Of the four Franciscans who were thrown into prison during this persecution only one, Venerable Francis Levison, is known to have at last succumbed to his sufferings. He died in prison on February 11, 1680, after fourteen months of close confinement. Fr. Marian Napier was tried and sentenced to death; but, in 1684, the sentence was commuted to banishment

---

³ He went by the assumed names Francis Webb and Francis Johnson. Dodd in his *Church History of England* (Vol. III, p. 400) mentions him by the latter name.

for life.[4] The other two Franciscans, FF. Bernardine Langworth and Francis Osbaldeston, after languishing in prison for six years, were set at liberty when James II ascended the throne.[5]

Despite these persecutions, the number of Franciscans in England increased from year to year, so that the sphere of their activity assumed broader dimensions. In 1687, nine new residences were established in different parts of the country. That same year, in November, it was decided that a friary should be erected next their chapel at Lincoln's Inn Field, in London. Work on the new building progressed rapidly, and the following spring ten friars were assembled there, wearing the religious garb and performing all the exercises of a well-regulated community. Soon after, the novices were placed there, and nine new members were added to the community. But the friars were to enjoy their peace and happiness only a few weeks. On Sunday, November 4, 1688, the very day on which William of Orange landed with his army at Torbay, on the coast of Devonshire, a mob attacked the friary and would have destroyed it and expelled its inmates had not the king sent a body of armed soldiers to disband the mob. Meanwhile, the Prince of Orange had marched northward, so that the king was compelled to leave London and rally his forces at Salisbury. Anxious for the safety of the Franciscans, he requested them to quit their friary for the present.

The fall of James II and the accession of William of Orange, a staunch adherent of Calvinism, spelled hard times for the Catholics in England. Together with their Belgian confreres, many of the Franciscans took refuge on the continent. "So great," writes Thaddeus, "was the rush to Douai, that there was not room enough for all the fathers who continued to arrive,

---

[4] On Dodd's list (ibidem, Vol. III, p. 400) he appears under the assumed name William Russel.

[5] FF. Charles Parry and Gregory Jones also are commemorated as having suffered imprisonment at this time for their priesthood; the former by Dodd (ibidem, Vol. III, p. 400), the latter by Hope (ibidem, p. 243) on the authority of Oliver. The matter is not mentioned by Thaddeus.

and the clerics had to be sent out to different houses of the Order in Belgium." Others, however, defying all danger, remained on the missions and continued to minister to their persecuted countrymen. Of these, six are known to have been seized and imprisoned. Fr. Gervase Cartwright, after being condemned to death and languishing in the jail at Leicester for twenty-eight months, was at last banished by the Prince of Orange. FF. Francis Hardwick and William Lockier were thrown into Newgate in the beginning of the revolution; they were still there in September, 1689, when the chapter appointed the former titular guardian of Canterbury and summoned the latter to Douai, where he was master of novices in 1691. FF. Daniel Selby and Lewis Grimbalson were confined for several months in York Castle and Fr. Bernardine Barras in the dungeon of Kidcote prison.

With the return of more peaceful times, many of the Franciscans went back to England and resumed their missionary labors. During the first half of the eighteenth century, the province prospered as perhaps never before or after. In 1756, it counted about 100 members, of whom, in 1758, at least 40 were active in England. Accordingly, many new missions could be taken over, to the great joy of the people who welcomed the friars with open arms and by generous benefactions sought to relieve their temporal needs. Thus the Franciscans were enabled to rebuild some of their friaries, notably those at White Hill and York. In the latter place and at Edgbaston they conducted a school for boys; while the one at Osmotherley was soon restored to its former flourishing condition.

Among the writers of this period we mention in particular FF. Antony Parkinson and Pacificus Baker. The former compiled a valuable history of the Franciscan Order in England, which we have had frequent occasion to consult in the course of our narrative. It was published in London, in 1726, under the title *Collectanea Anglo-Minoritica* or *A Collection of the Antiquities of the English Franciscans*. Fr. Baker wrote a number of ascetical treatises. One of his works, entitled *Scripture Antiquity*, is of a controversial nature. "Without much originality," Thaddeus observes, "all these works are remarkable for unction, solidity, and moderation."

Before recounting the decline and ultimate dissolution of the province, we must commemorate two friars who suffered and died in prison at this time. In 1698, Fr. Paul Atkinson was elected definitor of the province and was summoned to London to take part in the deliberations of the chapter then in session. But he failed to appear, and on further inquiry it was learned that he had been apprehended for being a priest, and on his refusal to take the required oaths he had been condemned to perpetual imprisonment in Hurst Castle. His death which occurred thirty years later, on October 15, 1729, is thus recorded: "In Hurst prison, Hants died the venerable Confessor of the faith and of Christ's priesthood, Father Paul Atkinson, formerly professor of theology, definitor of the province, and a jubilarian in the Order, who, during a continual martyrdom of thirty years, reflected honor on his prison, on our Province, and on the English mission; who, though not cut off by the persecutor's sword, still, as we piously trust, did not forego the palm of martyrdom. Wherefore we do not so much recommend him to the prayers of our brethren as propose him as a model for their imitation."

During the religious persecution revived by the Stuart rising, in 1745, Fr. Germanus Holmes was seized and cast into Lancaster Castle. The provincial necrology commemorates him in these terms: "The veneral confessor of Jesus Christ, Germanus Holmes, at one time professor of philosophy in our college at Douai, who, after suffering various insults from the insolent dregs of the populace on account of his priestly character, was consigned by the magistrate to Lancaster Castle and loaded with iron chains, where for four months he fought the good fight, and happily, as we hope, finished the course of his mortal life, having contracted the fever through the filthiness of the place; but not without suspicion of poison administered to him by the wicked woman who brought him his food."

The decline of the Second English Province became noticeable about the year 1770. In assigning the causes, Thaddeus points to the State laws then enacted against religious communities, which in turn necessarily meant a scarcity of vocations to the Order and a gradual falling off in men and means. In 1773, the French government, in its hostile attitude toward the Church and her institutions, prohibited youths from making religious profession before they had completed their twenty-first year; and in 1790, another law was passed, pursuant to which no one under French rule was permitted to take vows in a religious Order. Douai in Flanders, where the English Franciscans had their novitiate and house of higher studies, was at the time subject to France, and to their dismay the friars saw how these obnoxious State laws were beginning to effect the province. Already in 1779, they had no clerics to take up the theological course, and by 1790 the province numbered only forty-eight members.

Matters came to a head when the French Revolution broke out. On December 19, 1791, the Franciscans were placed under arrest in their house at Douai, and two years later, on August 9, an order was issued by the civil authorities giving the friars one day's time to leave the town. With a heavy heart, the sixteen resident friars departed for Belgium and took up their abode in a house at Tongres, which the Carmelites generously placed at their disposal. But darker days were yet to come. The triennial chapter of the province, held in London, on July 31, 1794, had just made provisions for the house at Tongres, when in the midst of the deliberations the friars of that place arrived with the sad news that their stay in Belgium was no longer possible, since French hordes had invaded the country and were threatening the lives of priests and religious.

Henceforth restricted to their mother country, the English Franciscans did all in their power to avert the total extinction of the declining province. Friends were not wanting to encourage them by offering them material assistance. A novitiate was opened at Osmotherley and later at Aston. But applications for the order continued to be few and far between. In 1813, the province numbered only twenty-one members, and, in 1838, but nine were left to attend the chapter held at Clifton. At this chapter, Fr. Leo Edgeworth was elected provincial. But for obvious reasons the minister general hesitated to confirm his election and appointed a commissary in the person of Fr. Francis Hendren. Meanwhile, the Sacred Congregation of the Propaganda had taken the matter in hand and, in January, 1841, Rt. Rev. Thomas Joseph Brown, O.S.B., Vicar Apostolic of the Welsh district, notified the Franciscans that the Holy Father had appointed him their visitor apostolic. With this provision, the English friars ceased to exist as a province.

It will be remembered that we set out to relate the story of the English Franciscans during the first century of the Protestant Reformation. The reader, we are confident, can now judge for himself how wholly unfounded, as far as the sons of St. Francis are concerned, is the charge that schism and heresy was possible in England because the so-called "old Orders" had degenerated and looked on with indifference when the great upheaval began. That the Franciscans were the first to feel the smart of Henry VIII's vengeful fury, can be accounted for solely by the fact that they were the first who dared to set themselves against his lawless policy, and that, on account of their traditional loyalty to the Holy See and their acknowledged influence with the masses, they were rightly designated by those in power as the most formidable and inflexible defenders of truth and justice.

With them imprisoned, banished, or executed, it was a comparatively easy task for Queen Elizabeth to complete the work of her father and sever the last tie that bound England to the Church of Christ. All during her reign, however, the few surviving Franciscans were waiting for an opportunity to rally their scattered forces. Hence, when James I ascended the throne and the Catholics began to breathe more freely, the friars banded together and established what is known as the Second English Province. We have seen how the members of this new foundation were imbued with the true spirit of St. Francis, and, like their forefathers of the first province, labored even unto imprisonment and death for the defense and propagation of the true faith. Five of their number died as martyrs during the terrible struggle that ended with the downfall of English royalty and the proclamation of the Puritan Commonwealth. Thus, throughout the century, from Henry's attack on the divine rights of the Holy See down to the nation's renunciation of the king's authority, the Franciscans never for a moment wavered in their defense of a just and holy cause. It is safe to say that, humanly speaking, Protestantism would never have gained the ascendancy in England, if in the beginning of the religious upheaval, the bulk of the clergy had been as faithful and fearless in defending the Catholic faith as the Franciscans.

The End

BIBLIOGRAPHY

ACTA MINORUM (Quaracchi, Italy), I-XXXVIII, 1882-1919.
ANALECTA FRANCISCANA (Quaracchi, Italy), I-V, 1885-1912.
ARCHIVUM FRANCISCANUM HISTORICUM (Quaracchi, Italy), I-VIII, 1908-1915.
Arturus a Monasterio, Fr., O.F.M.: MARTYROLOGIUM FRANCISCANUM (Venice, Italy), 1879.
Baumstark, Reinhold: THOMAS MORUS (Freiburg, 1879).
Bourchier, Fr. Thomas, O.F.M.: HISTORIA ECCLESIASTICA DE MARTYRIO FRATRUM ORDINIS MINORUM DIVI FRANCISCI (Paris, 1586).
Bremond, Henri: SIR THOMAS MORE—tr. by Harold Child (London, 1913).
Bridgett, Rev. T. E., C.Ss.R.: LIFE AND WRITINGS OF BLESSED THOMAS MORE (London, 1913).
Camm, Dom Bede, O.S.B.: LIVES OF THE ENGLISH MARTYRS (London, 1904), I-II.
Cobbett, William: REFORMATION IN ENGLAND AND IRELAND (New York, 1897).
Cuthbert, Father, O.S.F.C.: THE FRIARS AND HOW THEY CAME TO ENGLAND (London, 1903).
Digby, H. Kenelm: MORES CATHOLICI (New York, 1905), I-IV.
Dodd, Rev. Charles: CHURCH HISTORY OF ENGLAND (Brussels, 1537-1542), I-III.
Domenichelli, Padre Teofilo, O.F.M.: IL BEATO GIOVANNI FOREST (Prato, 1887).
DOUAI DIARIES, FIRST & SECOND in RECORDS OF THE ENGLISH CATHOLICS (London, 1878).
Du Boys, Albert: CATHERINE D'ARAGON (Paris, 1880).
ENCYCLOPEDIA BRITANNICA (Philadelphia), I-XXI.
Felder, P. Dr. Hilarion, O.Cap.: STUDIEN IM FRANZISKANERORDEN (Freiburg, 1904).
Gasquet, Cardinal Aidan, O.S.B.: ENGLISH MONASTIC LIFE (New York, 1904).
Gasquet, Cardinal Aidan, O.S.B.: HENRY THE THIRD AND THE CHURCH (London, 1905).
Gasquet, Cardinal Aidan, O.S.B.: HENRY VIII AND THE ENGLISH MONASTERIES (London, 1889), I-II.

Gasquet, Cardinal Aidan, O.S.B.: THE BLACK DEATH (London, 1908).
Gasquet, Cardinal Aidan, O.S.B.: THE EVE OF THE REFORMATION (London, 1905).
Gaudentius, P., O.F.M.: BEDEUTUNG UND VERDIENSTE DES FRANZISKANERORDENS IM KAMPFE GEGEN DEN PROTESTANTISMUS (Bozen, 1880).
Guérin, Mgr. Paul: Le PALMIER SÉRAPHIQUE (Bar-le-Duc, 1872-1874), I-XII.
Heimbucher, Dr. Max: DIE ORDEN UND KONGREGATIONEN DER KATHOLISCHEN KIRCHE (Paderborn, 1907), I-III.
Hill, O'Dell Travers: ENGLISH MONASTICISM (London, 1876).
Hope, Mrs.: FRANCISCAN MARTYRS IN ENGLAND (London, 1878).
Hope, Mrs.: THE First Divorce OF Henry VIII (London, 1894).
Holzapfel, P. Dr. Heribert, O.F.M.: GESCHICHTE DES FRANZISKANERORDENS (Freiburg, 1909).
Hudson, Rev. H. N.: SHAKESPEARE: HIS LIFE, ART, AND CHARACTERS.
Hueber, P. Fr. Fortunatus, O.F.M.: MENOLOGIUM (Muenster, 1698).
KIRCHENLEXICON, Wetzer und Welter's (Freiburg), I-XII.
Leon, Fr.: AUREOLE SÉRAPHIQUE; Engl, transl.: LIVES OF THE SAINTS AND BLESSED OF THE THREE ORDERS OF ST. FRANCIS—Vol. IV, containing a historical sketch of the English Franciscan Province. (Taunton, 1887.)
Lingard, John, D. D.: HISTORY OF ENGLAND (New York, 1879), I-VIII.
Little, A. G.: STUDIES IN ENGLISH FRANCISCAN HISTORY (London, 1917).
Magliano, Fr. Panfilo da, O.F.M.: St. FRANCIS AND THE FRANCISCANS, tr. from Italian (New York, 1867).
Mason, Fr. Angelus a S. Francisco, O.F.M.: CERTAMEN SERAPHICUM PROVINCIAE ANGLIAE (Quaracchi, Italy, 1885).
MONUMENTA FRANCISCANA, Vol. I, ed. J. S. Brewer (London, 1858); Vol. II, ed. Richard Howlett (London, 1882).
Ortolani, P. Cyrus, O.F.M.: DE CAUSIS BEATORUM ET SERVORUM DEI ORDINIS MINORUM (Quaracchi, Italy, 1905).
Parkinson, Fr. Anthony, O.F.M.: COLLECTANEA ANGLO-MINORITICA OR A COLLECTION OF THE ANTIQUITIES OF THE ENGLISH FRANCISCANS (London, 1726).
Pastor, Dr. Ludwig: GESCHICHTE DER PAEPSTE (Freiburg), I-VI.
Pocock, Nicholas: RECORDS OF THE REFORMATION (Oxford, Clarendon Press, 1870), I-II.
Roper, William: LIFE OF SIR THOMAS MORE, KNT. (London, 1905).
Sander, Nicholas: DE ORIGINE AC PROGRESSU SCHISMATIS ANGLICANI

(Coloniae Agrippinae, 1585; Rishton edition, 1690).
Sannig, P. Bernardus: CRONICKEN DER DREI ORDEN S. FRANCISCI (Prague, 1690), I-III (Parts I-VI).
Spillmann, Joseph, S.J.: KATHOLIKENVERFOLGUNG IN ENGLAND (Freiburg, 1900-1905), I-IV.
Spillmann, Joseph, S.J.: DIE BLUTZEUGEN DER TITUS OATES-VERSCHWOERUNG (Freiburg, 1901).
Staunton, Howard: THE GREAT SCHOOLS OF ENGLAND (London, 1865).
Stone, J. M.: FAITHFUL UNTO DEATH (London, 1892).
Stone, J. M.: MARY THE FIRST, QUEEN OF ENGLAND (London, 1901).
Strickland, Agnes: LIVES OF THE QUEENS OF ENGLAND (Philadelphia, 1899), II, III.
Thaddeus, Rev. Father, O.F.M.: LIFE OF BLESSED JOHN FOREST (London, 1888).
Thaddeus, Rev. Father, O.F.M.: THE FRANCISCANS IN ENGLAND, 1600-1850 (London, 1898).
Thaddeus, Rev. Father, O.F.M.: WALTER COLMAN, O.F.M. in FRANCISCAN BIOGRAPHIES (C. T. S., London, 1912).
THE CAMBRIDGE HISTORY OF ENGLISH LITERATURE (Cambridge, 1907-1911), I-VI.
THE CATHOLIC ENCYCLOPEDIA (New York), I-XV.
Timbs, John: ABBEYS, CASTLES AND ANCIENT HALLS OF ENGLAND AND WALES (London).
Wadding, Fr. Luke, O.F.M.: ANNALES MINORUM, first edition, I-VII (Lyons, 1625-1648); XIX (Quaracchi, 1914); XX (Quaracchi, 1899); XXI-XXV (Ancona, Naples, 1844-1886).
Wadding, Fr. Luke, O.F.M.: SCRIPTORES ORDINIS MINORUM (Rome, 1650).
Wright, Thomas: SUPPRESSION OF THE MONASTERIES (London, 1843).

www.ingramcontent.com/pod-product-compliance
Lightning Source LLC
Chambersburg PA
CBHW021437070526
44577CB00002B/204